# A Creole Experiment

# A Creole Experiment

## Utopian Space in Kamau Brathwaite's "video-style" Works

### Melanie Otto

Africa World Press, Inc.

P.O. Box 1892  
Trenton, NJ 08607

P.O. Box 48  
Asmara, ERITREA

**Africa World Press, Inc.**

P.O. Box 1892  
Trenton, NJ 08607

P.O. Box 48  
Asmara, ERITREA

Copyright © 2009 Melanie Otto
First Printing 2009

All rights reserved. No part of this publication may be reproduced, stored in a retrieval system or transmitted in any form or by any means electronic, mechanical, photocopying, recording or otherwise without the prior written permission of the publisher.

Book design:   Saverance Publishing Services
Cover design:   Ashraful Haque

Cover art by Janaina Tschäpe

Library of Congress Cataloging-in-Publication Data

Otto, Melanie.
  A Creole experiment : utopian space in Kamau Brathwaite's videostyle works / by Melanie Otto.
    p. cm.
  ISBN 1-59221-562-9 (cloth) -- ISBN 1-59221-563-7 (pbk.)
  1. Brathwaite, Kamau, 1930---Criticism and interpretation. 2. Brathwaite, Kamau, 1930---Political and social views. 3. Utopias in literature. 4. West Indies--In literature. 5. Caribbean Area--In literature. 6. Magic realism (Literature) I. Title.

PR9230.9.B68Z8 2009
811'.54--dc22
                              2009017913

*We must hold fast to dreams*
*We must be patient*
*from the crouching of those huts*
*from the sprouting of these fields*
*We can emerge*

*all revolutions are rooted in dreams*

**Grace Nichols**

# Table of Contents

| | |
|---|---|
| Acknowledgements | ix |
| List of Abbreviations | xi |
| INTRODUCTION: Kamau Brathwaite's Creole Experiment | 1 |
| CHAPTER ONE: *X/Self* and the (Re)invention of the "Creole Cosmos" | 19 |
| 1.1. "Your thunder has come home": The First Cosmology | 19 |
| 1.2. Carab the Filth Eater: The Second Cosmology | 40 |
| CHAPTER TWO: Death, Marriage, and Maroons: *The Zea Mexican Diary* | 51 |
| 2.1. In "the Blue Mountains of Kilimanjaro": The Irish Town Maroon Project | 51 |
| 2.2. "Succumbing to the Culture of Death": Brathwaite's Diary Entries | 58 |
| 2.3. "But my pain continues": Letters and Memorials | 66 |
| CHAPTER THREE: The Poet's Archive as *Houmfort*: Shar/ Hurricane Poem | 91 |
| 3.1. "Saving the Word": Epics and Archives | 91 |
| 3.2. "The knowledge is within": Incantation and the Survival of Memory | 97 |
| CHAPTER FOUR: Zombies and Messiahs in the Kingdom of this World: *Trench Town Rock* | 113 |
| 4.1. "Gateway to so sudden swiftly HELL": Kingston as Inferno | 113 |

4.2. "Mi hann come from God": Ananse's Triumph — 129

**CHAPTER FIVE:** *DreamStories*: The Far Side of the Mirror — 145

   5.1. "A most ancient place": Rift Valleys of the Psyche — 145
   5.2. "The Black Angel" — 147
   5.3. "Dream Chad" — 156
   5.4. "Dream Crabs" — 161
   5.5. "4th Traveller" — 166
   5.6. "Dream Haiti" — 173
   5.7. "Grease" — 175
   5.8. "Salvages" — 176

**CHAPTER SIX:** "Oceans within": *Barabajan Poems, ConVERSations with Nathaniel Mackey* and the Utopian Space of the Text — 183

   6.1. *Barabajan Poems* — 190
   6.2. *ConVERSations with Nathaniel Mackey* — 207

**CHAPTER SEVEN:** "The spirits of GOLOKWATI... have led me to this place": *Words Need Love Too* and *Born to Slow Horses* — 215

   7.1. "Write it upon my oumfô body": *Words Need Love Too* and the Spirit of Namsetoura — 215
   7.2. "Approaching the new life of Eleuthera": *Born to Slow Horses* — 232

Notes — 245
Bibliography — 277
Index — 301

# Acknowledgements

I would like to thank John Goodby of Swansea University for his supervision and his constant support and advice during the writing of my Ph.D. thesis, which forms the basis of this book, as well as Angela Ajayi, Kassahun Checole and others at Africa World Press for their help and guidance in preparing the manuscript for publication. I am grateful to family, friends and colleagues who have encouraged and guided me along the way. I would also like to thank Kamau Brathwaite for his correspondence and for giving me permission to cite large parts of his work, and the publishers listed below for granting me permission to reproduce copyright material. I am grateful for the support of the Arts and Social Sciences Benefactions Fund 2008/9 of Trinity College Dublin, which helped to cover the cost of the copyright permissions.

Excerpts from Brathwaite, Kamau, *Ancestors*, copyright © 1977, 1982, 1987, 2001 by Kamau Brathwaite. Reprinted by permission of New Directions Publishing Corp.

Excerpts from Brathwaite, Edward, *The Arrivants: A New World Trilogy*, copyright © 1967, 1968, 1969, 1973 by Edward Brathwaite. Reprinted by permission of Oxford University Press.

Excerpts from Brathwaite, Kamau, *Barabajan Poems 1492-1992*, copyright © 1994 by Kamau Brathwaite. Reprinted by permission of the author.

Excerpts from Brathwaite, Kamau, *Born to Slow Horses*, copyright © 2005 by Kamau Brathwaite. Reprinted by permission of Wesleyan University Press.

*A Creole Experiment*

Excerpts from Brathwaite, Kamau, *ConVERSations with Nathaniel Mackey*, copyright © 1999 by Kamau Brathwaite. Reprinted by permission of XCP: Cross-Cultural Poetics.

Excerpts from Brathwaite, Kamau, *DreamStories*, copyright © 1994 by Kamau Brathwaite. Reprinted by permission of the author.

Excerpts from Brathwaite, Kamau, *The Namsetoura Papers*, copyright © 2004, 2005 by Kamau Brathwaite. Reprinted by permission of the author.

Excerpts from Brathwaite, Kamau, *Save CowPastor*, copyright © 2004, 2005, 2006 by Kamau Brathwaite. Reprinted by permission of the author.

Excerpts from Brathwaite, Kamau, *Shar/Hurricane Poem*, copyright © 1990 by Kamau Brathwaite. Reprinted by permission of the author.

Excerpts from Brathwaite, Kamau, *Trench Town Rock*, copyright © 1994 by Kamau Brathwaite. Reprinted by permission of Lost Roads Publishers.

Excerpts from Brathwaite, Kamau, *The Zea Mexican Diary 7 Sept 1926 – 7 Sept 1986*, copyright © 1993. Reprinted by permission of The University of Wisconsin Press.

Excerpts from Brathwaite, Edward Kamau *X/Self*, copyright © 1987 by Edward Kamau Brathwaite. Reprinted by permission of Oxford University Press.

Excerpts from Brathwaite, Kamau, *Words Need Love Too*, copyright © 2000 by Kamau Brathwaite. Reprinted by permission of House of Nehesi Publishers.

Excerpts from Brathwaite, Kamau, *Words Need Love Too*, copyright © 2004 by Kamau Brathwaite. Reprinted by permission of Salt Publishing Ltd.

Excerpts from Nichols, Grace. *I Is a Long-Memoried Woman*, copyright © 1983 by Grace Nichols. Reproduced by permission of Curtis Brown Group Ltd.

# List of Abbreviations

## Titles by Kamau Brathwaite

| | |
|---|---|
| BP | *Barabajan Poems 1492–1992*. New York: Savacou North, 1994. |
| BTSH | *Born to Slow Horses*. Middletown, CT: Wesleyan University Press, 2005. |
| C | *ConVERSations with Nathaniel Mackey*. Staten Island, NY: We Press; Minneapolis; MN: Xcp: Cross-Cultural Poetics, 1999. |
| DS | *DreamStories*. Intro. Gordon Rohlehr. Longman Caribbean Writers. Harlow: Longman, 1994. |
| MP | *Mother Poem*. Oxford/New York: Oxford University Press, 1977. |
| "MR." | *Annals of Scholarship* 12.1–2 (1997): 1–28. |
| NP | *The Namsetoura Papers* <http://tomraworth.com/np.pdf>. 1–55. |
| Shar | *Shar/Hurricane Poem*. Mona, Jamaica: Savacou, 1990. |
| TTR | *Trench Town Rock*. Providence: Lost Roads, 1994. |
| Words [2000] | *Words Need Love Too*. Intro. Fabian Adekunle Badejo. Philipsburg, St Martin: House of Nehesi, 2000. |
| Words [2004] | *Words Need Love Too*. Intro. Stewart Brown. Cambridge: Salt, 2004. |
| ZMD | *The Zea Mexican Diary The Zea Mexican Diary 7 Sept 1926 – 7 Sept 1986*. Foreword Sandra Pouchet Paquet. Wisconsin Studies in American Autobiography. Madison, Wisconsin: The University of Wisconsin Press, 1993. |

X/S    *X/Self.* Oxford/New York: Oxford University Press, 1987.

## Titles by Ernst Bloch

PH    *The Principle of Hope.* Trans. Neville Plaice, Stephen Plaice and Paul Knight. 3 vols. Studies in Contemporary German Social Thought. Cambridge, MA: The MIT Press, 1995.

*Introduction*

# Kamau Brathwaite's Creole Experiment

◇◆◇

> say
> i
> not
>
> eye
>
> globe
> seeing word
> blue priest
> green voodoo doctor (*MP* 58)

In "Nametracks," from which the above passage is taken, Barbadian-born poet, critic and historian Kamau Brathwaite (1930 – )[1] illustrates the struggle that lies at the heart of his work and at the heart of the Caribbean experience. "Nametracks" describes a war of words between O'Grady, the plantation owner in *Mother Poem* (*MP*) (1977), and an unnamed enslaved mother, who calls O'Grady "the man who possesses us all" (*MP* 57). At the center of their struggle is a child, the slave mother's son. Implied in these characters are the personae of Prospero, Sycorax and Caliban from Shakespeare's *The*

*Tempest*, who re-enact the history of colonization and slavery in the Caribbean. O'Grady's/Prospero's insistence on Caliban's repetition of his words is symbolic of the erasure of Caliban's African heritage and the slave's enforced identification with the slave master's culture. Brathwaite illustrates this exercise in linguistic domination in Chapter XII of *Barabajan Poems* (*BP*) (1994), where "Nametracks" reappears and where, in connection, he cites a passage from the TV adaptation of Alex Haley's *Roots*. Brathwaite focuses on a scene where Kunta Kinte has his African name beaten out of him and is forced to accept an English name chosen for him by the overseer of the plantation.

Brathwaite's notion of the close link between name and identity is illustrated, again, in his concept of *nam*, which in his writing is synonymous with the submerged African culture of the Caribbean:

> ... the slave, the colonial, the oppressed – whoever – has a **n-a-m-e** and . . . that name is always under pressure from 'the man who possesses us all'. He is always trying to eat our identity/ name...
>
> Now in our name we have that 'e' at the end of it which is its little tail ... and that's the weak part of the name so that it is possible to lose your n-a-m-(e) – but then you are left – if you are properly blessed/ have been true to yrself to yr culture etc – with something much more powerful which is yr **nam** & the **nam** is yr **name** now protected by the two intransigent consonants (or continents) of sound... (*BP* 241)

It is this *nam* or secret name that Sycorax whispers to Caliban in "Nametracks":

> say *man*: she is tell muh
> say *man*: she is tell muh
>
> say *man*
> say *manding*
> say *mandingo* (*MP* 57)

Although *nam* is a concept that Brathwaite has invented, his perception of the word and the act of naming is influenced by African traditions, and in particular by the Nommo myth of the Dogon people of Mali. For the Dogon, the Nommo twins, who are half serpent and half human, are the life force of the universe and also the mediators between God and humanity — the offspring of God and the earth. They also bring language from God to humanity (Griaule 16–23). In analogy to the Nommo myth, Brathwaite's *nam* represents a creative life force within his work where it is frequently embodied by spirits such as Legba and Ananse and, more recently, by the spirit of Namsetoura, who has characteristics of both Sycorax and Ananse. Brathwaite further links his concept of *nam* to the Akan supreme deity Nyame or Onyame:

> So that when the right time comes or the crisis has to be faced...
>
> the *nam*
> reveals its *name* as *man*
> >yam >nyam >nyame >onyame >dynamo
>
> and in the end
>
> # Nomm0
> # The Word
> (*BP* 257)[2]

The concept of *nam* thus also includes the connection between God and the consumption of food. God becomes food.[3] In this sense, Onyame is related to the sacrificial nature of Christ, the Eucharist, whereas the Nommo echo the idea of Christ as the living word. Both aspects are present in the Haitian spirit, Legba, and emphasize the cross-cultural nature of Brathwaite's imagination. Most of all, the connection between the word and God implies the magical quality of language. It becomes an instrument of power because it has "the power to affect life," a belief that Brathwaite traces back not only to Africa but also to the oral cultures of the diaspora ("The African Presence" 241).

Brathwaite argues that *nam* is also an inversion of man, that "at moments or times of crisis, **man** goes into implosion, disguise, defence, maroon / profile, an alteration of consciousness — ***nam***" (*BP* 96). Significantly, it is mainly the male slave and his descendants who are crippled by colonial domination. In *Mother Poem*, the father is suffering from ill health, which is the result of poor working conditions, underpayment, and the exploitation of his labor. Hard labor literally and metaphorically crushes him; man becomes twisted, becomes *nam*. Women, on the other hand, are often presented as the keepers of ancestral memory, guardians of *nam*, and as links to the spiritual sphere from which they derive power.[4] Therefore, Brathwaite regards them as descendants of Sycorax. In "Nametracks," Sycorax attempts to prevent her child's sense of self from becoming twisted and submerged. She casts a spell on O'Grady/Prospero ("she is tell muh / e go day / e go dog / e go die" (*MP* 57)). Most of all, however, she tells Caliban to walk upright, straightening out *nam* into man.

In the mother's naming of her son in "Nametracks," the desire to live without masters, to be free of physical and spiritual domination, has been transformed into action and becomes an act of liberation. However, in order to convert *nam* to man, a mere return to an ancestral African self is not a solution for Caribbean-born Caliban. "The original 'Africa' is no longer there," as Stuart Hall argues (117). There can be no going back in time, only a moving forward into the future, which is what Brathwaite suggests: "In a colonial situation or post-colonial situation where we have been named by other people ... it is ... our responsibility to rename & redefine ourselves" (*BP* 240–41). *Nam* as the African past of the Caribbean becomes the point of departure for its creole future. Brathwaite points to the inbetweenness and admixture of creole culture by positioning it between "the two intransigent consonants (or continents) of sound" (*BP* 241), suggesting that Caliban's language and identity are a product of the coming together of Africa and the Americas.

Brathwaite's preoccupation with naming and renaming indicates that for him the struggle over language is symbolic of a wider conflict between dominating and dominated cultures. In the Caribbean, the language issue is particularly prominent as over time the slaves lost the memory of their original African languages (some suggest through a deliberate policy of language suppression in order to prevent the possibility of slave rebellions). Consequently, "the transplanted Africans found that psychic survival depended on their facility for a kind of *double entendre*": "They were forced to develop the skill of being able to say one thing in front of 'massa' and have it interpreted differently by their fellow slaves" (Ashcroft et al. 146). Out of this "radical subversion of the meanings of the master's tongue" (Ashcroft et al. 146) evolved the creation of a new language different from that of the slave master and indigenous to the Caribbean-born or creole Africans.

Although usually referred to as "creole" or "patois," Brathwaite distinguishes between "creole" and "nation language":

> We . . . have what we call creole English, which is a mixture of English and an adaptation that English took in the new environment of the Caribbean when it became mixed with the other imported languages. We have also what is called *nation language*, which is the kind of English spoken by the people who were brought to the Caribbean, not the official English now, but the language of slaves and labourers, the servants who were brought in by the conquistadors. (*History of the Voice* 5–6)[5]

In other words, "nation language" is Afro-creole, whereas creole is spoken by white, colored and black West Indians alike. "Nation" is a language that focuses on the African heritage of the Caribbean, "since Africans in the New World always referred to themselves as belonging to *nations* (Kongo, Kromantee, etc.)" (Brathwaite, "The African Presence" 219). Therefore, Brathwaite's Sycorax characters, including the spirit of Namsetoura, speak "nation" or Afro-creole.[6]

In the creation of this new language the act of moving beyond mere opposition is a vital step towards the formation of a Caribbean identity, a perspective Brathwaite shares with many other thinkers of the region. For Édouard Glissant, for example, opposition acknowledges a dominant other. Therefore, he suggests that "the most secure protection against self-destructive imitation is the process of creolization" or "cultural cross-fertilization," because it is a creative rather than a reactive process (*Caribbean Discourse* 46 n4). Glissant suggests that cross-culturality or creolization is "a productive activity through which each element is enriched" (*Caribbean Discourse* 8). There is a utopian element embedded in the notion of cultural cross-fertilization, pointing towards a dialogue that, as Wilson Harris suggests, "moves endlessly into flexible patterns, arcs or bridges of community" (*The Womb of Space* xviii). Cross-cultural dialogue then is the beginning of a world no longer divided into the dominating and the exploited. In this context, it becomes significant that Brathwaite calls his vision of a new world order "creole cosmos," which in his definition of "creole" includes the former oppressors.

The first book that deals with the notion of a "creole cosmos" is the 1987 edition of *X/Self*. Whereas in previous works, such as *The Arrivants* (1973), *Mother Poem* (1977) or *Sun Poem* (1982), Brathwaite focused on a particularly African-Caribbean identity, *X/Self* moves towards a vision that includes European, Amerindian as well as African elements, reaching beyond a specific ethnic focus. In *Caribbean Man in Space and Time* (1974), Brathwaite defines creolization as "a process, resulting in subtle and multiform orientations from or *twoards* ancestral originals" (7). The idiosyncratic "twoards" implies both the notion of "moving towards" and of "two ways," indicating that creolization is not just a hegemonic but a two-fold process of cultures moving towards each other.

Brathwaite introduces the "creole cosmos" as the underlying principle of *X/Self* in *ConVERSations with Nathaniel Mackey* (*C*) (1999): "... the poem is really 'about' two forces seeking to find a balance in what I regard as a new or *creole* cosmos, a cosmos which in fact begins to 'perdict'... the dissolution... of empire(s)" (*C* 117). Brathwaite voices this vision already in his "World Order Models: A Caribbean Perspective" (1985), indicating that the Caribbean experience may function as a model for a global world order:

> Based on my Caribbean experience, ... I would posit a World Order based not on politics or structures or institutions; but on a relationship of peoples, increasingly conscious of each other; increasingly influenced by each other — modern travel, modern technology has clearly made this a reality; but the essentiality of each culture must also be recognized and employed in the new transcendence. (63)

Since his first engagement with the idea of a creole society in his doctoral thesis *The Development of the Creole Society in Jamaica*, Brathwaite's definition of creole has moved towards a more global context.[7] However, his description of the "creole cosmos" in *ConVERSations* is in essence very similar to the one he proposes for the creole society of Jamaica between 1770 and 1820: "The single most important factor in the development of Jamaican society was ... a cultural action ... based upon the stimulus/ response of individuals within the society to their environment and — as white/black, culturally discrete groups

— to each other" (*Development of the Creole Society* 296). What links the Jamaican creole society of the late eighteenth and early nineteenth century to the "creole cosmos" of the twentieth and twenty-first century is the interaction of two or more distinct cultural and racial units in order to form "a 'new' construct, made up of newcomers to the landscape and cultural strangers each to the other" (*Development of the Creole Society* 296).

Brathwaite's political vision of a "creole cosmos" is mirrored in his cultural projects at Irish Town and CowPastor. Both are attempts to create alternative (or "alter/native" as Brathwaite has it) communities within the neocolonial capitalist world. Both projects envision communities that are economically self-sufficient and culturally independent, calling for the creation of local economies and local cultural institutions. His own archives play a vital role in realizing this vision. CowPastor in Barbados, for example, is to be the site of what Brathwaite calls his "Bussa Centre," a place for writers and artists to come together, where he can make his library accessible for public use. However, this endeavor has been challenged by the government's decision to build a road through his property, allegedly for better access to the airport. A similar project was aborted when Hurricane Gilbert destroyed Brathwaite's home and archive at Irish Town, Jamaica, in 1988 (Brathwaite sees CowPastor as continuing the Irish Town project). Both undertakings represent Brathwaite's vision of an independent Caribbean at large. In this sense, his work, in the form of his writing as well as the "outward poetry" of his life, contains a strong utopian element (McSweeney).

In *ConVERSations*, Brathwaite links his Irish Town project to the history of maroon resistance (*C* 121–27). In an attempt to enact his vision of an alternative to the neocolonial "plantation" and the various elements of exploitation and dependence that accompany it, he carries on the tradition of the historical maroon communities —communities of runaway slaves that retained a strong orientation towards their African heritage. In "An excerpt from Limbo," Brathwaite refers to maroon societies as unique "Caribbean efforts at self-realization and independence" (97), whose "nam self radiating outwards would help to create the new world" (102). In a sense, maroon societies can be classed as successfully enacted utopias and radical experiments in establishing an independent Afro-creole culture, a potential equal to Euro-creole culture.[8] As such, maroon communities are a prerequisite for the balance needed in Brathwaite's "new or *creole* cosmos."

## A Creole Experiment

The New World has figured as a utopian space in the European imagination ever since Columbus first set eyes on it, be it as the location of the earthly paradise, the realm of the noble savage or the source of the fountain of youth. In this respect, the New World contributed to the development of a whole range of utopian literature in Europe, Thomas More's *Utopia* (1516) being just one work among many. What most fictional utopias have in common is the depiction of an ideal elsewhere. Brathwaite's approach to the notion of utopia is of an altogether different nature. His concern is to work towards a world free from domination. Consequently, he emphasizes the need for the present situation to change in order to anticipate this better world. Philosopher Ernst Bloch calls this "concrete utopia" (*The Principle of Hope (PH)* 1: 17).[9] He believes that utopian possibility is latent or submerged in the present historical moment and needs to be accessed and activated by a form of creative dreaming. In this context, creolization emerges as a twofold process:

> ... the recognition of an ancestral relationship with the folk or aboriginal culture involves the artist or participant in a journey into the past and hinterland which is at the same time a movement of possession into present and future. Through this movement of possession we become ourselves, truly our own creators, discovering word for object, image for the word. (Brathwaite, "Timehri" 42)

Here, in his essay "Timehri," Brathwaite describes a movement from the past into the utopian space of the future. Crucial to his thinking about past and future, exile and home in this context is the concept of "tidalectics." In *ConVERSations with Nathanial Mackey* he describes how, during a stay on the north coast of Jamaica, he observed the landlady of his residence sweeping sand from her yard:

> And then one morning I see her
> 
> body silhouetting against the
> 
> sparkling light that hits the
> 
> Caribbean at that early dawn

>           and it seems as if her feet,
>           which all along I thought were
>           walking on the sand. . . were
>           really. . . walking on the wa-
>           ter. . . and she was tra
>           velling across the middlepass
>           age, constantly coming from wh
>           ere she had come from — in her
>           case Africa — to this spot in
>           North Coast Jamaica where she
>           now lives. . .     (C 32–33)

"Tidalectics" describes, above all, the movement of the ocean, "the movement of the ocean she's walking on, coming from one continent/continuum, touching another, and then receding ('reading') from the island(s) into the perhaps creative chaos of the(ir) future . . ." (C 34). In her *Raintaxi* interview with Brathwaite, Joyelle McSweeney calls the sea a "cognitive space . . . in which perhaps Caribbean peoples can think outside the Western mode of the dialectic." In "New Gods of the Middle Passage," Brathwaite argues that if the original Middle Passage is dehumanizing, the Middle Passage in reverse is a healing experience, a journey back to *nam*, from where the journey forward begins anew (52).

In a sense, the "creole cosmos" itself is subject to "tidalectic" movements. On the one hand, it is situated in the here and now of a world subject to an increasing globalization, which implies new, neocolonial dependencies and conflicts. On the other hand, the "creole cosmos" points towards a future where a global growing together means the dissolution of such dependencies. At this intersection between reality and possibility, the "creole cosmos" is both created in and emerges from what Bloch calls "the darkness of the lived moment . . . in which everything that is both drives and is hidden from itself" (*PH* 1: 12). As if paraphrasing Brathwaite, Wilson Harris touches on a similar "tidalectic" thought when he says: "Continuities running out of the mystery of the past into the unknown future yield ... proportions of the 'genuinely new'" ("Letter from Francisco Bone" 49). This idea of the genuine newness of the past gives Brathwaite's vision utopian qualities. Significantly, his essay, "World Order Models," is itself a response to a collection of essays, *On the Creation of a Just World Order: Preferred Worlds of the 1990s*. Its editor, Saul Mendlovitz, states: "Where our thinking is utopian, it advances what we call *relevant utopias*, that is, world order systems that make clear not only alternative worlds but the necessary transition steps to these worlds" (xii). This passage encapsulates the notion of "concrete utopia" and creates a link between Brathwaite's own concerns and Bloch's philosophy. Bloch himself is mentioned in Mendlovitz's book as a thinker who concentrates precisely on the "transition steps" rather than imagining a perfect society. I will concentrate on the investigation of three interrelated Blochian concepts in Brathwaite's work, "concrete utopia," *Heimat*, and "arrived-at Being," as they are most closely related to Brathwaite's own thinking.

For Bloch, *Heimat* or homeland signifies an instance of arrival rather than a place of origin (the latter of which is the common definition of *Heimat*) and has global rather than national, regional or ethnic dimensions. Utopia for him is not an idealized elsewhere but a state of being: "The subject has ceased with its truest attribute: the desiderium; the object has ceased with its untruest attribute: alienation.... At this place on earth of arrived-at Being, of world as homeness, homeness as world, it settles down, here both flight and message end" (*PH* 3: 1311). In other words, *Heimat* as "arrived-at Being" becomes a space of communion between subject and object. Brathwaite's own sense of Caribbeanness draws on just such a notion of "arrived-at Being." In *The People Who Came*, the three-volume history of the Americas for Caribbean secondary schools he edited, the Caribbean region is described as a place where people have come to rather than originated from, hence the title of the series.[10] For Brathwaite, the Caribbean becomes home when people regard themselves as Caribbean, rather than from Africa, Europe or India, as having arrived in the New World rather than originating elsewhere. This he considers a vital step towards the development of a creole society. Without this sense of arrival the process of creolization remains incomplete, turning the Caribbean into a place of exile.

In *Caribbean Man in Space and Time*, Brathwaite expresses this sense of cultural incompleteness in terms of geological fragmentation.

The Caribbean islands are seen as geological and cultural fragments, which, nevertheless, share a "submarine unity" (1) via a common submerged bedrock, the African presence. The reason for this sense of fragmentation and subsequent longing for unity and wholeness inherent in Brathwaite's understanding of the Caribbean condition is the experience of the Middle Passage: "I'm so conscious of the enormity of slavery and the Middle Passage and I see that as an ongoing catastrophe. So whatever happens in the world after that . . . , to me these are all aspects of that same original explosion . . ." (McSweeney). Throughout Brathwaite's work we find geological and geographical metaphors that express cultural and historical events and connections. Mostly, these connections form alternatives to colonial history. He creates "vernaculars by geography," as Timothy Reiss argues, a phenomenon that appears in the works of a number of Caribbean writers, most notably in Brathwaite's, Walcott's and Harris's ("Realisms of the Fictive Imagination" 254). These vernaculars create "a different 'memory' . . . from fragments of many histories cemented by a shared geography, 'renamings' by place" (255).

Although an intense longing for wholeness is there in Brathwaite's model of creolization, his notion of unity does not preclude multiplicity. He himself states: "I say you have to be everything to bring those fragments together because fragments by their very nature are everything . . . . They are in fact everything, little seeds growing throughout the scattered diaspora, throughout the Caribbean" ("Words by Kamau Brathwaite" qtd. in Torres-Saillant, *Caribbean Poetics* 18). This implied unity within the "scattered diaspora" is a unity in diversity, a microcosm of the "creole cosmos." The Caribbean as a region is open to the world. In this sense, Brathwaite's notion of creoleness complements Glissant's concept of *antillanité* developed in *Caribbean Discourse* (1981) and extended in *Poetics of Relation* (1990), which implies both a rootedness in the Caribbean and an openness to the world. Glissant expresses this apparent paradox in his own reading of Brathwaite's *Caribbean Man in Space and Time*, where he argues that the people of the Caribbean "are the roots of a cross-cultural relationship" (*Caribbean Discourse* 67). This cross-culturality of the region results, as Glissant states, in the "subterranean convergence" of the "diverse histories" (*Caribbean Discourse* 66) of the Caribbean or in what Brathwaite calls its "many ancestored" genealogy (*Caribbean Man in Space and Time* 1).

Brathwaite's work is characterized by a strong commitment to the Caribbean region and its people. The image of the root, of being rooted in that particular place, which appears throughout his work, symbolizes this commitment. However, his sense of belonging equally transcends the notion of root as ethnic origin and identifies with the Caribbean as space of cross-cultural interaction, a microcosm of the world. In this context, his emphasis on the utopian possibility of art, literature, music, popular and folk culture becomes significant; here his "Sycorax video style" begins to take shape. If the Middle Passage represents the collective trauma encoded in the Caribbean psyche, which nevertheless holds within itself the seed of transformation and healing, Brathwaite's own personal Middle Passage, or what he calls his "time of salt," has led to this innovative style ("An excerpt from Limbo" 105).

He frequently refers to three instances in his life that had a traumatic impact on his writing practice, leaving his writing hand "paralyzed" as he claims: the death of his first wife Doris Monica (Zea Mexican) in 1986, the destruction of his home at Irish Town by Hurricane Gilbert in 1988, and the burglary of his Kingston apartment in 1990 when he was bound, gagged and nearly killed. Whether or not his writing hand was literally paralyzed as a result of these traumatic events, the experience led him to use his first wife's computer: "I began to play with it and discovered Sycorax lurking in the corner of the screen and that's how the whole thing started" (McSweeney).

In *ConVERSations with Nathaniel Mackey*, Brathwaite relates how he attempts to reach out to a large audience by employing his "video style" as a public art form comparable to murals, cinematic or hypertextual techniques. Brathwaite himself describes this "video style" as "a mural, with the *video* . . . at last making the mural *go*" (*C* 207). Through a rapid change of font size, "the poetry gets closer . . . to a kind of cinema-painting" (*C* 207). Consequently, the poetry "will, thr (u) these senses, become more public in the sense of more shared, more part of the community? — large-scale statements shared at important visible levels by all (many? most?)" (*C* 207). This new open form that is now so central to his writing is not merely a tool for the recovery of lost memory and a lost life but an attempt to transcend the limits of conventional genre categories. The "video style" thus also expresses "discrepant engagement," a term employed by African-American poet and critic Nathaniel Mackey "in reference to practices that, in the interest of opening presumably closed orders of identity and signification, accent fissure, fracture, incongruity, the rickety, imperfect fit between word and world" (*Discrepant Engagement* 19). The "video style" effectively creolizes the technologies of the western world, here represented by computer and television, and infuses them with a spiritual significance that has its roots in African culture.

The central piece that deals with the origin of the video style and why it is linked to Sycorax is "X/Self's Xth Letters from the Thirteen Provinces," which appears in both versions of *X/Self* (the 1987 edition and the one published in *Ancestors* in 2001) and also as "Letter Sycorax" in *Middle Passages* (1992). In this poem, Prospero's machine, the computer, is inhabited by and engages in dialogue with Sycorax, the spirit of African survival. In a direct analogy to "Nametracks," the poem becomes an act of Caliban's self-definition against the background of his African heritage (Sycorax), on the one hand, and the computer as an icon of "prospero linguage" (*X/S* 84), on the other. The computer becomes the site of struggle. By the end of the poem Caliban succeeds in writing in "nation language." Through Caliban, Sycorax has indeed begun to enter into conversation with Prospero, which points towards the beginning of the "creole cosmos." In this sense, Sycorax enters Prospero. She possesses him in the voodoo understanding of the word. Their conversation becomes communion, and the dissolution of empires finds its utopian dimension in the dissolution of self and other.

The interaction between Sycorax and Prospero also mirrors the relationship between the oral and written tradition in the Caribbean. Moreover, Sycorax and Prospero can be seen to represent the Caribbean imaginary and symbolic respectively. Rhonda Cobham argues that Lacan's paradigms do indeed apply in the Caribbean context, but with a different emphasis. Whereas in the western framework power and language are gendered, aligning the mother with the imaginary and the father with the symbolic, in the Caribbean power is racialized. The symbolic becomes synonymous with whiteness and plantation culture, colonial society and its heirs; the imaginary with blackness, folk culture and the oral tradition. As in Lacanian theory, selfhood in the Caribbean context revolves around the loss of the mother, in this case of Mother Africa as a result of the Middle Passage, which marks the emergence of the Caribbean subject into the (Afro-)creole language of the oral tradition. Cobham goes one step further and argues that in anglophone Caribbean literature, there is a second moment of loss, "the ... voluntary abandonment of the oral tradition to wrest from the white father the literary prerogative of naming that catapults him/her into the text" (51). However, as in "Letter Sycorax," the "nation language" of the oral tradition (Sycorax) informs the standard written language of the master (Prospero) and disrupts its authority. In this sense, orality and writing are no longer polar opposites but situated in a "syncretic relationship" with each other, where the boundaries between the magical and the mundane are blurred (Cobham 44).

In *ConVERSations*, Brathwaite himself states that the "video style" is a fusion of the oral and the written, creating a magical space. In this sense, the "creole cosmos" itself is a magical space, where the Caribbean imaginary (Sycorax) and symbolic (Prospero) merge and commune. Whereas for Cobham only the imaginary is a utopian space, a realm of infinite possibility outside of social meaning (45), Brathwaite's utopia is a socially enacted one and therefore operates on the level of the symbolic. The "creole cosmos" is a magical space precisely because it creates social meaning on the symbolic level but draws its inspiration from the imaginary realm of folk culture and the history of slave resistance. The fact that Brathwaite finds it increasingly impossible to separate his life from his writing emphasizes the importance of the "video style" in his own experiment in "creoleness."

In her essay, "The Word Walking Among Us," Elaine Savory describes Brathwaite's "video-style" writing as a "decolonization of his own poetic style," as a breaking out of the restrictions of genre:

> ... [Brathwaite] has become more and more engaged in reaching an audience outside the Western-educated, and so his place as an icon of middle-class Caribbean literary culture has been questioned. Brathwaite's decolonization of his own poetic style has come at a great cost precisely because postcolonial writing has often affiliated itself in form, if not in content or accent, with prevailing Eurocentric identities of poetry, plays, fiction or criticism and theory. (125)

His works increasingly challenge western paradigms and the very idea of the book, creating "a testament of dissidence with respect to the West" (Torres-Saillant, *Caribbean Poetics* 143). In this sense, the project of the "video style" itself is a form of maroon resistance or of "concrete utopia." The "video style" is in many ways a means to "speak different ways of thinking, manifest changed histories and other environments" (Reiss, *Against Autonomy* 313). Moreover, the "video style" emerges as Brathwaite's own version of magical realism. His two-volume *MR* (2002), which won the Casa de las Americas Prize, provides an extended discussion of this topic. *MR* is based on a shorter essay, "MR," published in 1997, which summarizes his main ideas on the subject and will serve as the basis for my discussion.

Since the mid-1990s, Brathwaite has been reflecting on what he perceives are two literary traditions in the Americas, which are often thought of as separate: realism, which he calls the "Sisyphus" tradition, and magic realism, which he calls the "Eldorado" tradition. He argues that the split between realism and magic realism conventionally corresponds to the split between the anglophone Caribbean and Latin America, between islands and mainland. Sisyphus "represents our 'reality' of stasis & emprison — the literature of negative catastrophe" ("MR" 16). Eldorado, on the other hand, "remains close to the hope? the dream of a ?New World" ("MR" 2), which Brathwaite also refers to as "the optimistic creative rascal of (New World) encounter — the dream & pressure of metaphor breaking out of the prison s/hell to par ticipate in a literature (and in both cases orature) of optimistic catastrophe — catharsis. . ." ("MR" 16).

The negative reality of Sisyphus echoes Orlando Patterson's novel *The Children of Sisyphus* (1964), which describes life in the harsh and uncompromising environment of the Kingston Dungle. Eldorado refers to the myth of the same name that has been interpreted in vastly different ways among the writers of the region. V. S. Naipaul, for example, sees it as a metaphor for the colonization and exploitation of the region, whereas writers from the Spanish Caribbean recognize the utopian implications of the myth. One writer who for Brathwaite manages to bridge the gap between anglophone realism and Hispanic utopia is Wilson Harris. His work focuses extensively on the Eldorado story, but unlike other anglophone writers he explores its magical or utopian dimension and is, therefore, classed by many critics as an anglophone magic realist. In this sense, his example indicates that the division between realism and magic realism along language borders does not hold and that the relationship between the two is a lot more complex.

For Harris, Eldorado "possesses [an] archetypal equation between place and placelessness" (utopia meaning "no place") and thus creates a link between a magical and a utopian reality ("New Preface to *Palace of the Peacock*" 55). He argues that "El Dorado is fabulous but it is not only a legend of relived memory and the City of God one seeks everywhere"; rather, Eldorado always contains a shadow or Sisyphus aspect, which is the "grave and blood-stained canvas of greed for gold and territory across centuries" (55). In this sense, Eldorado has the quality of a "concrete utopia." Even though Brathwaite makes frequent reference to such well-established magic realist writers as Gabriel García Márquez, his own version of magical realism departs radically from that of Márquez and others. Whereas mainstream magic realism works largely within the boundaries of European prose forms, such as the novel and the short story, Brathwaite's magical realism is a radical formal as well as thematic experiment. It is, in other words, synonymous with his "Sycorax video style" as the **"surface of the txt reflexts the 'magical' . . . underground or submerged fracture of 'reality' in order to catch/xpress its wound & heel — its wound & healing nature"** ("MR" 18). The underground presence of Sycorax, Namsetoura, and other expressions of the imaginary, when rupturing the flow of the text on the page, creates the magical reality that is the result of a "COLLISION OF CULTURES" ("MR" 24). I want to argue that Brathwaite's work is magic realist in the sense that it attempts to create a new reality that draws on the magical powers of the Caribbean imaginary.

What is new about looking at Brathwaite's writing in terms of utopian thinking is that his life and work question the conventional meaning of utopian, which always resonates with the notion of impossible and unrealistic daydreams. In a very tangible and literal sense, his "work tries to create a world" (Brathwaite, "Forward" 5 qtd. in Torres-Saillant, *Caribbean Poetics* 139). His metaphors "are alive and manifest vital actualities: the actual process of cultural creation making new experience of place" (Reiss, *Against Autonomy* 296). Brathwaite's writing is not so much literature in the narrow sense of a text confined to the space between the book covers but rather an expression of what Timothy Reiss terms "fictive imagination" in the sense of "not fictional . . . but *making*" (*Against Autonomy* 183). Exploring the increasingly close relationship between his writing and his political and cultural projects becomes an important task. The "fictive imagination" is thus a vital component of Brathwaite's understanding of magical realism ("we can't in any meaningful way separate 'literary' from 'world'" ("MR" 6)).

This study of Brathwaite's "video-style" works is by no means exhaustive, nor can it be, given the amount of material produced by the poet. Rather, this book is an attempt to trace a development in his writing and remains selective in the choice of works discussed. Therefore, the reader will find no discussion of, for example, the new version of *DreamStories* or smaller "video" works such "Scapeghosts." I have also decided not to add individual sections on *MR*/"MR" and *Golokwati 2000*, which could have been placed in chapter six as they are similar in style and theme to *ConVERSations* and *Barabajan Poems*. I feel that this would have resulted in unnecessary repetitiveness.

Brathwaite's ideas on magical realism pervade the whole of my discussion of his "video style," and I refer to them throughout this study. The ideas that fed into the writing of *Golokwati 2000* are also dealt with in Brathwaite's *Born to Slow Horses*, and a discussion of the "Golokwati gathering" and its metaphorical echoes seems better placed in connection with this book as its difference in style throws a new light on the notion of "public gathering." As there is only so much space in a book, I have chosen an in-depth reading of selected representative works over an encyclopedic approach.[11]

# Chapter 1
# X/Self
# and the (Re)invention of the "Creole Cosmos"

## 1.1. "Your thunder has come home": The First Cosmology

*X/Self* (*X/S*), first published individually in 1987 and "reinvented," as Brathwaite puts it, in *Ancestors* (2001) together with *Mother Poem* and *Sun Poem*, is a transitional work that I would situate between Brathwaite's writing before the "time of salt" and his subsequent "video-style" books. Its publication in 1987 falls just within the "time of salt," which begins in 1986, but is not yet stylistically affected by its impact on Brathwaite's creativity. The first version of *X/Self* still belongs to what he calls the first or "that original ?edenic cosmology," the time before the onset of trauma ("An excerpt from Limbo" 110). However, the poem already shows signs of a more radical approach to the presentation of words on the page, especially in its final section, which anticipates the more open form characteristic of the "video style."

*X/Self* is also the first work in Brathwaite's oeuvre that reflects on the emergence of the "creole cosmos." Whereas *The Arrivants* (1973), *Mother Poem* (1977) and *Sun Poem* (1982) focused on a particularly African-Caribbean identity, *X/Self* moves towards a cross-cultural vision that includes a diversity of European, Amerindian and Asian/

Middle Eastern perspectives. *X/Self* thus marks the beginning of a new creative period in Brathwaite's writing, a reading of his work that he himself indicates in an interview with Stewart Brown: "In fact **X/Self** is the beginning of another series of things. It is a junction, and of course there are summation parts of it but there is also, for the first time, a significant Amerindian presence in **X/Self** . . . . Technically its not really so much summation as another possible direction into which we have to define ourselves" (86). Unlike Brathwaite's earlier work, *X/Self* sets the Caribbean into a global context, deterritorializing the idea of creolization and opening it to the possibility of becoming a world order model.

Structured in five sections, *X/Self* describes a journey through space, from the center to the margins of empire, which is paralleled by a journey through time, from the Roman empire to the neocolonial world. This movement, however, is not linear. In the first poem, "Letter from Roma," the journey begins in ancient Rome, from where the emperor's nephew is sent to the "thirteen provinces" (*X/S* 1) on the margins of the empire, echoing the thirteen provinces of Canada, Saudi Arabia, and various other parts of the old colonial and neocolonial world. There the emperor's nephew is to pacify "rebellious tribes," whose presence in the poem suggests the imminent collapse of Rome. The tribes are not referred to as such but are described as "glinting terrorists / . . . coiling new shining cobras among the paddy fields" (*X/S* 4), which associates them with the Vietcong. Consequently, the Roman empire, suddenly transported into the twentieth century, is indirectly identified with the United States, which throughout Brathwaite's work appears as a neocolonial power. As one version of the "thirteen provinces" is located in the Middle East, the poem also foreshadows the realities of the post-9/11 world and creates a link to Brathwaite's recent post-9/11 writing such as *Words Need Love Too* and *Born to Slow Horses*.

The "terrorists" appear again in section IV as the maroons. The association with modern guerrilla warfare, "terrorism" in the eyes of the west, links the rebelling tribes and the Vietcong of "Letter from Roma" with the maroons in the poem "Stone" of section IV of *X/Self*:

> we are not taken lightly in our cups
> or in our sleeping bags shocked by surprise
> the sentinels along our lifeline ledge of echoes
>
> come down the hill at sunrise with eyes that red the dark

> m16s that are not
> crutches
> though we might hold them o so casual against our sides (*X/S* 93)

Here the maroons, like the tribes of "Letter from Roma," have moved into the twentieth century. Although maroon societies still exist in the Americas today, the context here, as throughout *X/Self*, is global. Maroon resistance becomes part of a global resistance against neocolonial hegemony and the modern — capitalist — plantation. Thus in "Stone," the maroons are also associated with the Rastafarians whose messiah is the Ethiopian Emperor Haile Selassie I, the "Lion of Judah" ("at the bottom of this high world high above it all we draw / the lion" (*X/S* 93)). Despite their orientation towards Africa as a promised land, the Rastafarians, like the maroons, represent a genuine New World, i.e. creole, identity, since both relate to social and environmental conditions unique to the New World. As alternative communities they create utopian space within contemporary Caribbean society and also function on a wider scale as utopian world-order models. Both the maroons and the Rastafarians occur again and again in Brathwaite's work as agents of the world's dispossessed and, therefore, not as terrorists but as freedom fighters.

In "Salt," the first poem of section II, the rebellious tribes of "Letter from Roma" briefly appear in their original historical context, for example as the Visigoths, led by Caesar's Gallic opponent, Vercingetorix, "the arvernin creole / chieftain" (*X/S* 6), only to be taken back into the present where they are associated with twentieth-century opponents to western power, such as Che Guevara and Fidel Castro. This interlacing of different times in *X/Self* functions as a "labyrinth of past/present/future," a term Christine Pagnoulle borrows from Wilson Harris's novel *Carnival* (1985) (*The Carnival Trilogy* 28). In her reading of *X/Self*, Pagnoulle argues that "disregarding chronological succession, literature of this kind superimposes various layers of history and myth through allusions, borrowings or word plays" (449). With regard to his discussion of magical realism Brathwaite expresses a similar idea. He describes the Eldorado tradition as a "vision . . . which is not predictably 'clear', 'straight', . . . linear', but . . . lateral if anything, prismatic certainly. . . " ("MR" 7).

In his notes to *X/Self*, Brathwaite himself refers to this prismatic technique as "magical montage" (*X/S* 115), which combines the ideas of magical realism and modernist montage.[1] Using this technique, *X/Self* not only explores time as a continuum without any fixed center

## Chapter 1

but also describes a geography of empire in which the distinctions between center and margin gradually disappear. During the course of *X/Self*, the reader begins to realize that the emperor's nephew does not travel to the margins of the Roman empire or to any of the aforementioned thirteen provinces, but to the Caribbean. Thus the imperial map, too, becomes a labyrinth. By the end of *X/Self* we have entered a world of cross-cultural interchange in which there is no center or in which the center can be anywhere. In this sense, *X/Self* constructs a concept of time and space as "a labyrinth in which there is no fixed centre" (Pagnoulle 449), thus achieving the dissolution of empires that Brathwaite envisions as the heart of the "creole cosmos."

In the first instance, however, *X/Self* does not present the "creole cosmos" as utopia. Rather, as Brathwaite himself writes in *ConVERSations*, the dissolution of the old empires gives rise to new configurations of power, new empires and new forms of slavery:

> . . . as soon as the center of power begins to disintegrate, it does not follow, as we have since seen in the former Soviet Union's empire, that ancillary freedom follows . . .
>
> What often happens is that a new forum of feudalism, a new form of barbarity comes into the world . . . . (*C* 118)

"Salt" presents the "creole cosmos" as the beginning of a new imperial world order:

> Rome burns
> and our slavery begins
>
> herod herodotus the tablets of moses are broken
> the soft spoken
>
> whips are uncoiled on the rhine on the rhone on the tiber
> severus the unlocked tiger of wounds lacerate me (*X/S* 5)

## X/Self and the (Re)invention of the "Creole Cosmos"

Here the "creole cosmos" appears as an expression of the chaos that ensued at the collapse of the Roman empire when the (then known) world was momentarily decentralized in the breakdown of imperial order. In this context, section II of *X/Self* also anticipates Samuel P. Huntington's reading of the post-cold war world. In *The Clash of Civilizations and the Remaking of World Order* (1996), Huntington criticizes the notion of a post-cold war global harmony suggested by Francis Fukuyama in his vision of the "end of history." Huntington observes the opposite, an increase in conflict and fundamentalism and new formations of power relations:

> The illusion of harmony at the end of the Cold War was soon dissipated by the multiplication of ethnic conflicts and "ethnic cleansing," the breakdown of law and order, the emergence of new patterns of alliance and conflict among states, the resurgence of neo-communist and neo-fascist movements, intensification of religious fundamentalism.... (32)

In a similar way, this is what happens in section II of *X/Self*. The fall of Rome gives rise to new forms of oppression: the Holy Roman Empire, modern imperialism, industrialization and global capitalism. Of course, implicitly Huntington's statement also anticipates the post-9/11 world.

Brathwaite's work is fundamentally concerned with alternatives to these forms of oppression, and the presence of Vercingetorix in the poem points to a vision of an alternative world order with potentially utopian qualities. The Gallic chieftain is one of many personae who appear as creole or of non-European origin in *X/Self*. In his notes to "Salt," Brathwaite writes:

> Many of the personae from 'the Ancient World' who appear in this sequence (and in the poem generally) are black, African, slave, brown, creole, Latin, Asian, Alexandrine or Byzantine (or reputedly so; though sometimes, for various reasons, denied of this in some cahiers), for instance:
> *herod, moses, severus . . . , nikarios, saladin, othello, vercingetorix; che, kismet, ho chi minh, julia, aaron, nancy* (ananse); *naphtali, tutankhammen, aesop, alcmar* (alcman), *socrates, mohammet; ayub khan,*

# Chapter 1

> *shiva, mahatma gandhi, legba l'ouverture, hirohito.*
> (*X/S* 113)

As Brathwaite reclaims these personae from western historiography, they assume the function of the imaginary as outlined in the previous chapter, whose presence unsettles the authority of the dominant culture.

Another creole persona not mentioned in the above list but of crucial importance to the poem is Hannibal. Hannibal, who set off from Carthage in northern Africa to cross the Alps with his elephants and invade Rome, represents the most poignant intrusion of the imaginary in *X/Self*. The poem "Alph," the last poem in section II, describes "Hannibal heavily crossing the alphs" (*X/S* 51). This is not only an allusion to the historical Hannibal's crossing of the Alps but also to the subversion of the imperial language, here represented by the Greek letter *alpha*, by Brathwaite's version of Hannibal. This crossing or creolization of the imperial language is elsewhere in *X/Self* described as the ascendancy of the "dialect of the tribes" (*X/S* 29). This ascendancy of marginalized languages and their movement to the center is linked to the rising of the tribes described in "Salt" ("the tribes are arising like mulled wine" (*X/S* 6)), which marks the decline of the Roman empire and by extension the end of any form of imperial control. Consequently, the monolithic imperial language is broken up into a continuum of lects.[2]

During the course of the poem, Hannibal becomes a Caribbean persona,[3] the descendant of slaves mutilated by plantation work, seeking spiritual empowerment in voodoo:

> was his father born lame bit by machines crushed by a god
> would the handclaps of vodoun have roused
> him could his drums dream these empires
>
> ump (*X/S* 51)

In the 1982 version of *Sun Poem*, "Alph" appears under the title "Blue Loa." A *loa* is a spirit of Haitian voodoo, which is itself an example of a creolized religion, fusing African and Christian elements. The association of Hannibal with voodoo demonstrates Brathwaite's perception of creolization as a global phenomenon. Hannibal also foreshadows the coming of the African-Caribbean god, Xango, at the end of the poem, the messiah of *X/Self*. The creole presence in *X/Self* subverts the west's assumption of cultural superiority and creates a space for cultural crossfertilization. In this sense, the creole personae transcend their roles of both agents and antagonists of empire and become genuine alternative models, anticipating the utopian persona of Xango. The reading of "Salt," therefore, shows how the "creole cosmos" lies at the intersection between reality and possibility. The chaos that ensues at the fall of Rome is an instance of Bloch's "darkness of the lived moment" (*PH* 1: 12), which utopian consciousness seeks to illuminate. In this sense, the creole personae represent such a utopian consciousness, directing it towards a world without domination.

Apart from the political vision of creolization, *X/Self* enacts in particular the polyphonic and "tidalectic" aspect of Brathwaite's thinking. The poem is largely presented as a sequence of voices. X/Self, the protagonist of the poem, assumes these voices as he journeys backwards and forwards in space and time in search of his "unknown undiscovered self" (Rohlehr, "The Rehumanization" 265). Whereas section II views imperialism from within, i.e. its speakers are all situated at the imperial center, section III moves to the "margins," to the Americas, to portray the effects of imperialism from the far side of the Atlantic. In turn, the center as a focal point disappears as the conquistadors' metropolitan identity becomes unmoored, deterritorialized, heterogeneous.

"Titan" depicts this poignantly. "Titan" identifies imperialism as one particular form of what Wilson Harris calls an "*imposed* unity that actually subsists on the suppression of others" (*The Womb of Space* xviii). The poem opens with the journey of the conquistadors across the Atlantic Ocean and proceeds to describe the destruction of the Aztec capital Tenochtitlan by the Spaniards. (Temixtitan or Temextitan are alternative spellings the Spaniards used (Cortés 207), so the poem's title is a reference to the city of the Aztecs as well as the Greek myth of the Titans — of which more below.) X/Self, who assumes the voice of Cortez, illustrates the conquistadors' notion of cultural superiority at the beginning of the poem in images of fire and drought penetrating the whole of the Americas: "Now they burn west / across the christian ocean humming high above the high drift / of the harmattan" (*X/S* 61). The idea of burning west implies "burning westward," from Europe to the Americas. It also implies the conquistadors' "burning" desire to possess the riches of the New World. Furthermore, the word "burning" has a very literal meaning, referring to the destruction of the Aztec capital by fire. The metaphorical fire that drives the conquis-

## Chapter 1

tadors across the sea becomes a very real instrument of destruction. In this context, the "christian ocean" resonates with the history of conquest and the slave trade, connecting Europe, Africa and the Americas across the centuries into the present.

In contrast to "christian ocean," "harmattan" functions as an alternative connecting meridian between Africa and the Caribbean, both as a meteorological and a cultural phenomenon. Brathwaite describes this connection on numerous occasions throughout his work. The following passage is taken from an interview with the poet, "Geological Connection/Poetic Perception," conducted by M. J. Fenwick and Vincent O. Cooper in 1995:

> When I returned to the Caribbean from Africa, I went to live in St. Lucia, and standing on the promontory there at St. Lucia on the morne, I saw this mist coming from the Atlantic towards the island. . . . And as this mist, or this cloud, approached, I could feel on my skin a dryness, a desiccation which I had been aware of in Africa, and in Africa they called it the "harmattan," this dry wind that comes up in the Sahara. And it suddenly occurred to me as a metaphor that this wind was the same harmattan from Africa which was, in fact, reaching the Caribbean. Now that's a very important discovery because it right away showed me or internalized for me the fact that there was a geological connection between Africa and the Caribbean. (82)

Throughout Brathwaite's work, the African-Caribbean connection represents an alternative world order to that of European domination. In *X/Self*, "harmattan" becomes the utopian possibility of "christian ocean," which stands for the Atlantic world at large. Moreover, the word "harmattan" presages the arrival of Xango in section V of *X/Self* and encodes, as we will see, an alternative to the history of imperialism.

At its first appearance, the fire in "Titan" is associated with Christian elements, and Christianity itself becomes an instrument of subjugation and dominance. The voice of Cortez describes the initial attempt to conquer Tenochtitlan in images that recall the Pentecostal experience:

> and so we fell upon them on the day of pentecost

> more than five. no fifty thousand perished in that lake
> alone along the saltway in the thirteenth year
> the cycle of the shears and crossroads. the parrots
> crying all night long
>
> and ever as i turned to face them. i
> came back full of arrows darts and stones
> for there was water all around & they could hit. us with impunity

(*X/S* 61–62)

The scene described here refers in part to the *Noche Triste*, the initial defeat of Cortez and his army at Tenochtitlan in 1519 (Todorov 54–55). The scene foreshadows both Brathwaite's fictional Cortez's catharsis through an embracing of his doubles later in the poem, here prefigured in his openness to the new, which profoundly affects him ("i / came back full of arrows darts and stones"). This defeat in turn is mirrored in the later defeat of the Aztecs in the face of the European war machine.

In the battle for Tenochtitlan, Cortez associates himself and his army with the Pentecostal tongues of flame, the Holy Spirit, and thus with the agents of divine authority. This identification implies not only an act of hubris but also of domination through the medium of language, through the *alpha* as yet uncrossed by Hannibal. In the biblical story of Pentecost, the Holy Spirit causes the disciples to speak the word of God in a universal language. Through this universal language imparted by God, which, in a colonial context, can be read as a form of divine authorization of the Christian world to rule over the non-Christian, Europe assumes a position of cultural superiority over "the people without history" (Wolf 4–5). Consequently, the only way "the people without history" can enter into history is through the agency of Europe. The poem "The visibility trigger," which appears in section II of *X/Self*, depicts this as a single violent act that begins imperialism. In the poem, the colonizers enter an African village and fell the silk cotton tree, the seat of ancestral spirits, to replace it with the Christian cross. The uprooted silk cotton tree "crashed / into history" (*X/S* 50), and African versions of history are obliterated and subsumed into the master narrative of European history.

Cortez's hegemonic action is intensified by the exploitation of his own deification by the Aztecs. In the poem, the voice of Cortez says: "i will let them worship the head of my horse / as they have worshipped mol and moon and white and yucatan / in the house of the dead landlord" (*X/S* 62). In his annotations to *X/Self*, Brathwaite points out that "Cortez thought (for some time, at least . . .) that the Aztecs he was conquering were deifying . . . him. There is some evidence . . . that they were making icons of his horses — never seen before in the Americas. And he himself became identified with *akbal*, god of death and the underworld . . ." (*X/S* 124). Brathwaite further suggests that Akbal is the "Aztec god of the underworld" (*X/S* 125), although this is only partially so. The god the Aztecs associated with death and the underworld is Mictlantecuhtli. Akbal, on the other hand, is the name of a day in the Mayan calendar. The Mayas identified each day and month with a certain deity whose traits, either beneficent or malign, influenced the day or month associated with them. Akbal is often translated as "darkness" (the god of death wears the glyph inscribed on his forehead), which would create a link between Akbal and Mictlantecuhtli in the poem (Sharer and Traxler 742).[4] The reference to Akbal indicates the presence of Mayan culture in the poem, further fracturing any form of homogeneous cultural identity.

In the poem, Cortez challenges Akbal's authority:

for i have determined
to destroy these mosques i call them. steps
leading down

to growl and grim and slaughter. steps
leading down
to mouth and growl and akbal. (*X/S* 62)

Cortez's challenge of Akbal becomes the ultimate act of hubris in "Titan." In Greek mythology, Cronus, king of the Titans, swallows his offspring in order to prevent the usurpation of his throne. In *The Greek Myths* (1955), Robert Graves points out that initially the king was annually sacrificed in the cornfield as part of a fertility ritual. However, "by the times to which these myths refer, kings had been permitted to prolong their reigns . . . and offer annual boy victims in their stead; hence Cronus is pictured as eating his own sons to avoid dethronement" (41–42). The aspect of human sacrifice links the story of the Titans and their dethronement by Jupiter to the conquest of Mexico. The Aztecs become equated with the Titans, the Spaniards, who found the Aztec ritual of human sacrifice abhorrent, with the Olympians. Moreover, the arrival of the Spaniards coincided with an Aztec belief according to which a world age was coming to an end. Cortez's challenging of Akbal, who in the poem comes to stand for the ritual of human sacrifice, mirrors the Olympian challenge of the Titans.

In the myth of the Titans, the Cyclopes coded into the poem with a special reference to their underworld habitat, the volcano, the realm of chthonic fire, are released from Tartarus by Zeus. The Aetna of the original myth here becomes the New World's Popocatepetl, and the god whom they serve is Akbal, the New World version of Vulcan, club-footed like his European twin. Brathwaite describes the chthonic realm in his notes to "Titan":

> *the house of the dead landlord*: the world of the dark was also the place of birth, being, bones, origins. Disease, disasters, death also came (escaped) from this Mictlan and it was the responsibility of the priests of this House to suck 'afflicting darkness' back down into the underworld. In the poem, Cortez is both searcher for bones and origins, and is himself the afflicting darkness (of conquest) .... (*X/S* 124)

Through this descent into the underworld Cortez becomes linked to Quetzalcoatl:

> ...Quetzalcoatl is depicted as...the restorer of human life through a cosmic dive into the underworld, Mictlan, where he outwits the lord of the dead, Mictlantecuhtli, to recover the bones of the ancestors. In this story, Mictlantecuhtli prepares a death trap for Quetzalcoatl. Quetzalcoatl falls to his death, but then he revives himself to escape Mictlan, meanwhile revitalizing the bones of the dead. ("Quetzalcoatl" 153)

Originally the "patron deity of the Toltec empire," Quetzalcoatl had to flee from Tollan but promised to return to restore his kingdom (153).[5] Whereas Quetzalcoatl releases life-giving energies from the chthonic realm of Mictlan, becoming a messianic figure, Cortez releases its destructive aspects by becoming an agent of Akbal, if not the god himself: "this club foot god that haunts me / makes me vomit out destroy" (*X/S* 62–63). In the myth of Zeus's revolt against Cronus, the destructive energies released are the Cyclopes freed from Tartarus. Cortez, similarly, unleashes the forces of the underworld on Aztec

*Chapter 1*

culture, thus effecting its destruction. In this context, the one-eyed Cyclopes become an apt image for imperial Europe's lack of cross-cultural, double, vision.[6]

In spite of this, Cortez's descent into the underworld, ultimately, has cathartic effects. He opens himself to the presence of the other, thus far eclipsed, when he becomes aware of the beauty of Tenochtitlan:

> and there was fruit and native   roses and great cisterns of
> sweet   water
> and birds of many breeds and colours that came into the lake and
> gold
> enough to
>
> build la scala and the eiffel   tour i swear i had not
> seen or heard   or even
> dreamed of lands more beautiful than these not in the whole of
>
> africa
>
> i stood there looking out as if i had discovered the pacific
> though there was yet no thought of andes inca atahuallpa darien
>
> and so i overturned their idols rolled
>
> them down the stairs and   stare out at you from your
> postage   stamps
>
> i
>
> cortez condor clubfoot
>
> evening star
>
> (*X/S* 63)

## X/Self and the (Re)invention of the "Creole Cosmos"

In *The Conquest of Mexico* (1993), Hugh Thomas points out that due to the fierce resistance of Montezuma's successor Cuauhtémoc (Guatomec), Cortez was unable to conquer Tenochtitlan without completely destroying it.[7] The destruction of the city, at least on the fictional level of the poem, becomes Cortez's revenge, not only for his defeat in the *Noche Triste* but also for his own openness to the other culture. The passage of the poem that begins "i swear / i had not / seen or heard / or even / dreamed of lands more beautiful than these" is an almost exact transcription from Bernal Díaz's *Discovery and Conquest of Mexico*: "I say again that I stood looking at it and thought that never in the world would there be discovered other lands such as these, for at the time there was no Peru, nor any thought of it. Of all these wonders that I then beheld to-day all is overthrown and lost, nothing left standing" (191). Hugh Thomas argues that the city "was not destroyed by chance": "It was the consequence of a deliberate policy, carefully and methodically carried through, with all the forcefulness of European war, and with no care for the ruin of a masterpiece of urban design" (503).

The destruction of the city can also be read as Cortez's attempt to destroy the unacknowledged other within himself. Brathwaite's fictional Cortez, however, is aware that there is no logic in his desire for destruction, and this lack of logic is expressed on a syntactical level in the passage immediately following the account of his descent into the realm of Akbal: "*and so I overturned their idols*" [emphasis mine] (*X/S* 63). The broken logic in the syntax — there is no reason why the recognition of beauty should be its destruction — reflects the fracturing of Cortez's personality, his opening to the "arrows darts and stones" of New World culture. In this sense, "Titan" reflects Harris's notion of "cross-cultural capacity" or cross-cultural dialogue (*The Womb of Space* xvii). Cortez is in constant dialogue with his doubles, Akbal, Cronus and Quetzalcoatl, through which he finally arrives at an awareness of self.

On a formal level, Cortez's transformation of consciousness is rendered in an open field composition.[8] The conquistador's descent into the underworld is mirrored in the typescript of page 63 of *X/Self*, reproduced above, which Brathwaite describes as Cortez's "'descent' into my pictopoem of the temple of Akbal" (*X/S* 124). The "pictopoem" is rendered as a conical structure, suggesting a downward movement. Words such as "gold," "africa," "evening star" are isolated from the syntax. In an analysis of a poem by William Carlos Williams, Nathaniel Mackey refers to this technique of singling out words on the page as "disrupting ... a tightness that would stress each word's value not as an entity in and of itself but as a placeholder, a cog in some larger pattern (sentence, phrase, line, and so on)" (*Discrepant Engagement* 124). In "Titan," isolated words function as "an assault on whatever routine narcotizes perception," as do the line arrangements that disrupt the linear reading process (*Discrepant Engagement* 125). Thus the lines can be read horizontally as well as vertically, giving the impression of simultaneous perception.[9] This interaction of form and content plays a vital part in Brathwaite's font and layout experiments that characterize his "video style" after *X/Self*.

The reference to Keats in the same passage points to another vital component of the "video style": that of the subterranean, intertextual echoes or of "magical montage." In his notes to *X/Self*, Brathwaite cites Keats's poem "On first looking into Chapman's Homer," where Keats speaks of Balboa, the first European to set eyes on the Pacific from a mountain peak in what is now Panama. Keats, however, replaces Balboa's name with that of Cortez:

> *darien*: Titan/Cortez is here thinking of John Keats's poetic error in 'On first looking into Chapman's Homer', mistaking Balboa for Cortez:
>
>> Then felt I like some watcher of the skies
>> When a new planet swims into his ken;
>> Or like stout Cortez when with eagle eyes
>> He star'd at the Pacific—and all his men
>> Look'd at each other with a wild surmise—
>> Silent, upon a peak in Darien. (*X/S* 125)

The reference to Keats reveals Brathwaite's interest in stories, traditions of storytelling and their relationship to one another, which the notes attempt to illuminate. By fast-forwarding Cortez from Bernal Díaz's account to Keats' poem, Brathwaite emphasizes a "tidalectic" movement between texts and intertexts, plunging them into "the labyrinth of past/present/future" to achieve the prismatic — magical realist — effect he regards as the main component of the Eldorado tradition.

Cortez's encounter with the New World is an unsettling one, disrupting a system of perception informed by European notions of cultural superiority. Cortez succumbs to the New World as his person, which is an expression of the European fiction of the unified self, disintegrates and opens to embrace other, hitherto alien, identities.

## X/Self and the (Re)invention of the "Creole Cosmos"

In this sense, Cortez, too, becomes a creole persona, a micro "creole cosmos." I have devoted such a lengthy reading to "Titan" because the poem marks a turning point in *X/Self*. From here the "creole cosmos" moves towards its utopian possibility. Cortez goes beyond the creole personae of the Old World because we actually witness him undergoing a change of consciousness and developing a New World identity. He moves from repressing otherness to someone who opens himself to otherness, whereas Hannibal and Vercingetorix undergo no such change. They are always already in a state of "arrived-at Being." Cortez, on the other hand, undergoes a process of transformation that takes him from the "darkness of the lived moment" to the light of utopian consciousness. Wilson Harris calls this potentially transformative openness to the other "[t]he wounds... of the Creole" and argues that "[c]reoleness... harbour[s] within itself a potential for the renascence of community" ("Creoleness" 238). In this sense, "Titan" moves from a conflict of origins, from totalizing cultural assumptions, towards the birth of a new, creole, community.

Section IV of *X/Self* describes this journey in detail. "Citadel," for example, offers a series of images that epitomize a "tidalectic" movement, on the one hand, and "arrived-at Being," on the other: the African-Caribbean deity, Yemajaa, "goddess of the waves, the salt waters, of the Middle Passage" (*X/S* 130), the coconut travelling across the sea in search of a space to take root in, the "cup" of the poetic word and the web of the African-Caribbean trickster, Ananse. As goddess of the sea and the Middle Passage, Yemajaa becomes a figure of exile. She reflects the "titalectic" movement of the sea that is reiterated, but also transcended, in the drifting coconut:

> a long way the one eyed stare of the coconut will travel
> steered by its roots what its milk teaches
>
> till its stalk with its flag and its cross
> sword its mailed head and chained feet
>
> walks over the arawak beaches (*X/S* 100)

With the coconut taking root on an island beach, the Caribbean becomes a space of "arrived-at Being."

The image of the "cup" of the poetic word represents the space towards which Yemajaa, the coconut, in fact all things adrift, travel and unravel:

> but here in the cup of my word
> on the lip on my eyelid of light
> like a star in its syllable socket
> there is a cripple crack and hobble
> whorl
> of colour eye
> at last   cool harbour
> ....................
> ulysses cuts his white teeth towards it
> as does my father and the caribs and yemajaa ...
>
> it is a beginning
>
> forests canefields move over the waters towards it
> seeds of our salt fruit cashew seagrape fatpork macca quickstick
>
> palm
>
> with its blind tendril freedom (X/S 99–100)

The root space towards which the unmoored islands travel is the beginning ("it is a beginning") of the Caribbean as a space of *Heimat*. The cultural fragments of the region are gathered together into the poet's vision, represented by the cup, like ingredients of a unique Caribbean dish. The cup of the word thus represents the cultural wholeness expressed in Brathwaite's *Caribbean Man in Space and Time*. The different elements that come together in his vision comprise all cultural components of the region. The cup is, therefore, an image of decentralized power or the dissolution of empires, reminiscent of the overflowing cup of the empire at the beginning of *X/Self* ("the tribes are arising like mulled wine" (X/S 6)).

The citadel of the poem's title mirrors the image of the cup. As "christophe's citadel" it is a reference to the Haitian revolution, which began as a slave revolt led by Toussaint L'Ouverture in the wake of the French revolution in the eighteenth century. It finally resulted in Haiti's independence from France in 1804.[10] Toussaint L'Ouverture was taken prisoner by the French in 1802 and deported to France where he died in prison. It was his successor, Jean-Jacques Dessalines, who finally defeated the French in 1804. Henri Christophe, to whom Brathwaite refers in "christophe's citadel," was Dessalines's successor. Christophe ruled the north of the island after its split into two separate states in the wake of a conflict between the mulatto minority and the black ex-slave majority. Christophe's regime was in many ways just as repressive as colonial rule:

> ... Christophe had himself crowned king and created a black nobility. He used military force in an attempt to re-invigorate the plantation system.... A type of feudalism was imposed, with large plantations run by military and state officers, and worked by strictly supervised labourers. This version of militarised agriculture generated large surpluses, and the revenue was used to strengthen the army and build extensive fortifications in preparation for an expected French invasion. The most spectacular of these was the formidable Citadelle of La Ferrière, built at enormous human cost. (Arthur and Dash 46)

Despite his obvious animosity towards France, Christophe reintroduces European power structures. For this reason, Brathwaite associates him with Charlemagne, arguing that "[b]oth Charlemagne and Henri Christophe were attempting post-imperial imperiums" (*X/S* 117). The citadel of the poem seems to enclose Haiti, isolating or unmooring the island from the rest of the Caribbean and the rest of the world.

The citadel already appears in "Cap," the first poem of section III. In his notes to this poem, Brathwaite, referring to Aimé Césaire's *Cahier d'un retour au pays natal* (*Notebook of a Return to My Native Land*, 1939), describes the fortress as an emblem of a utopian realm of freedom: "*cap*: Cap Haitien, N. Haiti site of Henri Christophe's cidatel.... Aimé Césaire in his *Cahier*, likened the citadel, one of the Seven Wonders of Our New World, to a ship of liberty fronting the Atlantic ('*itself still sailing where the islands float*'— ('Citadel')" (*X/S* 122). The citadel can, therefore, also be read as a stronghold that secures a magical space of freedom and independence, and it is this reading that Césaire, according to Brathwaite, seems to have had in mind.[11]

Finally, the cup of the word becomes the web of Ananse: "and from this tennament this sipple spider space we hold / we make this narrow thread of silver spin the long time of sand" (*X/S* 101). Ananse's web, made of "this narrow thread of silver," gathers together the diverse elements of the Caribbean into the utopian space of *Heimat*. In *Islands* (1969), Ananse figures as "world-maker, word-breaker; / creator" (*Arrivants* 167). Like Sycorax, he breaks the power of Prospero's lan-

*Chapter 1*

guage. In this sense, the magic web of Ananse and the cup of the poet's word foreshadow the dissolution of subject and object in the experience of communion that begins with the arrival of Xango.

Like section I of *X/Self*, section V consists of a single poem, "Xango." "Xango" itself is divided into five parts, mirroring the structure of *X/Self* as a whole. In "Xango," however, there is no more conflict. The poem becomes an expression of *Heimat* as "arrived-at Being." Xango is a spirit of the santería tradition, the Cuban equivalent to Haitian voodoo. African-based Caribbean or Latin American religions are the products of a process of creolization, fusing African, European and sometimes Amerindian elements. Voodoo, which Brathwaite often uses as representative of all African-Caribbean religions, is an inclusive religion and can be read as an expression of a magical — utopian — reality.[12] With Xango, who, as a creole persona, becomes a messenger of utopia, the root of "arrived-at Being" replaces the wandering movement of the quest.

In section 1 of "Xango," conflict, which characterized the beginning of *X/Self*, is replaced by the Xango's lovemaking with Erzulie, Haitian goddess of love:

*Hail*

there is new breath here

*huh*

there is a victory of sparrows

erzulie with green wings

feathers sheen of sperm

*hah*

there is a west wind
sails open eyes the conch shell sings hallelujahs

i take you love at last my love

(*X/S* 107)[13]

## X/Self and the (Re)invention of the "Creole Cosmos"

As he makes love to Erzulie, Xango becomes his own offspring: "a boy with knotted snakes and coffle wires / a child / with water courses valleys clotted blood" (*X/S* 108).

Due to the repression of voodoo in Haiti well into the twentieth century, the *loa* were often disguised and survived in the images of Christian saints. Erzulie is frequently depicted as the Virgin Mary.[14] In this context, the lovemaking of Xango and Erzulie echoes the immaculate conception of the Christian tradition. The *loa's* lovemaking, however, remains in the foreground, portraying voodoo, unlike Christianity, as a liberating and not at all repressive religion with regard to sex. Xango is both God the father and Christ the messiah. The messianic reference occurs at the end of the first part of the poem where the resurrection is invoked: "his childhood of a stone / is rolled away he rings from rebells of the bone his liberated day" (*X/S* 108). Xango acts as Christ the liberator of the oppressed in the poem.

In Christian belief, the messiah prophesies a new heaven and a new earth. The resurrected Christ anticipates the "next world," but this "next world" originally had a concrete utopian, rather than an otherworldly, connotation. Bloch points out that in Jesus' time, "this world" and "the other world" did not designate a geographical division, "but a chronologically successive one in the same arena, situated down here" (*PH* 2: 500). In this sense, the teachings of Jesus aim at liberating the dispossessed and transforming society, turning humanity's earthly existence into an effectively enacted utopia. In section 2 of "Xango," America appears as a new earth in this sense, as realm of freedom from oppression:

> the bison plunge into the thunders river
> hammering the red trail blazing west to chattanooga
>
> destroying de soto francisco coronado
>
> un
> hooking the waggons john
>
> ford and his fearless cow
> boy crews j
>
> p morgan is dead
> coca cola is drowned
>
> the statue of liberty's never been born

## Chapter 1

> manhattan is an island where cows cruise on flowers
>
> (*X/S* 109)

Finally, section 5 of "Xango" marks the end of *X/Self* and the beginning of communion. The section begins with an instance of arrival "after so many twists / after so many journeys / after so many changes" (*X/S* 110). X/Self's wanderings through time and space come to an end as he meets Xango. The poem ends as X/Self is invited to become one with the *loa* in an instance of spirit possession:

> greet
>
> him
> he speaks
> so softly near
>
> you
>
> hear
> him
> he teaches
>
> face
> and faith
> and how to use your seed and soul and lissom
>
> touch
> him
> he will heal
>
> you
>
> word
> and balm
> and water
>
> flow
>
> embrace
> him

## X/Self and the (Re)invention of the "Creole Cosmos"

> he will shatter outwards to your light and calm and history
>
> your thunder has come home
>
> (*X/S* 111)

In a voodoo ceremony, the act of spirit possession involves an exchange of a person's *gros-bon-ange* or personality for that of the *loa*. In the poem, X/Self's *gros-bon-ange* gives in to the voice of Xango and becomes the mouthpiece of the god.[15] The act of possession is a utopian moment, as it brings about the dissolution of the subject-object divide. Cobham argues that in anglophone Caribbean literature trance is used as a medium for accessing and integrating the folk/imaginary aspect of the culture: "The voices introduced in this way speak through the magical properties associated with the folk, but they do so in the service of socially realistic goals" (29). The arrival of the god functions as an act of healing, and the ruptured and fragmented personality of X/Self, indicated by the slash that separates the two halves of his name and mirrored in the voices that find expression through him, takes root in the divinity of Xango. But rather than experiencing the eviction of his soul, X/Self becomes one with the god in an instance of communion, expressed in the poem through the intimacy of "touch him" and "embrace him." In Brathwaite's reinterpretation of voodoo possession, the fragmented self expressed in X/Self's name is made whole through the merging of his X, the beginning of his selfhood, with that of Xango whose name is unruptured.[16]

The experience of communion also extends to the cross-cultural context of *X/Self* as a whole. The risen Christ of "Xango" is a creole messiah. The instance of possession marks the fusion of both personae, Christian and Afro-creole, creating the dissolution of the divide between self and other. As a variation of this dissolution, which represents an instance of "arrived-at Being" or *Heimat*, the merging of European and African-Caribbean culture overcomes the conflict of origins. The typeset of the last page depicts a cross, an image that again links Xango to Christ. Moreover, the cross is the icon of the Haitian *loa* Legba, "god of the threshold, of openings" (*X/S* 114), whose invocation stands at the beginning of every voodoo ceremony. Legba is also the guardian of the *poteau mitan*, the center pole of the sacred chamber of the *houmfort*, the place of worship in voodoo tradition. The center pole represents the *Grand Chemin*, the road that connects the mortal with the divine world. Therefore, like the Christian cross, Legba's cross represents the world axis or world tree.

Implicitly, Damballah, the serpent deity of the voodoo pantheon, makes his first appearance here. Throughout Brathwaite's work, Damballah symbolizes the *Grand Chemin* of cultural traffic between the Old World and the New and between the past and the future, a quality Maya Deren, too, ascribes to him: ". . . Damballah is himself unchanged by life, and so is at once the ancient past and the assurance of the future" (115). In this sense, the *Grand Chemin* describes the route from a place of origin to a place of arrival. The voodoo ceremony in *X/Self* marks the beginning of utopian communion not as a present that disappears again within the movement of time, but as a presence that is in no need of a future. This is an example of the illumination of "the darkness of the lived moment" by utopian consciousness. As an expression of both Christian and African-Caribbean culture the cross comes to stand for a cross-cultural intertwining of opposing elements. The "creole cosmos" can thus be read as a form of *houmfort*, a magical space where the utopian moment of *Heimat* as communion can be achieved. In this sense, Brathwaite creates a vision of the New World that manifests itself in an "aesthetics of hope, vitality and redemption, which may turn out to be the most valuable gift that the New World can offer the Old" (Rohlehr, "The Rehumanization" 290).

## 1.2. Carab the Filth Eater: The Second Cosmology

If the 1987 version of *X/Self* represents "the first cosmology," a vision of the "creole cosmos" before the onset of personal trauma in Brathwaite's life, *X/Self* (2001) represents the poet's vision after the "the psychic disaster slippages of Mexican (86) Shar (88) TTR (90)," as Brathwaite states in a letter to Gordon Rohlehr (qtd. in Rohlehr, "Dream Journeys," *DreamStories* iii). Brathwaite refers to the trilogy of *Mother Poem, Sun Poem* and *X/Self* as *Ancestors* long before its single-volume publication in 2001. The subtitle of this edition states that it is intended as "a Reinvention of *Mother Poem, Sun Poem*, and *X/Self*." This reinvention consists in part of a rewriting of the original poems in the "Sycorax video style" and of an increased use of Brathwaite's nation language idiom as well as a complete revision of the order in which the poems appear. The most significant change to *Mother Poem* and *Sun Poem* is the insertion of additional sections that did not appear in the original publication, altering the tone significantly and integrating the original *Ancestors* into Brathwaite's other "video-style" writings discussed in subsequent chapters of this study.

"Pixie," added to the 2001 version of *Mother Poem*, tells the story of Stephanie or Pixie, who, feeling neglected by her mother, runs away from home. "Pixie" is a montage of poetry, news items, and letters. This arrangement of the text on the page that questions and disrupts received categories of genre is one of the most vital innovations of Brathwaite's "video" writing. "Pixie" also takes the idea of "magical montage," developed in the first version of *X/Self*, one step further, lending the interpenetration of voices, texts and time spheres greater visual impact. Within the context of *Mother Poem* itself, "Pixie" represents a response to "Woo/Dove," which precedes it. In "Woo/Dove," we learn that Stephanie's father has gone to Canada to find work, but he fails to support his family and instead disappears from their lives altogether, while poverty at home in the Caribbean forces the mother to send her daughter into prostitution. In "Pixie," Stephanie is presented as prostituting herself in order to arouse her mother's attention *"whose only interest is to pose in front of the mirror using make-up"* (*Ancestors* 69), as Stephanie complains in a letter to her brother. In the news-item sections of "Pixie" that precede the letter, Stephanie's mother says she is disabled, having suffered from a stroke, and is herself in need of care from her children. In the opening poem of "Pixie," the poet himself gives his own version of events and pins the mother-daughter alienation down to a failure of communication, Stephanie being unable to admit that she keeps "missing the musing mother" (*Ancestors* 60) and the mother not being able to "raise a hand to hit or even kiss / her. because the way she love her" (*Ancestors* 60). The mother in "Pixie," as elsewhere in *Mother Poem*, is synonymous with the island of Barbados itself, as the frequent references to the mother's name, Coral, emphasize (the bedrock of Barbados is made of layers of coral limestone, so the island is Mother Coral).[17] Pixie, on the other hand, represents the Caribbean people, who cannot make their islands their home (culturally and economically) and consequently leave either for Europe or America or, within the islands, to the makeshift housing of the ghetto.

In English folklore, pixies are related to fairies and can be regarded as a European form of the trickster. Pixie thus functions as a trickster, tricking her mother into love and concern by running away from home, thus expressing her own desire to belong. The concern Pixie creates through her absence forces those left behind to search for her body in the "canefield trash" (*Ancestors* 59), which is reminiscent of the rubbish dumps of Brathwaite's and Patterson's Kingston ghetto, including the

## Chapter 1

notion of "human garbage" discussed in Brathwaite's *Trench Town Rock* (see chapter four). The idea of searching for a lost individual in the "canefield trash" implies a historical dimension in the form of a sifting through the fragments of history (the unrecorded splinters of colonial history) in order to arrive at a sense of restored community, represented in the poem by the hoped-for mother-daughter reunion. In the context of Lacanian terminology, the mother is, of course, an expression of the imaginary. As a daughter of the island, Pixie longs to tap into this mother/folk imaginary, and the poem implies that this would give her unmoored self a sense of security, wholeness and direction.

Frequent references to rubbish and pollution create a theme that pervades Brathwaite's whole work and that becomes increasingly urgent in his recent writing concerned with his home in Barbados, CowPastor, and the spirit of Namsetoura he encounters on the land. In line with the concerns of the first versions of *X/Self* and *Mother Poem*, mother and daughter in "Pixie" are part of the wider context of the region's neocolonial dependence on the west. Tourism and environmental pollution are linked to forms of prostitution and represent a concern that echoes not only in *Ancestors* and its earlier versions but also in *Islands, DreamStories, Trench Town Rock* and subsequent works.

As my discussion of Brathwaite's "video style" began with the 1987 version of *X/Self*, I want to focus on this particular revision in more detail rather than discuss *Ancestors* as a whole. *X/Self* (2001), too, has undergone considerable change and resembles only in parts the original edition of 1987. Apart from its arrangement in the "video style," which it has in common with the revised *Mother Poem* and *Sun Poem*, there are now only four instead of five sections. "Letter from Roma" still opens the sequence. Section II has three poems missing, including "Alph," which in *X/Self* (1987) illustrated the creolization of Europe via invasion and via the subversion of its imperial languages (the crossing of its Alps and *alphas*). "The visibility trigger" is also missing from the new version of *X/Self* and thus one aspect of the notion of the world tree or axis, which at the end of *X/Self* (1987) signifies the utopian space of *Heimat*. Sections III and IV have been merged and reduced to only four poems: "Titan," "Palmares" (which appears as "Stone" in *X/Self* (1987)), "X/Self letter from the thirteenth provinces," and "Troia" ("Ice/Nya" of the original part IV). Gone is the coconut that traveled across the Middle Passage towards the Caribbean shores to take root. "Xango," too, has disappeared to give way to "Carab," the last poem of *X/Self* (2001), comprising its fourth section. The structural changes that have been applied to *X/Self* (2001) also drastically alter the poem's message. The

## X/Self and the (Re)invention of the "Creole Cosmos"

remaining parts of this chapter will focus on "Carab," which, in replacing "Xango," elucidates this change in meaning most poignantly.

"Carab" is a revised version of "Crab," a poem that appears at the end of both *Black + Blues* (1977) and *Third World Poems* (1983), the volumes of Brathwaite's so-called "Kingston poetry" of the late 1970s.[18] "Carab" begins as a paraphrase of the creative writing process:

> From this cramp hand
> cripple by candlelight
> a crab scuttles
>
> its mail'd dragonish swords
> its clench armour
> rattle the lame mango leaves
>
> its rome burns the gravel drier
> as it xplores cliffs. lions of grasshopper voices
> shrieking the trees seas
>
> what murderous tomorrows
> salutations of the dead.
> faced ancestors. grey-headed
> knitting off to bed
>
> (*Ancestors* 465)

The poet's hand is cramped or petrified by the loss of creative vision that accompanies the three traumas of his life, as Brathwaite states in "An excerpt from Limbo": "... my writing hand begins to seize up and instead of being the curlew which writes it becomes a fist, and then like a fist of stone and the hand goes heavy like that..." (105). The unsteady light of the candle by which the poet begins "Carab" adds to this loss or dimming of creative vision.[19] The crab is also an animal that lives close to the ground, even in the ground, and in the liminal zone between sea and land. In other words, poetic imagination has become more earthbound and thus closer to lived reality than it was, for example, in *Islands*, where the image used is that of a bird.[20]

As a vessel for the poet's imagination, the crab proceeds to explore the history of European conquest and colonization in the middle sections of "Carab." The crab "stalks the inheriting ghosts" (*Ancestors* 466) of the region first in the form of Columbus-cum-slave trader:

*Chapter 1*

> i had set out. crack. footstep. dhow. carrack. caravel
> galleons of spain at my commandant masthead
> and there was music. serenes of slaves
> syracuses of their chains bound to the vision of my sail
>
> (*Ancestors* 466)

Then the crab becomes witness to the conquistadors' arrival at the lakeshore of Tenochtitlan:

> and the dawn to have set us down here
> by the lake of invisible heritage
> heroless savages civilizations
> reflected in mirrorless walls
>
> of flamingoes clouds of departing eagles
> zimbabwe tenochtitlan saguenay
> mouse eaten capitols palaces of torn silk
>
> (*Ancestors* 467)

This passage echoes "Titan" in that it invokes the beauty of Tenochtitlan at the same time as it implies its destruction by the conquistadors. The reference to "capitols" evokes Rome, the predecessor of later European empires in both versions of *X/Self*. The listing of "zimbabwe tenochtitlan saguenay," located in southern Africa, Mexico, and Canada respectively, illustrates that colonial destruction is random and "embraces all civilizations" (Rohlehr, "Songs of the Skeleton" 318).

The remaining parts of "Carab" explore colonial history from the point of view of the oppressed. In giving this double perspective, "Carab" functions as a microcosm of both *X/Self* editions, where oppressor and oppressed are equally given a voice. The crab explores "the booms of cenotes." *Cenotes* are natural water cisterns reaching deep into the ground, where they are connected to subterranean rivers. They are the main water resources of the Yucatan peninsula and facilitated the development of the Mayan civilization in the region. In other words, the crab explores the sources of Mesoamerican culture. In establishing a link between the crab and the *cenote*, the poem creates a network of recurring images within Brathwaite's writing, linking the "Kingston poetry," *Ancestors*, and, as we will see, *ConVERSations* and *Words Need Love Too*. Underground water resources often function as a metaphor

## X/Self and the (Re)invention of the "Creole Cosmos"

for alternative spiritual resources in Brathwaite's work (particularly in *Mother Poem*). They are the imaginary spaces where we find *nam*, the submerged presence of Sycorax and Namsetoura. In this sense, the crab explores cells of resistance to colonial (symbolic) rule, a reading which is supported by the appearance of a Sycoraxian figure in the following passage:

> crook: ed witch of the rain
> limping from ratoon to spinache
> crutched to her ancient whip. dreaming of stinks
>
> kneading herbs oracles words
> condemning all conquerors
> hieronymous dahomean babies
>
> (*Ancestors* 467)

Yet the *cenotes* in "Carab" are dry. The word "booms" implies a hollowness, a capacity for echo, which would not be there if the *cenotes* were filled with water. Moreover, Sycorax here only curses ("condemning all conquerors"). She is the "demented obeah woman" of "Hex" (*Mother Poem*), "who curses her children's blindness of materialism" (Rohlehr, "Songs of the Skeleton" 31) and does not provide an alternative way of expression outside the binary opposition of colonial oppression and indigenous resistance. Here Sycorax does not nurture or empower. The empty *cenotes* are also reminiscent of the hull of the slave ship, and the crab, together with Sycorax and the slaves, are "bleeding under the dungeons decks" (*Ancestors* 467). Thus the presence of Sycorax does not yield healing through magic but merely echoes the traumas of the past.

However, both Sycorax and the crab are depicted as limping and lame and are thus related to Legba, "the god of beginning" (Rohlehr, "Songs of the Skeleton" 315), and the ultimate message of the poem is that of new beginnings, urging the victims of conquest to remember that they "have survive these terrors" (*Ancestors* 468). The crab of "Carab" represents an active part of the imagination of the poet, who is aware of the terrors of the past but also of the need to move beyond them, as the following passage suggests:

> the crab knows it all
> kernel of grit

*Chapter 1*

knowledge of the eaten edges of disaster

he walks carefully over stones. dreams
cradles of childrens skeletons
all these new mother poems

drinking the world at the drip of my skull
crippled knuckle of bone
crustaceous epitaph
scavenging slowly through hackles of grass

(*Ancestors* 468)

At first, the act of scavenging seems to evoke the image of the crab as parasite. "Carab," however, presents the other side of scavenging, that of sanitation and cleansing. He is sifting through "the canefield trash" in search of what has survived and needs space to be nurtured. The crab creates that space by eating the garbage of history that pollutes the present and prevents a movement towards reconciliation. In this sense, the crab's scavenging becomes an act of healing. Through the act of eating filth, the crab, which feeds on dead matter, merges with the scarab, the Egyptian dung beetle, which collects excrement and dead matter in its dung ball.

Although the scarab primarily evokes associations with Egyptian culture, its scavenging aspect is more prominent in pre-Columbian traditions. In the *Books of Chilam Balam*, the chronicles of the Yucatecan Maya, the scarab is described as the "filth of the Earth," both in its material and moral form, but despite its association with human filth, the scarab "is called to become divine" ("Scarab" 833). Similar to the *Popol Vuh* of the Quiché Maya of Guatemala, the *Books of Chilam Balam* were written after the Spanish conquest in the language of the Yucatecan Maya but in Latin script. They depict the conquistadors as dung beetles, thus appropriating a pre-Columbian metaphor to comment on the new colonial situation, perhaps in particular on the divine nature that the Europeans claimed for themselves. The ambivalent interpretation of the dung beetle in the *Books of Chilam Balam* mirrors the ambiguous nature of the crab in Brathwaite's writing.

In Aztec tradition, Tlazolteotl, the goddess of sexuality and childbirth, is also referred to as the "Filth Eater" (Cisneros 49 qtd. in Caputi 19) because "she is able to absorb the sins, ego, corruption, disease, and waste of human beings" (Caputi 19). Tlazolteotl "takes filth (pol-

## X/Self and the (Re)invention of the "Creole Cosmos"

lutions of all types, psychical as well as material) back into herself and cosmically recycles it, transforming and energizing the cosmos, and rebirthing matter" (Caputi 19–20). Although the Aztec goddess is anthropomorphic, her association with filth links her to the Mayan dung beetle. In her energizing of the cosmos and her cleansing and rebirthing of matter, Tlazolteotl functions as a link between the Mesoamerican dung beetle and the Egyptian scarab, whose rolling of a dung ball represents the cycle of the sun and thus the cycle of death and rebirth ("Scarab" 833). Both the filth eater and the sun symbol reflect an understanding of natural and human history as cyclical, which echoes Brathwaite's notion of "circle" or "ecosystem cultures."

In Brathwaite's writing, the "circle" cultures represent traditional African societies, whereas the *cenote* describes a particularly American culture paradigm (*C* 115).[21] In *ConVERSations*, but also in the earlier "World Order Models," Brathwaite links these cultural paradigms of circle/*cenote* and missile (an image of European imperial expansionism) to the notion of ecosystems and biosphere. In "World Order Models," he refers to terms used by American poet Gary Snyder in his essay, "The Politics of Ethnopoetics" (*The Old Ways* (1977)). Snyder distinguishes between "ecosystem cultures" and "biosphere cultures":

> Ecosystem cultures being those whose economic base of support is a natural region, a watershed, a plant zone, a natural territory within which they have to make their whole living. Living within the terms of an ecosystem, out of self-interest if nothing else, you are careful. You don't destroy the soils, you don't kill all the game, you don't log it off and let the water wash the soil away. Biosphere cultures ... are cultures that spread their economic support system out far enough that they can afford to wreck one ecosystem, and keep moving on. Well, that's Rome, that's Babylon. It's just a big enough spread that you can begin to be irresponsible about certain specific local territories. It leads us to imperialist civilization with capitalism and institutionalised economic growth. (20–21)[22]

"Ecosystems" would thus be local, self-sufficient, and sustainable economies, which Brathwaite also describes as cultures of the "circle," since, in their preservation of the environment that sustains them, they have no need for expansion in order to survive ("World Order

## Chapter 1

Models" 54). "Biosphere" systems, on the other hand, rely on expansion, thus Brathwaite calls them "missile" culture, a term that emphasizes the idea of a projection outwards ("World Order Models" 54). In other words, "ecosystems" are based on dialogue not only of the human community with the environment but also within and between human communities, they are manifestations of the "creole cosmos." "Biosphere cultures," on the other hand, create wastelands, not only in an ecological but also in a societal sense; they lay waste the spirit of community as well as the spirit of the land.

The notion of circularity is repeated in the shape of the scarab's dung ball and the crab shell. It is also reflected in the circular structure of "Carab" itself. The poem begins and ends with a reference to the ancestors. At the beginning of the poem, the sleep of the ancestors is disturbed by the terrors of history. The reference to "floorboards of cured wood" (*Ancestors* 465) in the opening lines of the poem implies the floorboards of the slave cabin and also function as an intertextual reference between "Carab" of *X/Self* and "Hex" of *Mother Poem* where the mother's children are said to have been buried under the floorboards of the slave hut:

> she will remember the floorboards of a cabin
> how there was a grave there
> where she bury her children
> their skin drilled to screams like the soft of guavas. (*Ancestors* 75)[23]

The connection to these slave ancestors has been lost. It is the task of the crab, of poetic imagination, to restore this lost link: "and alone / my hand following the crabs poem / stalks the inheriting ghosts" (*Ancestors* 466). As the crab's journey ends, the ancestors have entered living memory and come alive in the last stanzas of the poem:

> and the grass flesh
> and the flesh memory
> and the memory nodding
>
> grey haired and ancestral verandahs
> rock/ing rock/ing slowly to sleep
> and the sleep soft wide circling circling
> coming in with the birds and the wind and the steep stars
>
> (*Ancestors* 468)

The ancestors are portrayed as nodding, which implies a nodding off to sleep as well as a nodding in consent (Rohlehr, "Songs of the Skeleton" 321). The poet's imagination has released them from their graves underneath the slave hut. He has also established a link between the slave past and the more recent past that extends into the poet's and his readers' living memory. To the creation of this link the ancestors nod their consent. At the same time, the implication in the last stanza is that of a day coming to an end. The ancestors nod off to sleep in the knowledge that they, unlike the dead slaves with whom the poem opened, can rest in peace and that a new cycle of time can begin. In its journey between sea and land, the crab succeeds in restoring the world axis (the link between the living and the dead) at the end of "Carab." Thus the image of the crab embodies the tension in Brathwaite's work between "tidalectics" and communion, between exile and *Heimat*, despair and hope, and as both modes of existence coexist in the Caribbean, the crab also represents the region, "Caribbean" being another connotation encoded in the word "Carab."

Bloch compares the "darkness of the lived moment" to an absence of fulfillment or an emptiness that wants to be filled (he calls this the "Not"). As opposed to "Nothing," which is synonymous with dystopia and the total annihilation of hope, the "Not" implies a "not yet" and thus the promise of fulfillment (*PH* 1: 306–7). In other words, the "Not" is potentially utopian: it suggests an empty space that has yet to be filled and recalls the empty *cenotes* the crab explores in the poem. The crab itself can be seen as an empty shell that, as a vehicle for the poet's imagination, sets out to seek its subject matter. At the end of the poem, the crab has united the Mesoamerican, African and European heritage of the Caribbean in the form of the Amerindian filth eater, the Egyptian scarab, and Christ, who, although not mentioned in the discussion of the filth deity above, is implied, since his power to purge humanity of its sins is a form of filth eating.[24] The lowly crab of *X/Self* (2001) is, therefore, the direct opposite to the divine Xango of *X/Self* (1987). Unlike Xango, the crab renounces its divine nature and associates with the human and animal world. This change in emphasis from the heavenly to the earthly aspect of divinity echoes Bloch's notion of the "humanization of religion" (*PH* 3: 1196), which plays an important role in other books discussed in this study. At the same time, the crab metaphor shows that Brathwaite may have acquired a more down-to-earth and realistic approach to his vision of a "creole cosmos," one more firmly anchored in the here and now. The crab metaphor also introduces a new kind of tension into the second cosmology of his post-1986 work between the dystopian reality of the Caribbean and its utopian potential, between the reality of Sisyphus and the hope and potential of Eldorado. "Concrete utopia" begins in the here and now, in the space of the "Not." The circular space of the crab's shell can be read as a mundane *houmfort*, where, for as long as the poet's imagination lasts, the vision of the "creole cosmos" as a communion of cultures is achieved.

## Chapter 2

# Death, Marriage, and Maroons: *The Zea Mexican Diary*

◇◆◇

### 2.1. In "the Blue Mountains of Kilimanjaro": The Irish Town Maroon Project

In *ConVERSations with Nathaniel Mackey*, Brathwaite explains how his perception of the Jamaican landscape and his own situation in that landscape influenced the writing of the first *X/Self*.[1] Mt Blanc, an image that appears in *X/Self* as a signifier of European hegemony, which is more fully explored in the earlier essay "Metaphors of Underdevelopment: A Proem for Hernan Cortez" (1984) as well as *ConVERSations*, has its counterpart in Kilimanjaro, which Brathwaite introduces as an icon of African consciousness:

> **N**ow the image that keep
> (s) recurring between th-
> ese two motions of power
> and powerlessness, and th
> (e) image — which I'm al-

*A Creole Experiment*

> so always aware of — is a clump of bamboo which grows outside my window at a place where my/self and family have move to (in Jamaica) into a cool little 3-000 ft mid/air village call Irish Town [IT], with the Blue Mountains of Kilimanjaro on one side — one aspect of the vision — and the green hole of Mt Blanc or what would / could become Mt Blanc — certainly result and victim of Mt Blanc — the grey, rusty and off-white waste(s) of Kingston — on the other (C 119–20)

In "Metaphors of Underdevelopment," Brathwaite explores the "historical and cultural equilibrium/disequilibrium" (238) between north and south or first and third world, for which the two mountains stand. In this context, we also first come across ideas that later develop into "creole cosmos" and "tidalectics." A cultural equilibrium between north and south is created through a balance and equality between the partners in question, which includes a balance between matter and spirit. In the images of Mt Blanc and Kilimanjaro we find this balance upset, with material wealth and spiritual poverty gravitating around Mt Blanc and spiritual wealth and material poverty gravitating around Kilimanjaro. The two mountains thus represent the disequilibrium or the dystopian aspect of the "creole cosmos" as neocolonial world order. Brathwaite frequently refers to the spiritual impoverishment of European culture as beginning during the sea voyage across the Atlantic. He calls this process "alter-Renaissance" ("World Order Models" 58). During this sea voyage European spirituality is lost and only the materialist base of the culture arrives in the Caribbean:

> While Columbus sailed west, Da Vinci and Michelangelo reached other worlds. . . . By the time the slave trade was underway, Palestrina was writing his *Mass of Marcellus*.
> But none of these spiritual forces was exported by Europe. Botticelli was not here, nor was Cellini; no sign of Kepler, Grotius, Harvey or Descartes. Where was Voltaire and Cervantes? How did the Calvinists see the New World? The European missile was mercantilist. And as, at the apogee of orbit, the capsule/culture bearing rocket must turn upon its own axis for re-entry into the earth's atmosphere, so did the missile of the European Renaissance, its most magnificent achievement within Europe, alter itself high up over the Atlantic to bring us not Shakespeare, Milton, Hamlet but Cortez, Crusoe, Simon Legree. The geo-political fragmentation of the Caribbean was completed in the psyche of the alter-renaissance. ("World Order Models" 59)

As discussed in the previous chapter, Brathwaite describes European cultures as "missilic" because their expansionist desire projects them outwards, whereas traditional cultures, "ecosystems," are for him cultures of the "capsule" or "circle":

> The African capsule or circle culture . . . was concerned with equilibrium, and was inward looking and conservative: drum, round mud hut, village, sense of time. It was not designed for conquest, but survival; and it was the capsule powered by that rocket of the slave trade, middle passage transplantation, that brought miraculously intact — more intact than missile-culture writers would instinctively perceive — what we now call the culture of the slaves; with *kumina* the

core, atomic nucleus and colonel. ("Caliban, Ariel, and Unprospero" 56)

Brathwaite merges the symbolic landscapes of Africa and Europe in the geography of the Caribbean to illustrate the global struggle between power and dependence which repeats itself in the radius of his own personal experience. In this sense, his metaphors become much more than literary devices. They become lived experience. Within this poetic landscape, the bamboo, an image taken from the poem "Flute(s)" (*Middle Passages*), becomes "the symbol of the possibility of a new life new words a new world of writing endeav or" (*C* 153), the symbol, in fact, of the first cosmology.

During the course of *The Zea Mexican Diary* (*ZMD*) (1993), Brathwaite's wife Doris Monica (Mexican or Zea Mexican) emerges as the keeper of memory, committing Brathwaite's work, his written life, to the computer before Brathwaite himself has learnt to use it.[2] In this sense, she is related to Sycorax of "Nametracks." Moreover, Brathwaite portrays Mexican as having a deep connection to the Caribbean as a place of *Heimat*, and at the end of the *Diary* she is transformed into the land itself, which links her to the mother persona of *Mother Poem*, with the exception that Mexican also has a strong connection to the pre-Columbian Amerindian presence. For Brathwaite, *Heimat* is connected to the idea of community. For him, a sense of community, of sharing a communally acquired wealth, represents the basis for an alternative to the Euro-American plantation, which focuses on the accumulation of individual wealth, thus atomizing western society. Already in *X/Self*, he presents maroon culture as such an alternative model.[3] In *The Zea Mexican Diary* and more clearly so in *ConVERSations* and other "video" writings, the maroon model emerges as a lived reality. Brathwaite attempts to create a self-sufficient community in Irish Town:

```
but we move into these hi

lls because I have become

by this time very involve

with the notion of maron-

age, that great alterNAti

ve which some people in
```

> the Caribbean discover si
> nce the 17th century and
> even before with the Car-
> ibs of course — all those
> resistances against Mt Bl
> anc —
>
> and with this moving into
> the hills of Irish Town I
> would be able to set up
> some kind of co-operative
> some kind of subsistent,
> self-contain — [to the audienc
> (e)] Do I hear you say 'that same
> own dream-on 'utopian'?] comm
> unity where we would grow
> our own food . . . (C 123-
> 24)

Hilltops, swamps and jungles are typical locations for maroon settlements. Historically, maroons were runaway slaves who sought independence from plantation life and the bondage of slavery. Therefore, their settlements had to be situated in areas inaccessible and inhospitable to their pursuers. The Cockpit Country and Blue Mountains of Jamaica mentioned above by Brathwaite are such historical maroon locations. Irish Town itself becomes a modern day maroon settlement modeled on those that have survived into the present day.[4] The house at Irish Town becomes a maroon refuge, a space of independence, where Brathwaite attempts to "devote all/the rest of my blk puddin & souse to that worldpool of writing" (*ZMD* 130). In this sense, the Irish

## A Creole Experiment

Town project described in the above passage from *ConVERSations* is a critique of the distinctions between the social status and the social acceptability of the academic and the poet. In the bourgeois world experienced by Brathwaite, the poet has no function and no place. On the contrary, creativity is stigmatized as social deviance, a transgressive act challenging existing structures of thought and behavior. Brathwaite devotes a great part of the *Diary* to the defense of the poet. At the same time, his maroon project is a critique of received notions of genre. Brathwaite tends to blur genres in the period beginning with the *Diary*, where personal account stands side by side with poem, letter and social analysis, creating, as Silvio Torres-Saillant argues, "a testament of dissidence" (*Caribbean Poetics* 143).

Within the landscape of his creative vision, Brathwaite situates Irish Town between Mt Blanc/Europe and Kilimanjaro/Africa, intimating that maroon societies are a syncretic product, a creole experiment in fact. Therefore, long before American and Haitian independence from Europe, maroon communities constituted the first autonomous creole (as opposed to the aboriginal Amerindian) societies of the New World, which, through trading connections throughout the Caribbean region as well as with the South American mainland formed an alternative world order to that established by the plantation. In "Nanny, Palmares & the Caribbean Maroon Connexion," Brathwaite writes:

> ... Maroons are not 'people isolated' — *marooned* on a hilltop & trapped (hopefully not *moróned*) into their own communities. Because of their independence they were able to achieve, they were able to xploit, whenever possible, that independence to create connections with other Maroon — & other — communities. And that is one of the ways in which they so successfully, more than 'survived'. (127)

Here he also refers to overseas trading relations of the Brazilian maroon republic Palmares, the most famous maroon community in the Americas:

> ... **Palmares** (1599-1694) — the 98 year-old Black *kilombo* Republic in Bahia, Brazil – the most dynamic, the most dramatic [perhaps — rather — the one most dramatized/romanticized by Portuguese modernismo &

negrismo writers (see also the utterly lovely film on Palmares, A deusa negra by the Nigerian Ola Balogoun . . .] w/ a lot of connexions w/ trade into Venezuela and, some claim, across the Atlantic into Benin & Yoruba . . . (128)

Whether these trading connections with Africa actually existed may be questionable, but part of Brathwaite's argument in the essay is that a lot of maroon history was falsified or edited out of colonial documents. In a sense, it does not exist within colonial historiography. The reason for writing this essay and his earlier study *Wars of Respect: Nanny and Sam Sharpe* (1977) was to dispel the myths and silences associated with maroon resistance, in particular those surrounding the Jamaican maroon leader, Nanny. What matters to Brathwaite in the above passage is the idea behind the claim that the maroons had trading links with Africa, which points to the possibility of maroon resistance as a form of "concrete utopia," an alternative world order to the plantation.

Maroon leaders such as Nanny became cultural figureheads during Caribbean independence movements and have since become icons of national identity. Moreover, in the wake of national independence during the 1960s, 1970s and 1980s, many Caribbean intellectuals and artists styled themselves as maroon figures (Fleischmann 565-79 qtd. in Price xiii), among them Brathwaite himself. In this sense, the concept of *maronage* is extended beyond its immediate plantation context. It includes what Brathwaite calls "psychological maronage," a form of resistance within the global neocolonial situation:

> . . . there should have been a redefinition of maronage — the term itself — & a widening of the notion of it to include things like *psychological maronage* which we in the present day & kind of world [Third, Developing, underDeveloping, neoColonial/ suppressed / down-pressed Cannibal & Calibanistic etc] are very much part of & certainly very much involved with / in one way or the other ("Nanny, Palmares & the Caribbean Maroon Connexion" 120)

In this new form, *maronage* becomes an alternative way of thinking. Brathwaite's own Irish Town maroon project represents, in part, such a redefinition of the original maroon experience in the sense of "psychological maronage." *Maronage* becomes a transgressive act.

In his introduction to *The Principle of Hope*, Bloch writes: "Thinking means venturing beyond" (*PH* 1: 4). For Bloch, figures of transgression, or "figures of venturing beyond the limits" (*PH* 3: 1033), represent the epitome of utopian consciousness: ". . . all figures of venturing beyond the limits . . . want to escape from the other world of the wish into its this-world. Into power over the moment, where more is plucked than the given day, into the powerfulness of a conquered being-here" (*PH* 3: 1033). Likewise, Antonio Benítez-Rojo refers to the maroon society as a "transgressive community" in that it moves away from or moves beyond the repressive space of Caribbean plantation society and creates a new space of freedom within the hilltop, swamp or jungle settlements (252).[5] Thus maroon communities create utopian space, an alternative reality within the reality of the plantation system. Accordingly, Brathwaite's Irish Town community in the foothills of the "Blue Mountains of Kilimanjaro," represents a creation of utopian space set apart from the neocolonial world of Mt Blanc that creates the social, economic and spiritual "wasteland" of Kingston.

In Brathwaite's personal life, however, Mt Blanc prevails over Kilimanjaro, an experience he refers to in images of landslide and natural catastrophe. In 1986 Mexican dies. Brathwaite's house at Irish Town is buried in a mudslide during the hurricane season in 1988. His carefully assembled library is almost completely obliterated, and the Irish Town maroon project disintegrates. Brathwaite employs the image of the mudslide that obliterates the bamboo to illustrate that the "creole cosmos" has, despite the vision of *X/Self*, not yet emerged from, or has sunk back into, the darkness of poetic vision. In this sense, the mudslide represents another, more personal, manifestation of the disequilibrium discussed in "Metaphors of Underdevelopment" that expresses itself in broader cultural and historical terms in *X/Self*. Just as geological memory extends into human memory in *Caribbean Man in Space and Time*, in *The Zea Mexican Diary* personal devastation and natural catastrophe interpenetrate.

## 2.2. "Succumbing to the Culture of Death": Brathwaite's Diary Entries

*The Zea Mexican Diary* is the first in a series of autobiographical works in which Brathwaite records personal trauma. The book centers on Mexican's terminal illness from cancer and Brathwaite's attempt to come to terms with his grief when she finally dies. Her death marks the end of the first cosmology and functions as a catalyst that causes the poet to review his vision of a "creole cosmos." However, despite the loss of a sustained vision, the idea of the "creole cosmos" manifests itself on several occasions in the *Diary* as an attempt to give meaning to the emotional devastation of bereavement.

In her foreword to *The Zea Mexican Diary*, Sandra Pouchet Paquet points out that Brathwaite's work prior to his wife's death is characterized by a "sweeping collectivization of personal experience" (vii–viii). She maintains that in *The Arrivants* and *Mother Poem, Sun Poem* and *X/Self* "personal experience of mother, father, and native landscape is metamorphorized to reflect the collective inheritance of a people and a culture" (viii). *The Zea Mexican Diary* reflects how Mexican's death shatters this poetic vision and develops "a different aesthetic personality: the persona of the public poet as cultural historian and critic... appears instead a lonely individual talent, isolated and alienated from the community in which he had encased and defined himself" (Paquet viii). On the whole, *The Zea Mexican Diary* depicts an isolation of the poet as individual, which reflects Brathwaite's notion of "psychological maronage" as a radical dissociation from society.

The *Diary* is structured in twelve chapters, comprising a journal section, a selection of letters, and three individual closing chapters (an "Epigraph" to Mexican's life, a burial ceremony and a vision of the afterlife). The journal was begun shortly after Brathwaite learned that Mexican was terminally ill with cancer. It was originally not intended for publication (and only later edited and extended). Through publication, however, individual trauma becomes again collective experience. Therefore, despite the isolation of the individual, the book also yields "intimations of restored community beyond the alienation and marginalization imposed by grief and loss" (Paquet x).

Within the body of Brathwaite's work, *The Zea Mexican Diary* functions as a rite of passage from the collective voice of his poetry up to and including *X/Self* (1987) to the more experimental pieces that foreground the poet's individual, yet often autobiographical voice. Rites of passage also occur as a theme within *The Zea Mexican Diary*. The first four parts of the book, the journal section, describe Mexican's rite of passage from life to death. The following six chapters, the "Letters" section, represent Brathwaite's rite of passage, his "Time of Salt" (*ZMD* 11), during which he attempts to come to terms with his loss and grief. This period outlasts Mexican's death by many years and ends only when the poet finally plans to settle at CowPastor. The concluding chapters XI and XII, entitled "The Tulip Tree" and "The Awakening," read as Brathwaite's return to the human community and reveal instances of communion with the spirit of his dead wife. A quotation from the *I Ching*, which precedes the book as a motto, intensifies the notion of passage. Brathwaite cites "The Second K'un — Oppression," which begins by showing "its subject with bare buttocks straitened under the stump of a tree. He enters a dark valley, and for three years has no prospect (of deliverance)" (*ZMD* 14). In "Dream Journeys," Gordon Rohlehr suggests that "Brathwaite's choice of this quotation from the *I-Ching* indicates his interest in divination, his belief too that life is governed by spiritual forces to whom the human subject is ultimately responsible" (*Kamau Brathwaite: 1994 Neustadt Prize for Literature* 766). In the *Diary*, this responsibility to spirit becomes poignantly personal.

In the first two chapters of the *Diary*, "Irish Town 1" and "Irish Town 2," Brathwaite records the period from Mexican's being diagnosed with cancer up until the day before her death. Being advised by the doctor not to break the news to her as knowledge of her illness might accelerate its fatal course, Brathwaite uses the journal to come to terms with her inevitable death. In his reflections, Mexican's individual disintegration appears as an extension of the natural devastation caused by incessant rainfall during May 1986 when the entries begin, which foreshadows the rainfalls that cause the mudslide of *Shar/Hurricane Poem*:

> **Ever since the doc's news there has been rain here in Ja: 2 weeks of ruin that has claimed *30 lives* (& is still continuing) w/ *40,000 people* they say home-less in S Clarendon alone Roads gone Bridges wash away etc etc etc Right here at home the mud came down the hill down the front steps into the house and all her newly planted garden beds are wash'd away What a metaphor for what must be going on inside her . . . .** (*ZMD* 31)

He even establishes a link between her "nightmare **X**/ray lungs toiling toiling away" and from which he fears "to hear some like **nuclear disas-**

ter" (*ZMD* 30) to the nuclear catastrophe of Chernobyl that happened earlier that same year. His vision of global devastation thus serves to emphasize the extent of his personal devastation and his darkening vision of the "creole cosmos." This vision is also an extension of his notion that the Middle Passage is an ongoing catastrophe that manifests not only in cultural but also in environmental contexts. Natural catastrophe mirrors human catastrophe and vice versa (McSweeney). Again this is an example of what Reiss calls the "geographical remaking of history" ("Realisms of the Fictive Imagination" 265), and Brathwaite makes increasing use of this connection not only in the *Diary*, but also in *Shar* and in *Trench Town Rock*.

The nadir of the *Diary*, chronicled in the third chapter, "Mona," is reached as Brathwaite gives up hope for a miraculous cure of his wife's cancer. He describes this as "succumbing to the Culture of Death":

> **But this morning seeing her ramble like that** [effect of all those pain-killing drugs, they said] – **after such a good day yesterday – a good sleeping day, that is – no visitors – I begin to doubt** [to despair of] **the miracle & in fact succumbed to** [what I was calling] **the Culture of Death by asking Mary to read some 'Religious Philosophy' (Words for the Day) to her; & I played my Poems tape which is full of death & requie quiem music** – (*ZMD* 63)

At the same time, "succumbing to the Culture of Death" also extends to Brathwaite's creative sphere. When Mexican his muse ceases to exist, he will, as he says, "forever lose the light the light — the open doors" (*ZMD* 78), and eventually her death does result in the aforementioned temporary loss of his writing hand ("An excerpt from Limbo" 105). In the course of the *Diary*, Mexican not only emerges as the muse in the European sense, but also as an incarnation of the Haitian *loa* Legba, guardian of the threshold between the worlds.[6] Consequently, with her death, Brathwaite fears that he may lose his link to the spirit world from which he derives his "gifts of àshe" (*ZMD* 78), *ase* (*àshe* or *àxé*) being the life force that in Yoruba culture is believed to flow through all creation (Duerden 48). In her association with Legba, Mexican herself emerges as a figure of transgression, being able to mediate between the male and the female, thus functioning as an agent of communion, and between the physical and the metaphysical plane, bringing the spiritual presence from beyond the boundaries of mortal life into this world. The communion of the human and the divine foreshadows the experience of death as the end of physical existence. Death, in this sense, functions as a utopian space, an aspect of "arrived-at Being," and it will emerge as that later in the *Diary*. With Mexican's death, the door to the divine world, which Legba guards, closes, and Brathwaite loses his creative direction: "It's as if the light of the bamboo goes out . . . and what happen to me . . . is that of course you cd not find > the pathways . . ." ("An excerpt from Limbo" 105). Thus his creative vision sinks back into "the darkness of the lived moment."

There is also a sense in which Brathwaite feels that Mexican's death is an act of spiritual punishment in response to the poet's adultery:

> How God has come to punish me for not cherishing enough: the long nights I sometimes/ too too often surely/ was a-way/ the smell of other muses on my breath/ the tales she must have heard the agonies of doubt/selfdoubt her love might well have tried to justify xplain/xplain away forgive & must have caused her generosity to hide & harbour like a pearl inside her heart/her hurt until it built itself into this tumour and how I feel Olorun/God has now withdrawn from me because I did not preciate ijs gifts of àshe: the always possibility: creative cross-roads: open doors: Mawu Ogou the Eshu/Legba: loas
>
> (ZMD 78)

Brathwaite considers himself guilty of being unfaithful to Mexican, and the spiritual forces that have endowed him with this link to creative inspiration now demand atonement. This sentiment coincides with Rohlehr's observation regarding the *I Ching* and Brathwaite's belief "that life is governed by spiritual forces to whom the human subject is ultimately responsible" ("Dream Journeys," *Kamau Brathwaite: 1994 Neustadt Prize* 766).

The creative and spiritual significance Brathwaite ascribes to his life with Mexican hints at a utopia of marriage that has turned into its opposite with the death of the beloved partner, so that death appears not only as the negation of Brathwaite's vision of the "creole cosmos" but also as the end of personal happiness. Bloch describes marriage as an "experiment of communion which finds no equal either in sexual love or *in any social community which has previously appeared*" [emphasis mine] (*PH* 1: 327). The utopia of marriage points towards the realization of communion in a new society where distinctions between the private and the communal have become obsolete. In other words, marriage is "the nearest manifestation of solidarity" (*PH* 1: 326). The family or married couple are thus the nucleus of a utopian society. In this context, the maroon community, where distinctions between the private and the communal have become obsolete, anticipates utopian *Heimat*. Thus, the historical phenomenon of *maronage* is an example of how the "future still exists in the past . . . as something brooding in an *undischarged, undeveloped, in short, utopian* way" (*PH* 1: 102). In this sense, the marriage of Kamau and Mexican acquires a communal dimension, as Rohlehr points out in "Dream Journeys": ". . . Kamau and Zea Mexican are not merely individuals but, transcending individuality, have become social essences, whose work relates to the awakening of an entire civilization" (*Kamau Brathwaite: 1994 Neustadt Prize* 766).

With Mexican's death, however, the vision of the "creole cosmos" at Irish Town abruptly ends. Brathwaite's subsequent isolation from his family is a repercussion of Mexican's death and the death of his vision at the same time, as both his family and friends refuse to recognize his project of creating an alternative society as well as creating poetry. In the *Diary*, the failure of vision is accompanied by a change in setting. The Brathwaites leave their house in Irish Town (here referred to as the "Dump"), "because she couldn't take the hills anymore or the stairs at the 'Dump'" (*ZMD* 65), and move to the house of Brathwaite's sister Mary Morgan at Mona (thus the title "Mona" given to the third section of the *Diary*).

Section IV, "Middle Passages," which follows "Mona," opens with the announcement of Mexican's death:

## A Creole Experiment

> Tonight – at midnight [just before midnight]
> Mexican died – peacefully, thank God
> I was not there
> Had gone to Irish Tn to finish Jah Music& her
> Bibliography ... (*ZMD* 85)

The first part of "Middle Passages" is a reconstruction of Mexican's last hours of life during Brathwaite's absence. Brathwaite introduces a rapid change of font that is sustained throughout the remaining sections of the book. Sandra Pouchet Paquet suggests that "[l]ines and fonts are varied to achieve rhythmic effects, to mirror emotional states, and for thematic emphasis" (x). These font changes and alternative line arrangements also reflect Brathwaite's unorthodox dealing with the experience of death and grief. Brathwaite presents the first section of "Middle Passages" in centered typescript, which concretizes the sense of Middle Passage as the writing is aligned down the middle of the page. Rather than the collective rite of passage on the slave ships, the image of the Middle Passage here signifies an individual rite of passage, the passage of the dying subject through the strait path and narrow gate of the Sermon on the Mount to deliverance in death. Mexican is thus also the "straitened subject" of the Second K'un.

The second and third section of the chapter recount Brathwaite's hours of work at Irish Town. All three parts, in fact, happen simultaneously. Section 2 begins: "Up at Irish Town I must have just dotted the last i of her Bibliography (of my work) I was typing for her" (*ZMD* 89). The completion of the bibliography and Mexican's death are presented as coinciding, and Brathwaite, indeed, regards his working on her words as a bulwark against death: "I began to tell myself that as long as I was doing this — for her — she wdn't — cdn't — somehow — die ... & I had just I suspect dotted the last i of it that night — when she died ..." (*ZMD* 89–90).

Section 3 describes how Brathwaite is woken from sleep by "someone like a voice calling me ... like a high mournful cry" (*ZMD* 90). This cry reminds him of a "white owl that had startled us on our first night up there ... & this white owl must have been sitting on this huge dark passionfruit tree when we opened the door & came flying towards us w/ out sound just the white flashing" (*ZMD* 90). The cry that wakes him and the sighting of the owl are presented as spanning their married life at Irish Town, as if the owl had foreshadowed the end of the couple's life together from its very beginning. In this context, the owl becomes associated with the jumbie bird, a small brown owl regarded as a bird of ill omen in Caribbean folklore.[7] In the following passage from the *Diary*, Brathwaite describes a white owl flying out of the darkness. The ghostly appearance of the bird and the wailing cry also call to mind the jumbie bird's Irish cousin, the banshee (*beán sí*):

> ... this white owl ... came flying towards us w/ out sound just the white flashing like the mournful cry that now wake me up w/ like Michael's voice now somehow calling out
>
> 'Daaaaaaaaaaaaaaaaaaaaaaaaaaadeeeeeeeeeeeeeeeeeeeeeeeeeeeeeeee'
>
> like long & mournful in the dark like that & I decided right then & there to get back down to town as fast as possible ... (*ZMD* 90)

The personal catastrophe of death becomes a multi-accentuated sign in the interplay of Caribbean, Celtic and Chinese tradition (the jumbie bird, the banshee and the *I Ching*). Thus even the dystopian aspects of the *Diary* retain elements of the "creole cosmos."

Section 7 represents the most crucial passage of the chapter "Middle Passages" in that it marks the end of Mexican's rite of passage towards death and the beginning of Brathwaite's rite of passage, his Middle Passage (hence the plural in the chapter title) towards a new awareness of self and community. The section presents Brathwaite standing at his wife's deathbed, pondering the paradox of her body being still so close but her spirit moving away into the afterlife: "... i am walking to/ toward(s) her to that almost stone & still the love & **person** i had known but somehow gone away & silent from me though it was as if she cd still speak & perhaps did but now so distant/ near me/ distant..." (*ZMD* 93). As he realizes that she is moving further and further away from him, he attempts, and fails, to follow her in spirit: "... i never reach where she is floating from me on my naked feet/ i feel the clicks the stones the thorns the plimplar & the weed (s) cutting me & catching at me as i toil & toil towards her w/out moving as she moves/ as i move forward as she does not move ..." (*ZMD* 93–94). Brathwaite, in fact, enters the valley of the Second K'un as Mexican leaves it. For her "the earth [is] already on its curve towards the sun towards the stars" (*ZMD* 93), whereas Brathwaite is in the middle of the dark valley the *I Ching* describes. He is the "subject straitened, as if bound with creepers" (*ZMD* 14). His inability to move and follow his wife into the afterworld becomes synonymous with the "straitened subject's" inability to proceed through the dark valley. The mentioning of *Trench Town Rock* in the following passage suggests that Brathwaite considers all three traumatic experiences, the death of his wife, the destruction of his house, and being burgled and almost killed in his Marley Manor apartment, as happening under the influence of the Second K'un:

And is only today (15 March 92 + 15 August 92) after so much more unhapp

has happened happened happened & still a doan reach yet [see for xample Trench

Tn Rock' **Hambone** (Aug 1992)] & recognize this Middle Passage passage that a li-

mbo/lembe thru is what the **Second K'un** has said me all along like no like

n/ like yes/terday a thousand years away . . . (*ZMD* 95)

Brathwaite's journey into symbolic death begins at a dystopian moment in his personal and creative life. In the course of the *Diary*, however, this dystopian moment acquires a utopian connotation. The journey into the unknown region of death mirrors the journey to Eldorado, which for the first European explorers lay beyond the boundaries of the known world. For Wilson Harris, Eldorado is an altered state of consciousness, often associated with death, as in *Palace of the Peacock* (1960), rather than an actual place. Moreover, against Brathwaite's expectation that he will "forever lose the light the light — the open doors" (*ZMD* 78) to inspiration, Mexican's death functions, paradoxically, as a new source of inspiration, as the later chapters of the *Diary* reveal.

## 2.3. "But my pain continues": Letters and Memorials

"Middle Passages" concludes the journal section of *The Zea Mexican Diary*. The "Letters" section begins with a letter addressed to Mexican, written on 14 September 1986, the night before her funeral service. In this letter, Brathwaite summarizes their life together in a shorthand sketch, highlighting certain episodes that reflect her character. This sketch mirrors Brathwaite's impression that in retrospect it "seems such a short time we were together In fact feels like no time at all **Contracted to a Span**" (*ZMD* 110–11). With hindsight, too, their life together becomes what he calls "the golden time" (*ZMD* 111), an Eldorado or Eden to which he once had access, but which he loses with her death:

> **Doris was gold Do ris is gold...**
>
> And yet I have 'blasphemed' again st you – because I love you so so utterly...
>
> ... So that you gave me the energy even to be 'unfaithful' though I was never that/ sharing the munifi cence you gave w/ others though it was that/not that/ but it must ha ve hurt/ you always said you cdnt understand . What worries me (*is too late now*) is that I don't kn ow how & how far deeply down it really hit you hit you hurt you – & if it cause the cancer
>
> (*ZMD* 119–20)

This infidelity is pictured as the poet's fall from grace, and thus from his direct union with the spiritual sphere.

## A Creole Experiment

Brathwaite frequently refers to the Aztec capital Tenochtitlan as a version of the city of Eldorado as both are associated with gold. At one point, he calls Mexican "Tetemexticanl" (*ZMD* 123), a name that echoes the various alternative spellings of Tenochtitlan, such as the Temixtitan or Temextitan used by the Spanish. Thus Mexican herself can be read as a personification of Eldorado. In this context, Mexican's death becomes synonymous with the destruction of Tenochtitlan by the Spaniards.[8] At the end of the chapter, Brathwaite invokes her name in an almost incantatory fashion:

**yes yes yes**
**yes yes yes**
        **yes**
**She is the**
**one is the**
**one is the**
**wonderful/**
**my lady of**
**the gold of**
**the gold of**
**the golden**
**w a r a k u n a**
**skin: my tê**
**my tê my**

**T e t e -**
**mexti-**
**c a n l**

(*ZMD* 123)[9]

## Death, Marriage, and Maroons: The Zea Mexican Diary

Mexican, who was Guyanese of African and Amerindian ancestry, embodies his idea of creolization (Walmsley 747). She combines the spirit of Africa with a sense of the Americas as *Heimat*, a space of arrival for the uprooted soul of Africa. Thus, together with her connection to the spiritual sphere, Mexican acts as a transgressive figure by transporting the desire to feel at home in the Caribbean into the reality of the Irish Town maroon project.

"Ayama's Letter," which follows the letter to Mexican, is the most curious piece in the *Diary*, as the "letter" gives no clue as to who Ayama is. In "Her Stem Singing: Kamau Bratwhaite's *Zea Mexican Diary: 7 Sept 1926 – 7 Sept 1986*," Anne Walmsley suggests that "Ayama [is] the poet's alter ego" (747). In his introductory note to the *Diary*, Brathwaite himself refers to her as "daughter of Obatala" (*ZMD* 11), and the figure of the Yoruba deity can be read as Brathwaite's alter ego. In *Myth, Literature and the African World* (1976), Wole Soyinka recounts the African myth of Obatala, whose function is to mold human beings out of clay and into whose forms life is breathed by the supreme deity Olodumare. Soyinka argues that common to all Yoruba gods is an act of excess or human weakness that places them under an eternal obligation of some practical form of penance which compensates humanity. Obatala's error is his weakness for drink. On one occasion he drinks too much palm wine, his fingers slip and he creates "cripples, albinos and the blind" (15). As punishment he is captured and incarcerated but finally redeemed. Thus Obatala reflects the suffering spirit of humanity. Especially in his Brazilian version, Oxala, which Soyinka also refers to, Obatala's suffering becomes synonymous with the suffering of Christ. Soyinka emphasizes that "morality for the Yoruba is that which creates harmony in the cosmos" (156). Consequently, penance and retribution are not primarily seen as acts of punishment but rather as first acts of resumed awareness.

In the *Diary*, Ayama embodies such an act of awareness. The chapter is presented as a dialogue between Brathwaite and Ayama on the day of the funeral service (15 September 1986). Passages of her letter or conversation, appearing in large bold print, are intersected with Brathwaite's own observations presented in small print to reflect an almost whispered and increasingly weaker resistance to his wife's death. The letter begins with Ayama's words: **"Today is the day. When they Lay her to rest. And may her soul Rest in PEACE. For she Completed a cycle"** (*ZMD* 129). Brathwaite contradicts this by saying:

[But she did not, my love. The cir-

> cle knew its curve, was coming round w/ verve & confidence & the 'completion' was it seemed another thirty years away...] (ZMD 129)

Brathwaite's objection to Ayama's acceptance explains itself out of his understanding of having entered a new creative phase that accompanied his vision of an alternative, utopian world order in the form of the Irish Town maroon community:

> ... we went up to IT to create like a Maroon community/independent & subsistent likethat/with enough land & space & shall we say SPIRIT POWER for people to work/ to 'find' / develop ourselves & from/to where I cd eventually resign from the University [HOW GOD DISPOSES, eh?] & devote all/the rest of my blk puddin & souse to that worldpool of writing... (ZMD 130)

In such an alternative society, being a poet would not just be a "hobby," as his family and university colleagues call Brathwaite's vocation, but would elevate him to the status of spiritual leader or *houngan*. In voodoo culture, the *houngan* engages in what Brathwaite calls "the grapple w/ the loa" (ZMD 130), thus acting as a channel through which the community can engage with the divine. The following passage makes clear, as do the letters to his sister, that his family and colleagues, looking to western cultural models, re-enact the destruction caused by colonial rule, shattering his vision:

> so that it hurt when people don't seem to understand this, the grapple w/ the loa, they seeing the writing as a 'hobby'/ **my 'hobby'** as one of our Vice-Chancellors once told me! & call me un-/or anti-/social because as things stann now I find I must defend the what-happens-when-we-say-writing – that kind of 'catness' in a way – when others are out visiting or laughing or

> drinking or debunking or partying or just ST/ing – which is what I'd like to be doing too – why not! –but you can't do everything, since this loving in the spirit', as you put it, comes first first first/ the thousand hour days or years you have to spend upon the pound or poem of the flesh to make it into LIG HT)
>
> & all this time Death there aroun (d) the corner, in the shadows, sit ing down w/ us at supper or our birthday dinner, slipping in our very cup So that me can't even **s p e a k** Aya of **cycle completed** o n ly of circle mash up & circle des- troyed in the very middle of our fortune] (ZMD 130–31)

In Brathwaite's notion of history, the destruction of subsistence cultures and the environment that sustains them results in a feeling of being uprooted, of fragmentation and alienation, particularly evident in the Middle Passage, in the actual severance of people from their homeland. In Soyinka's account of the suffering of Obatala, there is also a sense of fragmentation. According to Soyinka, Obatala is often equated with the primal deity of Orisa-nla, who was shattered to pieces by a boulder rolled onto his back by his jealous slave Atunda. Orisa-nla's fragments created the Yoruba pantheon. The gods are also called *orishas* in memory of the first deity. Obatala's suffering and loneliness epitomize the Yoruba gods' longing for the primal oneness of Orisa-nla. Soyinka describes Obatala as "the serene womb of chthonic reflections (or memory), a passive strength awaiting and celebrating each act of vicarious restoration of his primordial being" (143). Obatala's suffering complements Ogun's experience of transition. In Soyinka's account of the story of the gods, Ogun forges a road through the abyss of transition, which the gods have to travel in order to join their mortal counterparts and re-experience the primordial oneness. The abyss of transition stands for the changeability of human life, as opposed to divine eternity, which is unchangeable. As in a rite of passage, the experience of transition implies the death of the old and the birth of a new self, and Ogun is the first deity to experience death and rebirth (143).[10] The union of the divine and the human becomes an instance of communion. Thus Orisa-nla is at once a mythic and utopian space of oneness, spanning, like Damballah and the *Grand Chemin*, the distant past and the as yet unbecome future. In claiming Obatala's and Ogun's experience as relating to his own, Brathwaite goes beyond the merely personal. Brathwaite's own understanding of the role of the poet is that of a public persona, a voice and guide of the people, although his environment sees in him merely an isolated, self-obsessed individual.[11]

In this context, the image of the broken circle in the quotation below can be read on both a personal and a communal level. Through Mexican's death and his subsequent isolation, Brathwaite becomes unfocused and unmoored:

> [But my pain continues, Aya, for the very reason that I just tellin you A circle has been broken & I & what was once the friends & people of the cycle/circle have so disintegrated/ centre gone/things fall a/part/ . . .] (ZMD 131)

The circle is a metaphor that links Mexican with the Irish Town maroon project, the maroon community being an example of "circle" or subsistence culture. In "An excerpt from Limbo," Brathwaite describes the maroon project as a series of circles with Mexican as their center (104). The circle echoes images from the poem "Veridian" (*Middle Passages*), which describes the maroon community as "looking inward to this centre," the center of communal activity (33–34; "An excerpt from Limbo" 98–99).

With Mexican's death, the center of this maroon life disappears, "the centre cannot hold," and Brathwaite's world "falls apart." The "anarchy" that "is loosed upon the world" echoes the fall of Rome and the rising of the tribes in *X/Self* that implode the empire. In the above excerpt from the *Diary*, Brathwaite, of course, alludes to Chinua Achebe's novel *Things Fall Apart* (1958), which in turn takes its title from W. B. Yeats's poem, "The Second Coming" (1921). In his introduction to the Everyman edition of *Things Fall Apart*, Kwame Anthony Appiah argues that what connects Yeats's poem and Achebe's novel is the notion of historical cycles, another echo of the circle (viii–ix). In using the intertextual reference to Yeats and Achebe, Brathwaite represents personal trauma as a comment on the postcolonial situation. In Achebe's novel, an African community disintegrates with the arrival of the Europeans, and the focus or center of African tradition is fragmented by the introduction of European cultural values. The African community Achebe describes becomes unmoored and exiled in its own country, from its own way of life.

The breaking of the circle in *The Zea Mexican Diary* is a disruption of continuity, both in the personal sense of the end of marriage and in the communal sense of the cultural fragmentation of the Caribbean. Whereas the maroons, in their orientation towards Africa, are able to uphold a sense of cultural continuity, the slaves on the plantation remain unmoored in this way, their traditional way of life falling apart as they are forcefully separated from Africa, family, and native language. The ignorance and unconcern that Brathwaite perceives in his family towards his suffering as well as his vision may thus also be read as a denial of the history of slavery, which at the same time conspires with colonial historiography.[12] In this context, Ogun's experience of annihilation corresponds to the cultural fragmentation induced by the Middle Passage, whereas Obatala's confinement parallels the literal confinement of the slaves on the ships.

At the end of the chapter, Ayama makes a statement that urges Brathwaite's work away from a mere existence as text: "**For, I am with you Kamau. And feel even richer in the quiet commun ication. And give thanks for you. And give thanks to Jah for your creation. And give thanks to your Parents for you And give thanks to [Mexican] for preserving the inner You. But words, Kamau, words are not enough...**" (*ZMD* 139). The insufficiency of words addressed by Ayama can be linked to the change of style in Brathwaite's work, the shift from conventional typescript to the experiment of the "video style," together with the shift from a narrow western definition of poetry to a montage of different genres. Both of these stylistic phenomena make the text appear fragmentary, mirroring the fragmentary nature of Caribbean experience. Mexican's death functions as a further, personal, experience of fragmentation, as the end of communion and a plunging back into the "darkness of the lived moment." The absence of closure that accompanies the "video" texts is enhanced by their interconnectedness, which will become evident in subsequent chapters. Brathwaite's creation of the alternative space of the Irish Town maroon society is an attempt to explode the idea of art and literature as separate from life. His creative and spiritual crisis following Mexican's death represents the final trigger away from "fiction" and towards "fictive imagination." In the course of this development, the utopian aspect of his vision, the "creole cosmos" as a manifestation of *Heimat*, shifts from the content of his writing to express itself also on the formal level of the "video style" as well as in a defense of his belief in the artist as maroon.

The chapter entitled "The working muses," which follows Brathwaite's conversation with Ayama, continues his defense of his maroon existence as poet and visionary.[13] The section begins as a display of letters of condolence, which frequently refer to Mexican as Brathwaite's inspiration and muse, for example:

> Who will there be to share [yr poems] with/
> who will there be to write them for?
>
> (*ZMD* 148–49)

These statements trigger Brathwaite's own reflection on "the **CREATIVE EKB** the poet" (*ZMD* 149). As "creative EKB," Brathwaite is Ogun, god of creativity. However, Ogun or Ogoun, a spelling Brathwaite uses in *Barabajan Poems*, is also god of war, and Brathwaite's practice of adopting African personae and thus an African-orientated consciousness can be read as a form of maroon resistance. Further on in this section he even refers to his defense of himself as poet-seer as the "'battle' of&for Identity," which is conducted against the "willful definition of the I against the xpress wishes of the I/ this downing of the art & writer" (*ZMD* 151). Brathwaite alludes here in particular to his wish to be addressed as Kamau during the funeral service, and his family's uneasiness with, and at times open rejection of, the name he acquired in Africa. Edward, his European name, is preferred by everyone except Kamau himself. Kamau consequently becomes the poet-persona in resistance, more precisely in maroon resistance.

Ngũgĩ wa Thiong'o also describes this renaming of Edward as Kamau during the latter's visit to Kenya as an act of self-definition and resistance against colonial rule:

> I invited Brathwaite to my rented home in Tigoni, Limuru.
> ... Tigoni was fairly central to Kenya's history, because it

*Death, Marriage, and Maroons:* The Zea Mexican Diary

was one of the earliest bones of contention between the British colonial settlers and Kenyans. The demand for the return of the stolen lands of Tigoni to their original owners was one of the key elements in the anticolonial militancy which in the fifties erupted into the Mau Mau armed struggle.... So the peasants from the villages and the men and women of letters from Nairobi ... now gathered in this rural outpost to celebrate Brathwaite's presence.... It was during the ceremony, with the women singing Gĩtiiro, a kind of dialogue in song and dance, that Edward Brathwaite was given the name of Kamau, the name of a generation that long ago had struggled with the elements to tame the land and make us into what we now were. Edward, the name of the British king under whose brief reign in the 1920s some of the Tigoni lands had been appropriated by blue-blooded aristocrats who wanted to turn Kenya into a white man's country, had now been replaced by Kamau. (678)

This renaming by Africans in Africa intensifies Brathwaite's sense of the African legacy in the Caribbean by being ceremonially reconnected to the ancestral continent. Kamau becomes the Caliban of "Nametracks," and the Tigoni women act as Sycorax figures, reminding Caliban of his African name. Brathwaite recounts this naming ceremony in Chapter XII of *Barabajan Poems*, where he also gives a cultural reading of the name Kamau, arguing that it contains both male and female elements:

**K**

is the signal of *the male elements* and ...
the **U**
at the 'end'
marks the beginning of the name's female meaning because in traditional African culture names like everything else are totally integrated so that a name is both male and female....

**ama**

... female spirit, anima ...

(*BP* 239–40)

In other words, the name read from left to right embodies the male principle, and read from right to left, from "the other beginning of its damballa" (*BP* 240), the female. Thus the name "Kamau" is akin to a snake biting its tail (Damballah being a snake deity) and represents the communion of male and female. In this sense, Kamau becomes Mexican's twin, as Mexican, too, incorporates both male and female elements as both European muse and African-Caribbean Legba.

As a maroon figure and figure of transgression, Brathwaite regards the poet as the core of an alternative world order (and here again Kamau is twin to Mexican, who is the center of the circle). For him, writing is a spiritual process, an act of communing with the divine. In this sense, the poet functions as a transgressive figure and follows the invitation of the muse who opens the door to the other side of mortal life. In describing writing as "the 40 days in the wilderness" (*ZMD* 151), Brathwaite compares himself to the biblical prophets, who went to the desert to struggle with temptation but also to seek enlightenment in communion with God. For Brathwaite, the act of writing represents such a process of struggle, not with God but with the *loa*. The text itself, the final outcome of this struggle, is a product of the poet's communion with the *loa*. The act of writing thus mirrors the act of spirit possession. Also in "The working muses," Brathwaite writes that some of his friends and family regard Mexican's death as a punishment for his maroon project and his desire to be a poet: "Indeed one 'formerFriend' said . . . that I am being **punished** (her choice of word!) because I'd gone to live 'up in' Irish Tn **pretending to be a poet** . . ." (*ZMD* 149–50). Brathwaite sees himself, like Obatala, as an ostracized individual, which, within the *Diary*, is expressed in a variety of ways, his creative isolation being perhaps the most poignant.

In Chapter VIII, "This obeia business," Brathwaite discovers that Jamaican folk culture, contrary to his own understanding, provides a variety of rituals that serve to estrange the dead from the community of the living:

> **from time to time wherever I go wh-**
> **erever I am . . . the odour of Miss**
> **Mac's sulphur . . . the dirty-looking**
> **fistfulls brought up here & lit & pl-**

> aced in tins in every corner of the house/ to burn her out as if she was in hell. . . .
>
> And Jean say how I muss repaint the house & change th(e) furniture around so she cyaaa(n) recognize the place – *my love my life my darling Mexican! – your house your care your love your home always your smile of welcome* . . . (ZMD 163)

This driving out of the dead contradicts the idea of community and communion Brathwaite witnessed when he lived in Africa, where the dead are encouraged to join the community of the living either as beneficent, advising spirits or by being reborn. But in the *Diary*, Brathwaite himself seems at a loss as to what kind of ritual to perform:

> [. . . I know there is some ritual I've not performed/ which I don't even know/ & no one that I know/knows how to bring it/ help me/ with it to/wards it Which the Africans know Which the Greeks knew . . .
>
> I have not even **seen** her yet She has not even **dreamed** me yet Has sent no whisper of a message – bird or butterfly or curse – not even rat-bat owl or johncrow/**Why is dat?**]
>
> (ZMD 131–32)[14]

Brathwaite's personal inability to establish contact with his dead wife points to the wider cultural situation of the Caribbean. Brathwaite seems to imply that the ability to commune with the dead has been lost during the Middle Passage. On several occasions in the *Diary* he attempts to recreate this link between the mundane and the numinous or magical. This will become more pertinent in the tree planting ceremony later in the *Diary*.

In section IX, "Letters to MaryMorgan," written by Brathwaite to his sister Mary, the poet appears in another form of isolation: as the isolated widower, separated from the community of women:

> I mean widows we know how to deal with 'in
>
> the culture'/ & they seem to know only too well
>
> (if I may say so) how to signal for **HELP**/ how to
>
> ensure/ even **ensnare** protec-
>
> tion/reconstruction
>
> – & I cannot mean any of this unkindly –
>
> & in any case they are usually more
>
> physically& mentally prepared & independent
>
> & have steadied themselves somehow for these
>
> 'eventualities' – ...

## 2

> But the widow's Other? *the widower?* in a-we-
>
> culture? Depending on his age/con- dition he's

> either useless cock or hot new une**X**pected
>
> 'property'/ the newly 'eligible "bachelor"'. In
>
> either/neither case
>
> **NO**/**BODY** bizness wid im grief &
>
> dislocation . im is suppose to **cope**
>
> ('real man' na cry etc etc etc)/
>
> **& stann up pun im one two feets**
>
> as VP rather harshly told me when I ask for
>
> help
>
> (ZMD 174–75)

For Brathwaite, this gender division expresses itself as spiritual isolation, as the loss of communion between male and female implied in the name Kamau and in the male-and-female muse Legba. The spiritual support he craves is made impossible by what he calls a second Middle Passage:

> ... **The Middle Passage** – but not th
>
> at first one  from  the  golden coast & co
>
> st of Guinea  but this still salter one ...
>
> ... this **Middle Class-**
>
> **age Passage** into 'dish' & 'dis'/ dis/str
>
> ess dis/crimination  the  lack & lost of but
>
> terflies & green & trees/ ...
>
> (ZMD 176–77)

Caribbean society has moved away from the life of the circle culture towards more western models of individualism that destroy community. This social fragmentation is a mirror image of the uprooting of the original Middle Passage and another example of its "ongoing catastrophe" (McSweeney). For Brathwaite, the "Middle Classage Passage" is an epitome of the contemporary world that has deprived itself of the possibility of *Heimat*.

In the second part of "Letters to MaryMorgan," added for the published version of the *Diary*, Brathwaite comes to see his exclusion from company as a rite of passage, "these **mysteries** I sometimes have to call them" (*ZMD* 183–84), similar to the confinement of Obatala, which results in heightened awareness and catharsis:

> **. . . the loss the pain the absence like an abscess or abyss the questions questions questions the problems problems problems may be one day resolved if not revealed . . .** (*ZMD* 184)

The "Letters" section thus ends on a note of hope for restored community and of reconciliation in particular between Brathwaite and his sister: "and so I hope that perhaps long after I have written this . . . & ridden these events . . . you will be walking back across this broken ground towards me . . ." (*ZMD* 185). Individual isolation finally gives way to a renewed sense of community. The remaining part of the *Diary* can be read as a rejoining of the individual with the community, which completes Brathwaite's rite of passage.

In this context, the dialogic nature of this process of rejoining is an important factor to note. Mary did indeed walk back across the broken ground to meet her brother by writing two essays that connect with his work. The first one, "Highway to Vision: The Sea Our Nexus," is a commentary on the importance of the sea in Brathwaite's writing and how it dominated the imagination and daily life of the siblings' childhood. Mary's own words are frequently interspersed with quotations from Brathwaite's poetry, creating the impression of a dialogue. The second, called "This Silver Feather," published in Timothy J. Reiss's *For the Geography of a Soul* (2001), is a reflection on Brathwaite's receipt of the Neustadt Prize for Literature in 1994. The issue of *World Literature Today*, in which "Highway to Vision" was published, was itself a special issue on the occasion of Brathwaite's receipt of the award. "This Silver Feather" frequently cites Brathwaite's own contribution to the issue. Mary Morgan's essay also reflects on his development of the "Sycorax video style" and how it emerged out of his own personal crisis. She particularly mentions — and quotes at length — *The Zea Mexican Diary*, as well as *Shar* and *DreamStories*, all of which record her brother's time of trauma or "time of salt." "This Silver Feather" also imitates the "video style," so the essay is a dialogue and a walking back across broken ground on a formal as well as personal level.

The "Letters to Mary Morgan" form the last part of the "Letters" section. They are followed by an "Epigraph," a short account of Brathwaite's and Mexican's life together, in a form reminiscent of an African praise poem. The "Epigraph" is read by Edward Baugh as part of the funeral service and written in centered typescript. Mexican is described as having

>            . . . a **conscience** made so strong so
> strong & I repeat so generous that it is **caritas** & always time
> for friends & all the names of trees & plants & flowers at her
>         fingertips (so very rare in Caribbean people)
>                 . . . . . . . . . . . . . . . . . . . .
>                        To her, then,
>        Queen & Keeper of our modern Caribbean literature
>                    – one of them, surely –
>                       I call her out
>                    **- *ohemmaa* -**
>
>                         (ZMD 192)

In *Wars of Respect: Nanny and Sam Sharpe*, Brathwaite relates the concept of *ohemmaa* to the maroon leader Nanny. The historical Nanny lived in the late seventeenth and early eighteenth century and was the leader of the Jamaican Windward maroons.[15] The name Nanny itself has, as Brathwaite's research shows, many connotations, most of them linked to motherhood in concrete as well as metaphorical terms:

> There has been some speculation about the origins of the name Nanny. Roderick Ebanks in a radio broadcast, October 1975, . . . says that the name comes from an aboriginal Ni, a kind of First Mother or Ancestor ready

like the Ashanti ohemmaas, to lead the nation to restoration in times of crisis. Alan Tuelon (*Caribbean Quarterly* 19:4: p. 21) claims that the name may well be 'a corruption of the Ashanti word, Ni, mother'. These could lead us to Nana NI, nana being the Ashanti form of address reserved for chiefs, spiritual leaders, ancestors and the venerable. In fact, in the Caribbean even today, some of us still call or refer to our grandparents as nen, nenne or nana, the first two of which are connected with another Ashanti form for mother, *na ni*. (41–42 n73)[16]

Among the Ashanti of West Africa, the *ohemmaa* or Queen Mother appoints the king (*ohene*), thus giving birth to the state: "... she owns the state, as a mother owns her child, and ... she is regarded as the mother of everybody.... Her chief duty was, and is, to care for the women, for their welfare, and for everything connected with birth, marriage and family life" (Meyerowitz 27, 38 qtd. in Brathwaite, *Wars of Respect* 13).

In *Barabajan Poems*, Brathwaite describes Caribbean women as cells of resistance, indeed a recurrent theme in his work:

>                ... & we/these
>     Calibans ...
>            ... had no power, no real
>         real power, really/&merely
>         did what was demanded of us
>                                  by
>             **'The Man Who**
>             **Possesses Us**
>                      **All'**
>
>     & it was these women – the
>                       mothers &
>       godmothers/grandmothers of
>       tradition, the protectors of *nam*

## who warned against this ...

(*BP* 134–36)

Contrary to the gender division Brathwaite experiences in everyday Caribbean reality, women in his writing emerge as defenders of community and keepers of ancestral memory. Glissant argues that among Caribbean slaves "collective dependence reinforced the 'reproductive' machismo of male slaves but did not authorize the appearance of femininity as a spiritual counterforce, even if women were frequently centers of resistance" (*Poetics* 60). Brathwaite's work frequently attempts to do just that — "authorize the appearance of femininity as a spiritual counterforce."[17] Moreover, he invents Stark, Caliban's sister, who represents the visual and audible presence of woman in Caribbean society, "a black woman w/ firm feet, sensitive/aggressive breasts and a space & plan if not always a room of her own" (*BP* 316).[18] In this context, the reference to Virginia Woolf's seminal essay, *A Room of One's Own* (1928), is no coincidence. Caliban's sister echoes Shakespeare's sister. Woolf's idea of the woman artist's androgynous mind is in many ways reminiscent of Brathwaite's male/female muse. As an image for independent creative women in the Caribbean, Stark is mirrored in Mexican. In "Caliban's Guarden" (1992), Brathwaite stresses that Sycorax, on the other hand, is not an acting but a "submerged" presence in Shakespeare's *The Tempest*, i.e. she is present through her absence, just as in the Caribbean context Mother Africa is present in the people's memory but absent as a reality (4).

In death, however, Mexican is no longer Sister Stark but becomes a Sycoraxian presence through absence. In being planted at the root of the tulip tree, she merges with the island of Jamaica. In this sense, Sycorax reclaims the island that was hers before Prospero took it from her. Thus in Mexican/Sycorax, Africa becomes rooted in Caribbean soil. At another level, Mexican/Sycorax gives birth to Brathwaite's/Caliban's maroon identity as the *ohemmaa* gives birth to the state in the form of the *ohene*. In this sense, Mexican is a utopian persona, embodying both the notion of origin, as *ohemmaa*, and of "arrived-at Being," as Nanny of the maroons.

"The Tulip Tree" describes the burial of Mexican's ashes, which are, even before their burial, perceived not as human remains but as part of the Caribbean landscape: "There was plenty of ash & the box that contained it was quite heavy with it but it wasn't wood-ash-white but a kind of (I was surprised) pink/brown w/ white flecks in it – like coral sand w/

little clips of fingernails of shells & conchs & perhaps crab in there – that smooth & shine & hint of pink: the sand of sea & time our origins..." (*ZMD* 198). This description of her ashes as shoreline is reminiscent of the transformation of the mother at the end of *Mother Poem*:

> the ancient watercourses
>
> trickling slowly into the coral
> travelling inwards under the limestone
>
> widening outwards into the sunlight
> towards the breaking of her flesh with foam (*MP* 117)

In becoming conscious of the Caribbean landscape as *Heimat* for himself as diasporic African, Brathwaite becomes native to the Americas and ceases to be an exile from Africa. As Mexican fuses with the land, she enters the realm of geological memory and connects human life to the history of the region. She thus functions as an antidote to the mudslide mentioned at the beginning of this chapter. In other words, she becomes an agent of the "submarine unity" Brathwaite envisions in *Caribbean Man in Space and Time* (1).

The vision of the *Diary* is in many ways more personal than the one expressed in his earlier writings. Likewise, the agents that link him to the land are not the Haitian *loa* in their spirit form, but people who are close to him and who reveal at times traces of the divine. Thus Mexican undergoes an apotheosis, but not in the Christian sense of an ascension to heaven. Rather she is "grounded" like a *loa*, i.e. invited into the human community to infuse it with divine spirit. This aspect of grounding, after some of her ashes have been planted together with the tulip tree, is addressed in the statement of one of the ceremony's participants: "... Bärbel spoke & prayed, pointing out that Mexican had now become part of the IT landscape that she loved & in this way she wd — as long as world was there — be with me/ with us always" (*ZMD* 200).

By planting her ashes at the foot of the tulip tree, Brathwaite creates the ritual he had craved and missed earlier. In the process, he also reinterprets Christianity. He not only transforms Mexican into a part of the landscape, but also into a part of himself, thus re-enacting the Eucharist: "... when I was going downstairs to get the second vessel, I put some of the ashes on my tongue & swallowed her" (*ZMD* 199). By re-investing the Eucharist with its literal meaning of eating the body of Christ, Brathwaite seeks the actual physical communion with the divine and not the symbolic communion practiced by the Protestant church. In Christian terms Brathwaite performs a sacrilege by elevating a mortal being to the status of the divine, undermining Christianity as an instrument of cultural hegemony. What is striking about the end of the *Diary* is that it moves towards an enactment of individual *maronage*. He thus reconnects with the initial Irish Town project.

Despite Brathwaite's reinvention of ritual, he feels that at the end of the tree planting, "**prayers sai (d) hymns sung the obsequies properly performed 'traditionals' observed the tulip tree in place — something was I still felt missing**" (*ZMD* 202). In connection with this missing rite, Brathwaite has an epiphany, not at the time of the ceremony, however, but when he was editing the *Diary* for publication. An Irish Town neighbor, a close friend of Mexican's, comes to join the ceremony:

This Mr Reid . . .

went down right away to the spot where Harry ha

(d) been digging & where the tree wd be & . . .

was . . . alone, looking out across the

landscape across the valley out to Kingston &

the sea - like . . . some kind

of sentinel - . . .

though I didn't recognize him then - we so seldom

do! -

# ELUEGGBA

god of the pathways - (*ZMD* 201–2)

## A Creole Experiment

As a trickster, Legba represents the African principle that "life achieves wholeness through a balance of opposites": "The trickster's acts of disorder prepare the way for new order; death gives way to birth" ("African Religions: an Overview" 64). Mr Reid becomes the master of ceremonies, performing the missing rite by saying words of farewell and commemoration to the deceased and shaking the stem of the newly planted tree. In the course of this ceremony, Brathwaite perceives the tree as becoming inhabited by the spirit of Mexican, and the shaking results in "her stem singing" (ZMD 207). Thus matter is infused with spirit.

Brathwaite depicts this ceremony in the layout of the typescript, presenting it in the shape of a cross, the cross of both Legba and Christ that also appears at the end of the first *X/Self*:

### O Mrs Brathwaite

hands working all the while, the earth being gently patted like a

comfort reassurance since it was now her body

### such a lovely person

&

he

### shook

the tree

### such a peaceful person

&

he

**shook**

the tree

(*ZMD* 203-4)

Legba is also the guardian of the *poteau mitan*, the center pole of the sacred chamber of the *houmfort*. The center pole is a representation of the *Grand Chemin*, the road which the *loa* travel to be united with their mortal counterparts. By merging the spiritual and the physical plane of existence, Legba restores order to the chaos of suffering and death. The dead and the living are each given their place in the cosmos, but they are also, as the world axis unites the dead, the living, and the gods, in constant communication with each other. In the act of the tree planting, Mexican becomes, in a very literal sense, a utopian space of arrival, mirroring the Xango persona of *X/Self*, a door for the imaginary to pass into the reality of the Caribbean and infuse it with magic. Moreover, the tree planting ceremony illustrates Mexican's transgressive nature with which the *Diary* began. Situated at the root of the tree, which in its cosmic dimension allows for the communion of all planes of existence, she has returned from the beyond of death to illuminate the "darkness of the lived moment" with the spiritual light of that other place. Mexican becomes again Legba's double or twin. Thus, as at the end of *X/Self*, the Caribbean becomes a *houmfort*, a magical and sacred space and a manifestation of *Heimat*.

The theme of rebirth that follows death appears again in the closing section of the *Diary*, "The Awakening" or "Anyaneanyane." It reads like a postscript to the original *Diary*, written some time after the tree planting. Brathwaite has begun a new cycle of life, represented by his new partner Beverly/Dream Chad, who will in time become his wife. He presents this section as a vision of the afterlife (which will reappear in *Born to Slow Horses*):

One late afternoon I drove Aunt May & Dream Chad up to Hardwar Gap &  the Park up there  Looking across from where we were there was a valley & beyond that on the same level w/ us a wood in mist & you cd see a road & the light under the trees in the distance but it was like over there & you couldnt see the connection how it got where it was how you cd get there & there was no one over there Only peace As if **there** was where she was walking away from us . . . (*ZMD* 213)

His depiction of the afterworld is presented as another epiphany. It deliberately avoids Christian references of heaven and hell and locates it instead in the geography of the New World, in the Blue Mountains of Jamaica ("I cd see her&not see her beyond that valley high/ up there in the Blue Mountains" (*ZMD* 214)), creolizing the notion of death and afterlife. The notion of death as dystopia as it appears early in the *Diary* is thus enlightened by those visions that fill Brathwaite with, at least a momentary, joy: ". . . I was suddenly & at last happy & very very sad & lonely at the same time . . ." (*ZMD* 214).

Although dystopian elements occur again in subsequent works, Brathwaite creates images such as Legba and the Blue Mountains that present death as "illuminated by still unguaranteed joy" (*PH* 3: 1180). Thus the book ends on a note of hope and healing and recognizes the need to let go of what has been painful in the past. The gap that appears in Brathwaite's vision of the afterlife, the valley that separates him from the Blue Mountains, represents this sense of closure on an individual level: he has to let go of Mexican, so that both she and Brathwaite himself can begin a new cycle of existence. This awareness is demonstrated in the title of the section.

The "Awakening" ceremony or "Anyaneanyane" first occurs in *Masks* (1968), which chronicles Brathwaite's experience of living in Ghana and forms the second book of *The Arrivants* trilogy. In *Pathfinder* (1981), Gordon Rohlehr describes the "Awakening" ceremony as conducted by the drummer of the Ashanti court on the morning of the Adae festival: "Adae festivals occur every twenty-one days, and are occasions for remember-

*Death, Marriage, and Maroons: The Zea Mexican Diary*

ing and paying reverence to the ancestors" (126; Lewis 65–69). In *Masks*, the ceremony is associated with the poet's awakening consciousness that acknowledges not only the African heritage in Caribbean culture but also Africa's own contribution to the slave trade. This acknowledgement functions as a remembering of the ancestors. However, Africa cannot be transplanted to the Caribbean, and new, creole forms of expression must be sought instead. The analogy to Mexican's death lies in the need to sever oneself from the past. The dead person is remembered, but grief, as a form of hanging on to the past, must not be allowed to take over the lives of those who survive her, so that the deceased can pass on into the afterworld, "each day getting more & more distance & getting more & more involve w/ what was happening over there" (*ZMD* 213).

In this context, the Blue Mountains of "The Awakening" function as a double metaphor. In the first instance, they recall again the maroon community of Irish Town, the center of Mexican's and Kamau's life together, as well as Jamaican maroon history in general, to which the Irish Town project was connected. In "Nanny, Palmares & the Caribbean Maroon Connexion," Brathwaite describes *maronage* as a form of Zionism, which in its original context embodies the yearning for a Jewish homeland. In the context of plantation slavery, this yearning for a homeland or *Heimat* represented a challenge to the plantation system:

> . . . as long as the Maroons occupied the space at the height & centre of the island — as long by militantly & successfully occupying the mountains & by cutting off easy & dependable communication between the North & South coasts where the major plantations were located & by their 'Zionism' were creating a kind of NewAfrican heaven & haven & kingdom at the visible heart of the island (in those always visible & (to them) viable Blue & John Crow Mountains) which would increasingly be an attraction to hundreds perhaps thousands of the enslaved & therefore a threat or cut-throat to the whole xpensive & would-be xpansive Plantation System from Port Antonio through MoBay right around to Morant Bay — there could be no guarantee that the Plantation would continue to be a profitable investment under such conditions . . . . (122)

In other words, Brathwaite suggests that the New World has the potential to become a form of new Jerusalem. In this messianic context, the maroon societies (both historical and contemporary) of *The Zea Mexican Diary* anticipate the Rastafarian worldview of *Trench Town Rock*.

# Chapter 3

# The Poet's Archive as Houmfort: *Shar/Hurricane Poem*

◇◆◇

## 3.1. "Saving the Word": Epics and Archives

*Shar/Hurricane Poem* (*Shar*) (1990)[1] represents Brathwaite's second account of personal trauma. It describes the destruction of his house and library at Irish Town by Hurricane Gilbert in 1988. The poem is also a commemoration of the death of his niece Sharon ("Shar") in 1990, when Brathwaite revised the poem for that purpose (Morgan, "This Silver Feather" 328). As Mary Morgan, Sharon's mother, points out in "Highway to Vision: The Sea Our Nexus," the poem

> is dedicated by Kamau to Sharon, my daughter, who spent the academic year 1989-90 between our home in Jamaica, hers in St. Lucia, and the University Hospital back at Mona, where she died in July 1990 after a triumphant fight with non-Hodgkins lymphoma — triumphant because of her shining faith (she sustained her pregnancy through chemotherapy) and the miracle of the birth of her second son, Richard (March 1990), beyond the expectation of her doctors. (668 n12)

For Brathwaite, Sharon's death echoes the trauma of Mexican's death four years earlier (Morgan, "Highway to Vision" 664). As a consequence, the two women merge into one person in the poem, and the death of one is commemorated in the death of the other. In another sense, *Shar* is also another way of "walking back across broken ground," a reconciliation between Brathwaite and his sister after the period of estrangement that characterizes much of *The Zea Mexican Diary*. In this context, *Shar* echoes Mary's own attempts at reaching out recorded in "Highway to Vision" and "This Silver Feather."

The poem itself has a two-part structure. The first part describes the destructive force of the hurricane and the devastation it leaves in its wake. As in *The Zea Mexican Diary*, natural catastrophe mirrors the emotional devastation caused by the loss of loved ones. The poet's state of mind is reflected in the landscape. Towards the end of the first part, however, there is a sense of acceptance and even of hope. The second part answers to this sense of hope by celebrating the power of human endurance and by anticipating a new cycle of life.

Brathwaite includes an introduction to the poem, which gives a rendition of a speech delivered by Carolivia Herron, Director of the Harvard University's Center for the Study of Epic Poetry (the "Epicenter"), on the occasion of its opening on 22 September 1988. Brathwaite was invited to the opening ceremony, where he read from his poem, the first version of which was "then very much 'in progress'" (*Shar* 1). Brathwaite's rendition of Herron's speech, entitled "Saving the Word," includes a description of his immediate reaction to the threat of the hurricane. "Saving the Word" also states the aims and concerns of the "Epicenter":

> **One of the. . major concerns of the Epicenter is the loss of words. . cultural words. . epic pieces. .by contemporary cultures that are lost because we don't have the capacity to save the words. . .and because many times the Western epics supersede the Third World epics to such an extent that there is not enough energy or interest in those of us who have the capacity to save words, to go to the places where these poems and epics are being spoken and sung, to save them. . .** (*Shar* 1)

This passage is followed by a definition of epic: "**I have called an epic (my own definition) a long narrative describing the origin &**

## The Poet's Archive as Houmfort: Shar/Hurricane Poem

nature & destiny of a race, group, tribe, nation or gender, depicting a hero or heroic ideal and incorporating the cultural world-view of that hero and his/ her people. . ." (*Shar* 2). Brathwaite's library comprises such a long narrative, the long narrative of the Caribbean, or as Brathwaite puts it himself:

> 'Irish Town' is one of the largest & most important archives of Cari bbean literature & culture in the Caribbean...It contains a record - since I keep almost everything - of many of our writers' progress (drafts unpublished manuscripts letters diaries artefacts books books books books thousands of miles of tapes LPs) – possibly one of the largest collections of Caribbean poetry in the world (*Shar* 3–4)

Brathwaite's library can thus be described as a cultural "epicenter," as the center of the long narrative of Caribbean culture and a storehouse of its words and history.

The passage ascribed to Herron also gives a brief introduction to Brathwaite's own life, referring to his personal migration from Barbados via Cambridge to Africa and back to the Caribbean as "a long narrative" (*Shar* 2). Moreover, the reference to *The Arrivants* suggests that the poet's life is an epic in itself, inseparable from the epic poems he writes and thus inseparable from the history of his people. Brathwaite elaborates on this idea:

> You have to be concerned with the sources of a poet's life a people's inspiration and try to protect care for as best you can, those sources...We have to be concerned with the poet's health well-being com fort. yes; but above all there are the **archives** - that written mem orialized recorded record of his/her life/hope/history/art. Because if you can applaud him /her ('clap a likkle') as he/she stands before you, if, as I assume, you feel that he/she has something important to say, then you've got to be concerned with the **whole thing**. (*Shar* 4)

For Brathwaite, a poet's life cannot be separated from his words. As was evident in the discussion of *The Zea Mexican Diary*, having access to the word makes the poet someone who has access to transcendent, revitalizing energies. Therefore, the poet is "a people's inspiration," and his library or archive can be understood as the people's soul. Brathwaite's library, above all, makes the Caribbean past accessible and thus makes possible the potential continuation of its culture into the future. However, Brathwaite laments contemporary Caribbean society's lack of interest in its own culture, which he sees as resulting in social indifference and even aggression ("our scavenge John Crow culture" (*Shar* 5)).[2]

The introduction ends with Brathwaite addressing a loved one, Sharon in the first instance, but the memory of Mexican is also very much present: **"Did you get out? where were you my love? and the baby? and of course I have to sit here helpless, not hear(ing) not know(ing) a thing..."** (*Shar* 5). He thus links both spheres, both readings, of the poem, the destruction of the house by the hurricane and his emotional devastation caused by the death of the two women. The appearance of this last section in bold print suggests its importance. It is, in fact, as important to him as the library, the description of which also appears in bold print. In this sense, the appearance of the text on the page, too, creates a bridge between the two layers of the poem. At times, the personal loss seems more prevalent than the environmental catastrophe and the devastation of communal memory mirrored in the loss of his archive.

The fact that Sharon's name appears fragmented in the poem's title points to a maiming of the individual in the first instance. Sharon does not complete the full cycle of her life. This links her to Mexican, who, as Brathwaite says to Ayama in *The Zea Mexican Diary*, had not completed the full cycle of her life either. The maiming of the name and, therefore, of the self connects Sharon (and indirectly Mexican) to X/Self, whose deprivation of selfhood is indicated by the slash that separates X from Self. In the context of the destruction of the archive, the fragmentation of the individual reflects the cultural fragmentation of the Caribbean, which Brathwaite describes in the opening paragraph of *Caribbean Man in Space and Time*. The force of the hurricane maims the Caribbean not only on a physical but also on a psychological level, destroying its storehouse of cultural memory for which the archive in Brathwaite's vision comes to stand. Later, in *ConVERSations with Nathaniel Mackey*, Brathwaite likens his archive to the library of Alexandria (*C* 153), the destruction of which is said to have obliterated most of the knowledge of the ancient world. Also in *ConVERSations*, Brathwaite reproduces the introductory remarks to *Shar*, both of himself and his rendition of Herron's, emphasizing the urgency of his appeal to the Caribbean community to concern itself with its archives (*C* 142–53).[3] He also includes a document entitled "Help," which lists

## The Poet's Archive as Houmfort: Shar/Hurricane Poem

the major works stored in the archive (*C* 298–302). By listing the titles of novels, poems, and LPs, Brathwaite attempts to rescue some of his library from obliteration, a task he takes on in *Shar* itself and in subsequent works, such as *Barabajan Poems* and *ConVERSations*.

Brathwaite's physical and spiritual homelessness as a result of the hurricane's destruction has deep existential consequences. In *ConVERSations with Nathaniel Mackey*, Brathwaite argues that Caribbean culture and literature have their roots in "pure little cas sava patch, yam plot, backdam, river-stream" rather than "dungles and . . . alleys. barracks, where bread and later bullet [see for xample, KB's **TTR** (1994)] increasingly become more important to the general than ballad or **beloved**" (*C* 131). Elsewhere in *ConVERSations* he refers to the house in Irish Town as "the *hoom* of psyche" (*C* 154), suggesting the connection of house and voodoo *houmfort*, the sacred space of communion between the human and divine. The house thus represents an aspect of *Heimat*, both in the physical sense of farming the "yam plot" and in the metaphorical sense of cultural belonging and "arrived-at Being." The house in the hills is also an alternative to the deprived city areas of Kingston (such as the Dungle), which in *Trench Town Rock* become the scene of violence, crime, and generally of Caribbean society's sense of alienation.

In "Houses in the West Indian Novel" (1976), Brathwaite argues that the image of the house is characteristic of the "English/European novel" where the "house suggests clearly defined boundaries: physical, emotional, traditional" (111). The motif of the house in West Indian literature represents, so Brathwaite argues, a European cultural referent. As examples he cites Phyllis Allfrey's *Orchid House* (1953) and Jean Rhys's *Wide Sargasso Sea* (1966), both of which describe "the descendants of the white plantocracy, living on their small island, at the top of a hill, hidden away among the scents of flowers" (111). The orchids' sweet smell leads Brathwaite to the conclusion that these novels "exposed the sweet/sick decay of what was once held to be 'life'" (111). In *Orchid House* and *Wide Sargasso Sea*, the presence of European culture in the Caribbean is at the point of disintegration.

In the same essay, Brathwaite cites a number of other novels by both white and non-white Caribbean authors, where the house functions as a place of sanctuary for the individual protagonist.[4] Brathwaite, however, also suggests that most novels by non-white, especially black, Caribbean writers focus on an absence of houses and on an absence of security and belonging. As an example of this type of writing, Brathwaite offers Orlando Patterson's novel *The Children of Sisyphus* (1964) with its setting in the makeshift ghetto of the Kingston Dungle (113–14). Brathwaite concludes: "Their concerns... are substitutes for houses, not alternatives" (115). Thus both white and non-white Caribbean writers experience and depict the Caribbean as a place of exile and not as a place of *Heimat*.

Brathwaite's writing shows a strong commitment to the preservation of African-Caribbean customs and traditions, offering an alternative to the European house as well as to the Kingston Dungle. In "Houses in the West Indian Novel," he suggests that voodoo represents an alternative to both the plantation and the ghetto:

> Now *vodun* is a Caribbean creation — along with pocomania, kumina, bongo, shango, the santeria, and other Afro-Caribbean religious dance dramas. It is the expression of a way of life, of looking, feeling and seeing, similar to the matrix which produced macumba, rhumba, samba and mambo in Latin America, the blues and jazz of North America, but it has not been secularized into entertainment forms as many of these latter now are. It is the expression of a folk sensibility that owes more to Africa than to Europe. From the point of view of the Caribbean artist, it is the basis of a possible alternative tradition; another way of exploring the world. (115)

Brathwaite suggests that in this alternative "way of exploring the world" the secular house of European tradition is replaced with the sacred space of voodoo worship, the *houmfort* or *tonnelle*.[5] He conceives of this space of ritual dancing and possession as a space of communion of all spheres of existence (the living, the dead, and the gods), as a "free moving from inner to outer reality and back again" ("Houses" 117). The dance thus corresponds to the voodoo notion of divinity as energy (Deren 187). In *Barabajan Poems*, Brathwaite describes this energy as creating a "choreography of sound inside the hounfort" (*BP* 180):

> ascending profile
> in reality the movement does not go 'one way' (i.e
> up) but creates a circle, the trump 'ascending', if you
> like, as the dove 'descends' and of course rather than
> being separate, the elements I try describe a
> 'collective/ communal polyrhythmic polyvalent
> tidalecttc 'jazz-voiced 'improvization'/engine

(*BP* 180)[6]

The space created by dancing is fluid and mirrors the structure of the *houmfort*. For Brathwaite, the Caribbean house as *houmfort* is "structurally wall-less in a hierarchical sense but corresponding to our Caribbean sense of community" ("Houses" 119).[7]

In this context, he perceives his own house at Irish Town, and especially his archive there, in precisely such spiritual and communal terms:

```
        . . . a hurricane hits Jamaica and the

house we build is practically totally destroyed. Here

are all the artifacts and all the archives all the manu-

scripts all these spiritual tokens and totems of the Car

ibbean sea and our trodden world we've been trying all

these years to find to keep to treasure to preserve to

hold against the precarious past and towards a future ca

ring : for our all-we community to share and overstand :

gone   .   suddem   .   flatten   .   just   like   that   .
(C 139)
```

Brathwaite regards his archive as something that belongs to the Caribbean community rather than to himself as an individual, since the Caribbean community in his eyes needs to create a cultural and artistic tradition independent of Europe (and by extension the United States). Art and literature created in the Caribbean thus function as totems or guardians that secure the region's spiritual wholeness. This is an ongoing concern in his life and work and has come to the foreground in his vision of the "Bussa Centre" at CowPastor.

## 3.2. "The knowledge is within": Incantation and the Survival of Memory

Characteristic of the introduction to *Shar* as well as of the poem itself is their presentation in a kind of shorthand style, a feature that already appeared in the "Epigraph" of *The Zea Mexican Diary* and will appear again in *Trench Town Rock*. The transcription of Herron's sketch of Brathwaite's life, for example, reads like a shorthand epic, an epic that contains only the most important nodal points in a history of migration. The poem, too, is structured as such a shorthand epic. It gives the impression of a desperate attempt to save the words of the poet's disintegrating library, and since the library also stands for the history of the West Indies, as a desperate recollection of the region's communal past in the face of disintegrating memory. Brathwaite's mind becomes an ark — the hurricane functioning as an image of the primal flood — that rescues, along with the history of the region, the possibility of a new beginning and the dream of a "creole cosmos." Situated at the involuntary watershed between past and present, the creation of a new poem out of the memory of the archive suggests an instance of moving "into the perhaps creative chaos of [the] future" (*C* 34), as Brathwaite puts it in his discussion of "tidalectics." This tentative movement into the future is ultimately a sign that he has not lost sight of his utopian vision.

The first section of the first part (each section is introduced with an enlarged initial, reminiscent of illuminated manuscripts) establishes the connection between the environmental devastation caused by the hurricane and the cultural uprooting of the Middle Passage:

wood
has become so useless. stripped. wet .
fragile . broken . totally uninhabitable
with what we must still build

a half-a-million shaved off from the auction block
curled & cut off from their stock

. . . . . . . . . . . . . . . . . . . . . . .

wasted wasted wasted all all all wasted wasted wasted
the five hundred years of Columbus dragging us here (*Shar* 7)

The poet links the Middle Passage to a history of migration that began long before the age of colonialism and the slave trade and which he sees as characteristic of the history of the African continent:

& the four thousand three hundred years before that
across valley & dune . dry river bed . gully & waddi . slip
scream of sandstorm . salt . mineral . glint . quartz

> cutting the soles of my feet . gold
> in the harrowed face of the rock . gold
> in what will become leaf . branch . gilt . eucalyptus . cocoa
>
> pod . odoum . tweneduru . chikichiki . even the evening man.
> grove
> at Golokwati Krachi & Pong
>
> &
> the spider arachne Ananse
>
> the sweet of your arms hollowed out at Anum (*Shar* 7–8)[8]

This passage represents a concise version of *Masks* (1968), where Brathwaite describes a people's migration from Egypt across the Saharan desert to the coast of West Africa and beyond, across the Atlantic in the bowels of the slave ships. As in *Masks*, the above passage from *Shar* also describes the poet's own journey back in time and place to this precolonial Africa; the poet becomes his migrating ancestors ("cutting the soles of *my* feet" [emphasis mine]). In this evocation of *Masks*, Brathwaite saves the memory of his own personal past (his life in Ghana), the history of the African-Caribbean population, as well as the words of the actual collection of poems entitled *Masks*, which he here sees as being destroyed along with the rest of his library.

However, at the same time as he saves the word/the past in this brief sketch, he laments the loss of the full-length epic, the archive at Irish Town, which could have continued to build endlessly into the future. The history/archive he has just reinvoked through an incantation of African place names is "reduced to all this / . . . to so almost nothing like this in the shattered cess of the storm" (*Shar* 8). Here we find the fullest exploration of Sisyphus in Brathwaite's work:

> up from the steep of the valleys of Marley & old Marcus Garvey
> their children
> clambering clambering clambering clambering over the land.
> slidering mountain like cease. less like cease. less like sense. less
>
> like Orlando Patterson's children of Sisyphus clam. or. ing out of the ghetto
>
> (*Shar* 9)

## A Creole Experiment

The reference to Patterson's *The Children of Sisyphus* implies an understanding of the Caribbean as the ghetto of the neocolonial world, trapped in the makeshift housing of the Dungle from which the islands try, but continually fail, to escape. In his introduction to Patterson's novel, Victor L. Chang points out the association of the Dungle with human waste, on the one hand, and the city-as-jungle metaphor, on the other, which in the novel serve to illustrate the inhumanity and hopelessness of ghetto existence:

> Patterson's Dungle is harsh and uncompromising. He transmits the literal and metaphorical meanings of the original source of the core word 'dungle' which is 'dung hill' and depicts a world in which dung — human and other — is constantly present. At the same time, associations which arise from the word 'dungle' such as 'jungle' and 'dump' are ever present. His characters live a kind of wild-animal existence, . . . savage, predatory and clawing out a kind of survival, amidst overwhelming odds. They are also the detritus, the remnants, the castaways of modern urban society. . . . Dungle and Back-O-Wall no longer exist today as depicted in the novel but have been replaced by a sanitised Tivoli Gardens. (xi)

In *Trench Town Rock*, Tivoli Gardens figures as a major site for crime, thus suggesting that, although the Dungle has disappeared, the "scavenge John Crow culture" continues.

However, mentioning Bob Marley and Marcus Garvey gives the above passage of struggle a more hopeful outlook. The children of Garvey, the Rastafarians (of whom Marley was, of course, one), attempt to make the ghetto a place not of deprivation, but of creativity: a third, utopian, space away from the binary opposition of neocolonial oppression and violent resistance. Marley alludes to this desire to sublimate aggression in his song "Trench Town Rock," which will be discussed in chapter four.[9] Sisyphus's continuous struggle can also be read as paralleling the apparently ceaseless migration of the African diaspora, who — like the Jews before them — wander restlessly in search of a new home. But whereas Patterson's Dungle dwellers are doomed to remain trapped in the ghetto, on the dung hill of human waste, Brathwaite's children of Sisyphus attempt to transcend the struggle, which is the focus of the second part of *Shar*.[10] In this sense, Brathwaite enacts rather than simply reflects on the shift he perceives as necessary from the "negative catastro phe" of Sisyphus to the "catharsis" that creates a space for the magical reality of Eldorado ("MR" 16).

In its first part, the poem moves between hope and despair, between utopian and dystopian vision, which is characteristic of Brathwaite's work of the "second cosmology." Again, natural catastrophe mirrors human catastrophe. The uprooting of trees and the tearing off of roofs both echo the poet's agony of loss, the final severance through death from those he loves:

> ... & and there was like this rip & roar & tattoo tear. ing out of elephants as if the lumbering prehensile thunders of the holocaust were trump. eting the roof right off & so they were &
>
> there was light &
> crazy colours of the leaves out. side
> like when the whole house rise to flash & plunder as it floated down the wind
>
>
> with all aboard & shingles (*Shar* 10)

The unmoored house not only refers to Brathwaite's actual house in Irish Town, but also to his sense of being existentially unmoored, adrift, in life after the death of his wife. In *The Zea Mexican Diary*, he experiences her loss as the loss of his "creative crossroads: open doors: Mawu Ogou the Eshu/Legba: loas" (*ZMD* 78). Legba facilitates the communication between the gods and humanity. The poet's wife as muse guards his access to inspiration. Moreover, Brathwaite claims in "Newstead to Neustadt," a speech given on the occasion of his receipt of the Neustadt Prize for Literature in 1994, that for him the "?phenomenon of possession ... increasingly ?coincides w/ the ?phenomenon of the writing of a poem" (657), which corresponds to the idea of the "grapple w/ the loa" in *The Zea Mexican Diary*. Writing, for Brathwaite, becomes ritual, a ritual that grants the poet access to a world outside the limitations of everyday language, which infuses his words with rhythm and meaning. However, traffic between the worlds can only happen with the agreement of the muse, or of Legba in a voodoo ceremony. Therefore, the loss of the muse is a threat to his creativity. In this sense, *The Zea Mexican Diary*, *Shar* and *Trench Town Rock* are mirror images of each other, enacting the trauma of loss, with the death of the muse, the destruction of the house, and Brathwaite's own near death in *Trench Town Rock* becoming interchangeable aspects of that trauma of loss.

Brathwaite's sense of being unmoored finds further expression in the frequent allusion to uprooted trees, as in the following lines:

> craters of outflung cherry & guinep & guava like they never knew what hit them
>
> the sacred lignum vitae stunned into a sudden sullenness of olive grey
> banana windmills broken (*Shar* 12)

These images are reminiscent of "The visibility trigger" in *X/Self*, where the European colonizers tear down a silk-cotton tree, the world axis and seat of ancestral spirits. In *Shar*, the felled tree becomes synonymous with the library and the unmoored house. With the destruction of the library, communication between the spheres of existence (the ancestors, the living, and the gods) and the spheres of history (past, present, future) has been disrupted. The possibility of ancestral Caribbean cultures continuing into the future and into the "creole cosmos" has been jeopardized.

The uprooting of the world tree also finds expression in an Amerindian belief according to which the felling of a food-bearing tree caused the primal flood. In *The Raw and the Cooked* (1964), Claude Lévi-Strauss records examples of this myth and relates how the discovery of the food-bearing tree is linked to the origins of human mortality:

> ...the myth about the food-bearing tree is found in great abundance among the Arawak and the Carib of Guiana, and even in Colombia; formerly..., only the tapir or the agouti knew the secret of this tree, which they refused to share with men. The latter used a squirrel, a bush rat, or an opossum to act as spies. Once they had discovered the whereabouts of the tree, men decided to fell it. Water gushed from the stump..., turned into a flood, and destroyed the human race.... The Wapishana and the Teruma of British Guiana tell... how Duid, the creator's brother, fed men with the fruit of the tree of life. But men found out where he was getting the food from and resolved to help themselves to it. The creator was furious at this act of insubordination and felled the

> tree, and the flood waters gushed from the stump . . . . (184)[11]

The Amerindian version of the fall not only illustrates how humanity lost its immortality and thus an aspect of its divinity, but also depicts a version of the "scavenge John Crow culture," which is the reality of Sisyphus. This "scavenge John Crow culture" describes a world in which individual interest and personal gain supersede the communal spirit of human society. The scramble for the fruits of the tree of life echoes the looting of crashed cars (with its dead or half-dead passengers still inside) that Brathwaite describes in *Trench Town Rock*.

The fall of humanity is also present in Mayan cosmology, where the storm god Hurakan destroys the first creation:

> Hurakan is the ancient Mayan god of wind and storm. He visits the anger of the gods upon humanity by bringing about the Flood. He is a creator god who according to legend dwelt in the mists hanging over the primeval flood, in the form of the wind, ceaselessly repeating the word "earth" until the solid world rose from the seas. When the gods became angry with the first human beings, Hurukan (sic) unleashed the deluge which destroyed them. From his name the word 'hurricane' is derived. Hurakan means "one-legged." ("Hurakan")

The devastation created by the hurricane in *Shar* parallels Hurakan's act of destruction, returning the solid world to the primeval waters. But his one-leggedness also relates him to Legba, guardian of life. This juxtaposition of destruction and life suggests that the image of the hurricane has apocalyptic rather than dystopian connotations. The apocalypse depicted in the Revelation to John creates a space for the new Jerusalem. The one-legged god Hurakan/Legba thus guards the gateway to the "new world," the "creole cosmos" of the future.

In Christian tradition, the tree of life is connected to the word of God and sometimes associated with the book of life mentioned in the Revelation: ". . . the 'Book of Life' in the Book of Revelation is set in the midst of Paradise and may be identified with the Tree of Life. The leaves of the tree, like the letters in the book, represent not only the totality of all created beings but also the totality of God's decrees" ("Book" 111). Brathwaite's library can be seen as encompassing a representative collection of literary and artistic creation in the Caribbean.

Moreover, the library represents a magical space of communion for the diverse expressions of Caribbeanness. Brathwaite laments the loss of the Caribbean word, the loss of this totality, and thus the severed communication between the human and the divine. However, since the Revelation to John presents a future vision of the world, the tree of life and the book of life spanning the beginning and the end of the world as it now exists, the loss of the written word stored in the archive may give birth to a new kind of word, in the same way as the complete destruction of this world or eon gives birth to the new Jerusalem.

Consequently, at this deepest point of despair, the tone of the poem begins to change and to suggest a more hopeful outlook. The frantic retrieval of the fragments of the disintegrating library, which characterizes the beginning of the poem, now turns into incantation. Where the poet saw himself alone in his despair at the loss of the word, its regaining is achieved through collective incantation. The children of Sisyphus begin to sing:

> song at last song
>
> from the throats of the five hundred thousand
> the hands
>
> clasped to bellies of pain & the rocking of agon
>
> but
>
> song . song . song
>
> (*Shar* 15)

The song evokes, like the recollection at the beginning, the "tidalectic" movement of the history of migration that Brathwaite sees as characteristic of the African continent and the black diaspora. The song begins with the journey into the past and, again, sketches the migration from Egypt across Africa to the New World (as depicted in *Masks*):

> & the songs of crossing the river & the dead & sea
> of the morning & the brass & bells of the water
>
> & more thunder of water & then it was louder like
> clambering clambering climbing the mountain

## The Poet's Archive as Houmfort: Shar/Hurricane Poem

> since Sumer since Akhad since Taë since
> the sun
> of Ankhnaton on Nubis on Nile on the western
> Sahara
>
> since Daaga since Mansa since Segu since
> Saheel since Sahell since
> Sokoto Sokoto Sokoto Sokoto
> since Bourkina Faso since Chad since
>
> guinea fowl Guinée since
> Gorée
> already a bougainvillea Atlantical island away
>
> . . . . . . . . . . . . . . .
>
> & pouring west . towards the years of wrest
> & wreck & space & time between the stone
>
> & Maya & the Aztec & the
> te & teh & touch of your face
> **Tetemexticlan**
>
> (*Shar* 16–18)

This collective incantation of the past represents a triumph of the oral tradition over the written tradition. Books can be destroyed, and memory and identity can be destroyed along with them. In his use of incantation, Brathwaite has recourse to his concept of *nam*. *Nam* represents the submerged memory of African culture in the New World, which can be brought to light by means of incantation. In this sense, *nam* is similar to the voodoo gods who reside in the abyssal waters and are raised into the world of the living through incantation and drum beat.[12] *Nam* survives the Middle Passage and makes possible the creation of creole cultures.

 Brathwaite's use of incantation as opposed to the western concept of the archive as storehouse of memory is a cultural comment. Oral cultures, he seems to suggest, are more fit to survive natural catastrophes, such as hurricanes, but also personal and collective trauma, such as bereavement and the Middle Passage. Brathwaite explains the reasons for this in *Gods of the Middle Passage*:

> The gods of Africa 'survive' in the New World/Caribbean not because they were carried ('Carrybean') there by missionary/theologian; no Augustine Mohammet brought them here; but because it is possible for god to dwell in man and man to be/come god ('the cosmic force within the flesh') not as epiphany, unique phenomenon, but ordinary as water in the hounsi's glass and all pervasive as its tides. That is why the most apparently humble and inferordinary slave-ship Akosua could, as she danced, outline the movements of the snake, the monumental majesty of wave-life Yemaaja. Why it is not necessary to read and writer to become a priest. In fact, it is the dispossessed, les damnés de la terre, who know <u>orisha</u> best. The knowledge is withim. <u>Dam dam damirifa</u>. The memory tra/verses centuries. The drum is organoncomputer. There could be no "forget" since there was 'nothing' to forget and <u>nam</u> is immemorial. The gods, therefore, do not 'survive', they wait they listen they remain as ancient and as modern as the morning star ... (7)[13]

In *Shar*, incantation re-establishes the communication between the human and the divine (in the human) and between past and present. Brathwaite retrieves his lost love and muse through an invocation of place, "Tetemexticlan" (implying both "Mexican" and "Tenochtitlan"). The incantation of New World place names, moreover, establishes a link between the migrating African self and the Americas as place where the journey of the African diaspora comes to an end. The retrieved communion with the divine through the muse thus also marks a renewed sense of *Heimat* as "arrived-at Being." The redemptive note on which the first part of *Shar* ends is emphasized by the pictogram of the "udjat" eye or eye of Horus, which is placed directly underneath the word Tetemexticlan. In Egyptian iconography, the eye of Horus comes to stand for restored fragmentation, a notion arising out of the context of the myth in which Horus and Seth fight over the rule of Egypt:

> In one contest, in which the two gods as hippopotamuses intend to see if they can remain submerged under water for three months, Isis refuses to take the opportunity of killing Seth with a harpoon. Horus, enraged, savagely attacks his mother and escapes

> into the desert. Seth finds him and cuts out his eyes.
> Hathor, using gazelle's milk, restores Horus's eyes....
> The restored eyes of Horus became, in singular form,
> the symbol for a state of soundness or perfection — the
> "udjat" eye. Its iconography consists of a human eye
> with a cosmetic line emanating from its corner below
> which are the markings of a falcon's cheek. It became
> the protection sign par excellence. ("Horus" 92–3)

The eye of Horus appears on a number of occasions throughout Brathwaite's work. In *The Zea Mexican Diary*, for example, it substitutes the letter "o" in "This obeia business" and represents both the trauma of Mexican's death and Brathwaite's belief that *obeah* should provide him with protective energy, which, however, *obeah* fails to do. In the context of *Shar*, the "udjat" eye epitomizes the physical devastation caused by the hurricane, the cultural fragmentation it draws in its wake (in the form of the destruction of Brathwaite's archive), as well as the emotional devastation and sense of being unmoored that Brathwaite experiences after his wife's death. The healed eye comes to stand for the redemptive possibilities of *nam* that end the first part of the poem.

The eye of Horus also becomes the restored world axis. In ancient Egyptian funeral rites, a pair of eyes was frequently placed on the side of coffins to allow the soul of the deceased to enter again into the world of the living. The eye becomes a door between the worlds.[14] The threat that Mexican's death previously posed to Brathwaite's creativity is now vanquished by the restoration of the word, the door to transcendence, through incantation. The "udjat" eye is thus another manifestation of the *houmfort* as place of communion. Moreover, the juxtaposition of "Tetemexticlan" and the eye of Horus closes the circle of migration. The journey that in *Masks* began in Egypt has come to an end in the Americas, thus providing a sense of closure. The acceptance of mortality (Sharon's and Mexican's death) and of the fragile texture of human creation (the archive that cannot be protected) at the end of the first part of *Shar* also gives a sense of the poet's cycle of suffering as well as the people's history of migration having come to an end. Now a new cycle can begin, and this is the focus of the second section of the poem.

The beginning of a new cycle of life in the second half of *Shar* is most evident in that no mention is made of either Sharon, Mexican or the destroyed library. The form of the poem also changes. The font becomes larger, directing the reader's eyes to only a few words at a time, and stressing, in particular, the words "song" and "singing," on which the second half focuses even more than the first. Its tone is that of celebration, praising a people's power of endurance and will to transcend their individual limitations in collective action:

> **sing**
> **sing**
>
> the glitter of
> voices
>
> des.
> chant. ing the
> rivers of silver.
> the shell^shale of
> noise of
>
> .
>
> des. troy. of des.
> troy. of des.
> troy
>
> ing the well you
> have. wall you
>
> have
> build you have
> build
>
> (*Shar* 23–25)

## The Poet's Archive as Houmfort: Shar/Hurricane Poem

The voice of the people proceeds yet again to recapitulate its history of migration and to retrace its African roots, this time in an even more concise form:

>             mover.
>             mover.
>             mover.
>             mover.
>
>      ing over the cut.
>        lash & wash
>        of the fields of
>
>          cassava &
>     indian corn. bread
>            & halt.
>
>         ing me pain.
>     ful & pen. ance &
>              ash
>
>      all. most dead in
>              the
>
>             pre .
>     tense of lust/re
>             less
>
>            Addis
>              &
>            Kano

A Creole Experiment

&
Ifa

(*Shar* 26–29)

The poem here gives the impression that the song/voice of the people rises over America and travels back to Africa for one last time. Then the memory of Africa is countered by a distinctly West Indian voice:

**but
looka me borrow a
cloud from de rain
wid it rain. bow
still wet when a
shine. when a
shine. in. wid. out
com. pen. sation
or. as I say. sorrow**

(*Shar* 31)

The rainbow, at the end of the poem referred to as "jah's / sym/bole & / flame in the rain / blow" (*Shar* 44), is another allusion to the biblical flood. As the flood recedes Noah sees a rainbow, the symbol of God's power to unite opposites, here fire and water, which represents a bridge between the human and the divine. In the context of *Shar*, the rainbow marks the end of the hurricane season and the idea of the primal flood associated here with it but also anticipates a state of "arrived-at Being," the end of all human questing. Like Noah, the people of the Caribbean have come to the end of their long history of migration and found a home in the New World. At the end of the poem, the children of Sisyphus do not slide back down the mountain, an image of their futile attempt to overcome their ghetto existence. Instead, their singing of "the song / of the morn. / ing" (*Shar* 41–43) rises together with the rainbow "out / of the tree / of / ijs / heaven" (*Shar* 45), "ijs" referring to Jah. The rainbow and the tree of heaven, both of which are also mirrors of Damballah, depict the restored world axis that points from the past into the future. The rainbow ensures the poet's access to the word and consequently the people's access, through the words of the poet, to regenerative energies.

The rainbow also echoes René Depestre's collection of poems *Un arc-en-ciel pour l'occident chrétien* (1967), translated into English as *A Rainbow for the Christian West*. In the collection, the Haitian poet invokes the power of voodoo in its "uncompromising spirit of revolt, predicting a complete revolution of human existence through the magic power of the mind and through its actual, positive power of synthesis," as Joan Dayan states ("René Depestre and the Symbiosis of Poetry and Revolution" 79). She further argues that "the 'magic realism' of his work resides in bringing the timeless elements of Voodoo into historical time" (79). But not only the reference to magic realism links Depestre's work to Brathwaite's. Dayan also detects a utopian element in *Un arc-en-ciel* that comes very close to Brathwaite's own as Depestre creates "a poetry that is precise and forward-looking, a political as well as psychic advance" (79). Brathwaite's *Shar* moves from the "negative catastrophe" of Sisyphus to the magical reality of voodoo, which offers Sisyphus release, both political and psychic.

In another of her articles, "A New World Lament," Dayan points out that the rainbow serpent Damballah is twinned with Shango/Xango, the liberating spirit of the first *X/Self*: ". . . the **sing./ing** conjures . . . the doubling of Shango and Damballa, '**the train./song of rain./fall,**' as we move through the '**slide./ering/ slide./ering/ slide./ering,**' which I take to be the snake's slithering '**over the pain & the valley**' . . . ." (339).[15] Shango/Xango is present in the form of the "train./song." In Appendix VII of *Barabajan Poems*, Brathwaite claims that Shango/Xango manifests himself in the New World as the noise and movement of the steam train, which finds expression in a number of blues and jazz pieces. The train played a vital part in the early decades of the twentieth century, when many black Americans left the poverty and racial segregation of the rural south and moved to the cities of the north in what has become known as the African-American "Great Migration" (Sernett 57). In a similar way, the Xango persona of *Shar* liberates the children of Sisyphus from the "darkness of the lived moment."

*Shar/Hurricane Poem* imagines the poet as the voice of the people. In *Shar*, as in the poetry up to and including the first *X/Self*, the poet's individual voice blends with the voice of the people. In *ConVERSations*,

Brathwaite describes his understanding of poetry as performance. The word comes alive "within a BREATHING houm or audience — retaining the tradition of the Oral Tradition's basis in individual/community call-and-response kinesis into collective *houm*" (*C* 222), "*houm*" echoing *houmfort* as well as home or *Heimat*. The society Brathwaite imagines is based on an idea of community as body whose members act in unison. Only this kind of society, so Brathwaite seems to suggest, is capable of rising unharmed out of trauma because individuals are not left on their own in times of crisis. Moreover, Brathwaite's reference to the oral tradition also implies, in the context of the second, incantatory half of *Shar*, that people of cultures with strong oral traditions rise more resiliently out of trauma, since they are not threatened by total amnesia. As the excerpt from *Gods of the Middle Passage* suggests, the body remembers because "the knowledge is within" the person (Brathwaite's "withim" suggests "within him") and not within the fragile walls of a library (7). The body of the slave and his/her descendants becomes at once *houmfort* and archive, a space in which Damballah is remembered as his undulating movements are enacted in dance. In this sense, the body itself is a magical and utopian space, where the Caribbean imaginary meets the Caribbean symbolic.

# Chapter 4

# Zombies and Messiahs in the Kingdom of this World: *Trench Town Rock*

◇◆◇

## 4.1. "Gateway to so sudden swiftly HELL": Kingston as Inferno

*Trench Town Rock* (*TTR*) (1994) represents Brathwaite's third rendering of personal trauma. At the heart of the text lies the burglary of his Marley Manor apartment in downtown Kingston in 1990, where he moved after the destruction of his house at Irish Town. During the burglary, Brathwaite was bound, gagged and almost killed. In a similar way to *The Zea Mexican Diary* and *Shar/Hurricane Poem*, *Trench Town Rock* shows a profoundly social concern as Brathwaite places his own ordeal within the context of other crimes committed in Kingston.

The book is structured in six chapters, each presenting one aspect of crime on the streets of Kingston. To emphasize that he is only one among many victims, the account of Brathwaite's own ordeal does not appear until Chapter 4. Other chapters focus on specific incidents, such as street fights of warring political factions, random police harassment of the Kingston population, and the murders of several people at the Marley Manor apartment complex, which Brathwaite witnessed firsthand. Most chapters are rendered as montages that combine Brathwaite's own eyewitness accounts and notes with newspaper clippings referring to these and other criminal incidents. As in "Pixie," these montage passages are employed to depict particularly fragmented and dystopian aspects of the city and the descent of the poet's own mind into that infernal cityscape. *Trench Town Rock* can, therefore, also be read as an underworld journey in the Dantean sense. The city as infernal landscape is described in images that echo Dante's hell. Chapters 3 and 6, on the other hand, comprise a poem and a folktale respectively and suggest an alternative vision or utopian glimpse of the otherwise dystopian reality of *Trench Town Rock*.

The crisis of political authority and the omnipresence of crime transport *Trench Town Rock* from immediate personal trauma into a wider context of urban reality. The book depicts the city of Kingston as a neocolonial wasteland. Kingston is a city "smouldering in garbage" (*TTR* 68), but it is also the site of human depravity, of "men & woman plundering that monstrous HELL of stench & detritus & death" (*TTR* 68). The city's population are described as "human scavengers" (*TTR* 69) preying not only on the city's garbage but also on each other, which is, again, evocative of Orlando Patterson's *The Children Of Sisyphus*. In this sense, the city of Kingston represents the exact opposite of the utopia of *Heimat* and reveals itself as "the grey, rusty and off-white waste (s)" (*C* 120) that Brathwaite perceived it as when still living in Irish Town.

In the context of neocolonial exploitation, the infernal journey exceeds Brathwaite's own personal experience and becomes collective trauma not only for the Jamaican population but also on a global scale. Brathwaite diagnoses the collective trauma witnessed in *Trench Town Rock* as loss of selfhood resulting from continued dependence on the west. The global scope of *Trench Town Rock*, which links it to the concerns of *X/Self* but also to more recent writings such as *Born to Slow Horses*, lies encoded in Brathwaite's reference to Marcus Garvey in the first chapter:

## 17 Aug is Marcus Garvey Birthday

the same day (1983) that poet Mickey Smith was stoned
to death on Stony Hill

(*TTR* 18)

In founding the Universal Negro Improvement Association (U.N.I.A.) at the beginning of World War I, Garvey, who was Jamaican by birth, attempted to challenge the exploitation of the black worker in the New World and the exploitation of natural resources on the African continent by the west. Garvey's program of emancipating black people included a strong orientation towards Africa with the possibility of resettlement. This went hand in hand with the creation of a cultural and spiritual autonomy from the west by identifying with Ethiopia and its ruler, Emperor Haile Selassie I, as an African head of state opposed to colonial oppression. The cultural agenda of Garveyism was to create racial pride, which influenced other black movements, such as Rastafarianism. Apart from initiating cultural autonomy, Garvey's Black Star Line Shipping Company attempted to provide the means by which to emancipate the black population of the world economically. In *Rasta and Resistance: from Marcus Garvey to Walter Rodney* (1985), Horace Campbell explains that with the Black Star Line "[t]he U.N.I.A. set out to establish independent economic ventures which would break the hold of the white capitalists over the black communities and over Africa" (61). The enterprise eventually failed, and Campbell stresses that the west did its best to prevent the U.N.I.A. from getting a foothold on the African continent: "The full threat of Garveyism to Western Imperialism was crystal clear, for the United States Government resorted to diplomatic pressures against Liberia to abort the U.N.I.A. settlement, and soon after the land earmarked by the U.N.I.A. engineers and surveyors was leased to the Firestone Rubber Company of Akron, Ohio" (62).

The alternative to western capitalism posed by Garvey is echoed in the reference to Jamaican dub poet Michael Smith, who was killed for speaking out against political oppression. Juxtaposed with Garvey's birthday and the utopian connotations that Garveyism had for many black people, Smith's death functions as the anti-utopian downbeat that prevails through most of the book. However, Garveyism and Rastafarianism remain utopian outlooks. That Brathwaite's text focuses on these movements is indicated by the title *Trench Town Rock*, taken from Bob Marley's song, part of which forms the book's motto.

Trench Town was one of the settlements that replaced the older Kingston slum areas.[1] Marley himself spent his formative years in Trench Town, which "even before the 1951 hurricane ... had ... become the main home in Kingston for the strange tribe of men known as Rastafarians, who had set up an encampment down by the Dungle in the early years of World War II" ("Trenchtown," The Life of Bob Marley). The Rastafarians regarded the place as "a spiritual powerpoint" ("Trenchtown," The Life of Bob Marley). Trench Town came to represent an alternative to colonial rule and colonial education.² Marley's song "Trench Town Rock" signifies political as well as spiritual liberation as it proclaims the liberating power of music. Music transforms ghetto life and wards off social violence by creating harmony and solidarity. In other words, music has the power to transform the ghetto into a *houmfort*:

> One good thing about music, when it hits you
> Feel no pain
> So hit me with music, hit me with music
> Hit me with music, hit me with music now
> I got to say trench town rock
> I say don't watch that
> Trench town rock, big fish or sprat
> Trench town rock, you reap what you sow
> Trench town rock, and everyone know now
> Trench town rock, don't turn your back
> Trench town rock, give the slum a try
> Trench town rock, never let the children cry
> Trench town rock, 'cause you got to tell JAH, JAH . . . .
>
> (*Bob Marley Sound Archives*)

The song emphasizes the need for communal responsibility ("never let the children cry") and responsibility before God ("cause you got to tell JAH, JAH"), both of which prevent the ghetto from plunging into "dread and carnage and despair" (Brown, introduction, *Words* [2004] xix). Campbell argues that reggae in particular "laid emphasis on Africa, black deliverance and redemption" (134). In other words, reggae encouraged an orientation towards alternative values that countered the materialism of the west. Reggae artists "were able to draw inspiration from the people and in turn stirred the physical and psychic energies of the people, which enabled them to withstand the pressures of poverty, unemployment, gun men and ganja enforcers" (Campbell 134). The slum thus becomes a utopian space, emphasizing spirituality and altruism as an alternative to western materialism and individualism. In this sense, Trench Town is related to Brathwaite's maroon project at Irish Town and to the history of *maronage* in general.

In the opening chapter of *Trench Town Rock*, "The Marley Manor Shoot/in," capitalist forces (for example, adverts for consumer goods) are identified as the cause of Kingston's crime, creating desires that most people in the Caribbean are too poor to satisfy.³ Brathwaite quotes an article from *The Sunday Gleaner* (November 1990), which notes:

> The two months June & July – the 'Independence holiday season' – totalled a high of 167 murders, because a/c to Dep Police Commissioner Bertram Millwood i/c of Crime, of the "existing high spirits and criminals' need for more spending money during the approaching Independence holiday season" (*TTR* 19)

Brathwaite implies that Jamaica's lack of independence from western cultural and economic systems renders its political independence, achieved in 1962, meaningless. Kwame Nkrumah, who led Ghana into independence in 1957, defined neocolonialism as "the stage in which the state has all the trappings of political independence, but is still economically dependent" (qtd. in Campbell 86).⁴ Brathwaite himself regards the Caribbean situation as neocolonial and resents "*the notion of 'post-colonial' applied so easily to our* **neo-colonial** *condition, its false premises of FIGMENT strategically (re)designed to continue the OLD STORY*" ("A Post-Cautionary Tale" 74). The utopian aspects of Brathwaite's *Trench Town Rock* can thus be said to reflect a very antiwestern stance, with Brathwaite deliberately representing European cultural referents such as the Dantean journey through hell as the dystopian influence in *Trench Town Rock*, whereas models of society based on an orientation towards Africa, such as Garveyism and Rastafarianism, are hailed as utopian alternatives.

The first chapter sets the scene for the descent into the underworld with the murder of three people at the Marley Manor apartment complex. The passage opens with Brathwaite waking up to the sound of gunshots and the voice of a man pleading for his life.⁵ The twilight of the opening section of *Trench Town Rock* introduces the underworld atmosphere. The observations following the gunshots add to this atmosphere. Brathwaite witnesses "a cry we couldn't see" (*TTR* 9) and "a soundless figure fleeing like on air" (*TTR* 10). The disembodied voice and the amorphous nature of the fleeing figure depict the city's inhabitants as shades reminiscent of those that people the Greek or Roman underworld.

Canto III of Dante's *Inferno* describes Dante and Virgil entering through the gate of hell. In the Marley Manor setting, this is reflected in Brathwaite's reference to the gate into the Marley Manor complex as "the Marley gateway to so sudden swiftly HELL" (*TTR* 11). The first chapter of *Trench Town Rock* thus functions as the beginning of the narrator's own underworld journey. Canto III of Dante's *Inferno* opens with the inscription on the gate of hell:

> Per me si va ne la città dolente,
> Per me si va ne l'etterno dolore,
> Per me si va tra la perduta gente
>
> . . . . . . . . . . . . . . . . . . . . . . . . . .
>
> Lasciate ogne speranza, voi ch'intrate.
>
> (Through me you enter the woeful city,
> Through me you enter eternal grief,
> Through me you enter among the lost
>
> . . . . . . . . . . . . . . . . . . . . . . . . . .
>
> Abandon every hope, you who enter.) (ll.1–9)

In *Trench Town Rock* the command to leave all hope behind is emphasized by the reference to imminent danger at a place called Hope Road, where "*three men*" are reported "*armed & dangerous*" (*TTR* 11). In this sense, the Marley gateway functions as an inversion of the original gate of hell. Dante journeys to a woeful otherworld. In *Trench Town Rock*, the shades and spirits spill out of the Marley gateway into the "kingdom of this world" (*TTR* 11) and turn Kingston into a "città dolente." As in "Titan" (*X/Self*), where the priests of the house of Mictlan lose control over the destructive aspects of Akbal, who subsequently possesses Cortez and makes him "vomit out destroy" (*X/S* 63), crime is out of control in Kingston. This is indicated in the inability of the police to protect the city's inhabitants. They arrive at the scene of crime too late ("these now were too late although they came" (*TTR* 11)), abandoning other victims of other crimes in other parts of Kingston, which the Marley Manor residents witness via the police car radio. The police forces that attempt to control crime are likened to ants ("and like ants, it sadly seemed . . . their cars to car/cases" (*TTR* 10)), which makes them appear powerless, mere scavengers arriving to clean up the scene of the crime rather than to prevent it. The loss of control is more drastically illustrated in the death of the Marley Manor night watchman who here appears as an ineffectual version of the guardian of the gate: "Now/at the wild white Marley gateway, there is a little matching dolly house where our 'security guard' — well — *sleeps*" (*TTR* 11), although it turns out that he has been shot himself. The guardian of the gate has become powerless against the forces he was appointed to control. Hence, they are free to "vomit out destroy."

In *The Divine Comedy*, both Dante and Virgil are shown to feel compassion with the suffering souls. Dante says of his first encounter with these souls:

> Quivi sospiri, piante e alti guai
> risonavan per l'aere sanza stelle,
> per ch'io al cominciar ne lagrimai.
>
> (Here sighs, laments, and loud wailings were resounding through the starless air, so that at first they made me weep.) (*Inferno*, Canto III, ll. 22–24).

Similarly, Virgil says to Dante:

> ... "L'angoscia de le genti
> che son qua giù, nel viso mi dipigne
> quella pietà che tu per tema senti...."
>
> (... "The anguish of the people here below paints my face with the pity that you take for fear....") (*Inferno*, Canto IV, ll. 19–21).

Likewise, Brathwaite in *Trench Town Rock* suffers with the victims of the Marley Manor shootings, especially with the victim named Early Bird, who is described as upholding Marley's legacy of peace. Early Bird's description makes clear that he is a Rastafarian:

**Was a young dreadlocks...**

**... his beautiful long hair like curled around his body making snakes like dance/like dancing. the seven bullet holes that walked us from our sleep all bleeding in the early morning light. One**

rebok trainer some way off. as if it had been cut off from his body in the terror.& his hair—some of his hair—his locks—beside him—pulled out by the very roots by some strange/ some strange strangar violence—the gunmen had been dragging him a- way like that by all his loveliness. his body now without its bones or muscleature. without its meat with- out its clutch & nomen of a face/ familiar creatures/that someone somewhere somehow knew/that someone/somewhere loved & be- cause the man himself had fled out through these leaking holes, his locks had whirled around him as the bullets made him dance his death & wrapped themselves around him as he fell. so now there was this eerie beauty in the barley light. his hair become his only perhaps comforter

(*TTR* 12–13)

*Zombies and Messiahs in the Kingdom of this World:* Trench Town Rock

The description shows Brathwaite's deep compassion for the dead man. Implicitly, Brathwaite also mourns the loss of Marley's legacy, which the murdered Rastafarian represents. In "A New World Lament," Joan Dayan suggests that the man named Early Bird also embodies Damballah, performing the *loa*'s dance in his final agony:

> ... the words make us see how the dance of death is turned, even if just momentarily, into another kind of dance, perhaps the *yanvalou*, the dance especially liked by Damballa: body sloping forward, the shoulders undulate and hands fall to the knees. The dead man's hair, as if possessed, comes alive in the poet's pursuit of foulness.... (339)

The death of Damballah symbolizes the death of utopian possibility as the children of Sisyphus, who in *Shar* achieved liberation, now slide back into "darkness of the lived moment," where their struggle begins anew. However, Dayan's reading suggests a manifestation of hope in the face of death, which will ultimately determine the course of *Trench Town Rock*.

The utopian alternative, which Damballah, Marley, Trench Town, and Early Bird represent, is mirrored in the Marley Manor architecture. The apartment complex is built around a courtyard which becomes the crime scene of "so sudden swiftly HELL" (*TTR* 11) in the early hours of the morning, "where just a world before there had been laughter splashing in the pool, reverb & ghetto-box, Red Stripe, bells softly sing/ing sing/ing, somebody sucking cane & shouting out dem dancehall business in the dark" (*TTR* 11). The courtyard as communal space again echoes "Veridian" of *Middle Passages*. "Veridian" describes a maroon community in terms of modern resistance fighters ("m16s that are not / crutches" (34)), thus linking the spirit of *maronage* to contemporary resistance movements that oppose the west. Brathwaite links the Rastafarian movement implied in the symbol of the "Lion of Judah," a synonym for Emperor Haile Selassie I ("above it all we draw / the lion" (34)), to the earlier forms of slave rebellion and maroon resistance.[6] He distinguishes these resistance movements as primarily alternative ways of living, stressing communal activity and communal space as the focus of daily life. In this sense, the Marley Manor courtyard, where people gather to spend the evening together, is related to the maroon village, in that it "looks inwards to this centre" (Brathwaite, *Middle Passages* 34) of community.

## A Creole Experiment

Jamaican Rastafarian culture, in particular its early stages during the late 1930s and the early 1940s, can be read as a continuation of the maroon tradition. In 1940, Leonard Howell, an ardent spokesperson of the Rastafarian movement, established the first Rasta commune, Pinnacle, in the hills of St. Catherine in Jamaica. Pinnacle was an attempt "to set up a cooperative enterprise outside of the exploitative relations of the society" (Campbell 94). The country's industry still largely consisted of sugar estates that owned most of the island's land and relied on the labour of the rural poor. Pinnacle presented a threat to the planters, in that the "Rastafarians were breaking some of the old capitalist habits which had become ingrained in the rural areas" (Campbell 96). Unlike those "who used their knowledge to exploit their fellow men, the Pinnacle settlement was attempting to restore to the society some of the spirit of communalism and collective work" (Campbell 95). Pinnacle was frequently raided by the police and its inhabitants finally dispersed, many into the Kingston ghettos. In their use of local produce, the Rastafarians of Pinnacle attempted to achieve economic self-sufficiency. Moreover, in using fruits, herbs and vegetables that the slaves had used before them, they also established a link with their slave past (Campbell 122). Therefore, despite their emphasis on African heritage, they also expressed a sense of *Heimat* as arrival in a new homeland. In their attempt to create economic self-sufficiency as well as alternative cultural values, the Rastafarians also continued Garvey's notion of black independence from the west. Moreover, the emphasis on communalism (also addressed by Marley in "Trench Town Rock") links Pinnacle, even beyond its dispersal into the downtown ghetto, to the maroon communities in other parts of the Americas, to the voodoo *houmfort*, and to Brathwaite's own Irish Town project.

The architectural layout of the Marley Manor apartment complex has to be seen essentially in connection with the burglary of Brathwaite's apartment, which is recorded in Chapter 4 of *Trench Town Rock*, and with Kingston's architecture in general. Looking in on a communal area, the Marley Manor complex is in many ways reminiscent of Brathwaite's idea of a wall-less house/*houmfort* discussed in the previous chapter. In contrast to this idea, the class-divided city of Kingston "appears in two paired images from Jamaican literature of the 1970s: the image of the grill and the gully" (Wheeler 228). Wrought iron security gates and window grills became a major characteristic of Kingston architecture as "[f]ear and security precautions multiplied during the political violence of the 1960s and 1970s" (Wheeler 228–

29). Elizabeth Wheeler argues that this period marks a turning point in Jamaica's perception of itself as a nation. Despite independence from Britain, the island still found itself in dependence: "Imperialism now appeared not only through British culture but also through North American advertising and the fluctuation of the U.S. dollar" (Wheeler 224). A second factor that affected the social division of the Kingston population was the major urban reconstruction during the period following World War II:

> As elsewhere in the 1960s, Jamaica's growing middle class tore down older buildings to replace them with modern concrete. Simultaneously, rural Jamaicans left the land in huge numbers and came to Kingston looking for work. In a city which could neither employ nor house all of them, many new residents created makeshift homes on undesirable gully land. (Wheeler 234)

In Brathwaite's Kingston poetry of the 1970s (*Black + Blues* and *Third World Poems*), the class divide is depicted as a direct result of North America's neocolonial presence, as "North American consumer goods appear in Jamaican literary works as signs of difference between rich and poor" (Wheeler 231).[7]

Although *Trench Town Rock* focuses on the early 1990s, it refers to earlier decades, for example, through the poem "Kingston in the Kingdom of this World," first published in the 1970s, to illustrate that Jamaica's social climate is still the same. That one's private space is threatened when one's house is ungrilled becomes evident in an observation Brathwaite makes in connection with the burglary of his flat:

*They come in thru a flimsy ungrilled deregulated balcon door (ply*

*wood & glass with
bolts no bigger
than small safety
pins at top of same
said door).* (TTR 55)

The seemingly utopian architecture of the Marley Manor complex, with its ungrilled windows and open courtyard, appears here as a fault in its security regulations. The openness of one's private space to the public sphere becomes a threat in twentieth-century Kingston, with the public sphere as the ultimate anti-utopian space. On the other side of the grilled window, in the streets of Kingston, there is carnage, signified in the mutilated corpse of Early Bird and another victim found at the crime scene of "The Marley Manor Shoot/in":

a police—big, dark, meaty guy whose job, it seems,
was checking on security at MMA
But I can't tell you what he looked like: features,
the human face, I mean: both eyes shot out/
stabbed
in, his nose unhinged, a huge gash in the right side
of the throat, his tongue there black & smooth &
half-leaf out his face as if he'd
strangled also
yet all his skin & flesh still firm & natural
like if he flash & living still & not a ant or insect
coming even near his blood & no one say a
prayer—at least out loud—nor paused—

O Sodom & Gomorrah—

> **nor raised a hum or hymn for anyone—for anyone
> of us—that night/that early morning sun/day**
> (*TTR* 16)

The loss of soul implied in the description of the mutilated body is enhanced by the onlookers' lack of compassion or concern for the dead man's soul. The repeated emphasis on the soulless mutilated body throughout *Trench Town Rock*, together with the strong influence of voodoo culture on Brathwaite's writing in general, invites a reading of the corpse as zombie, although Brathwaite himself never explicitly states this parallel.

In voodoo culture, zombies are the living dead, who are brought back from death by sorcerers who keep them as slaves. Their primary characteristic is that they lack a soul or will of their own. They are deprived of their selfhood and thus represent the ultimate form of alienated, enslaved humanity.[8] The zombie represents the loss of self — or loss of soul — encoded in the history of New World slavery and is thus one of the first genuinely creole paradigms. In the context of *Trench Town Rock*, the zombie becomes a cultural metaphor for Caribbean neocolonial dependence on the west, and the city of Kingston itself, together with its litter of corpses, can be read as a manifestation of the zombie.

Chapter 2 of *Trench Town Rock*, entitled "Straight Talk," views Kingston crime in relation to political authority. The chapter is presented as a transcript of the radio talk show "Straight Talk," in which McKenzie, the Jamaica Labour Party councilor for the inner city Kingston region of Rema, tells the host of the talk show, Wilmot Perkins, how the police and military harass the inhabitants of his district.[9] The harassment of the population appears to be a random act of intimidation and humiliation:

> **When the men were taken from their
> ouses, Mr Perkins... they were axed to
> drape each other in their pants waist**
>
> . . . . . . . . . . . . . . . .
>
> **You box me, I box you; I kiss you, you**

> **kiss me**
>
> . . . . . . . . . . . . . . . .
>
> **Kiss, Mr Perkins. Kiss like ow a man kiss/a woman. The soldiers/instruct/ the men/tokiss/each other**
>
> . . . . . . . . . . . . . . . .
>
> **Not only the kissing alone, Mr Perkins. They were axed, Mr Perkins, the men were axed to rub up themselves on each other** (*TTR* 30-31)

McKenzie relates this incident of harassment to the violence of the 1970s when the houses of these local residents were randomly ransacked:

> **... what was dun to de people in REMA yesterday M/M/Mr Perkin, is beyonn a all—no human be'en, Mr. Perkins deserve to be treated in dat way and a want to take you back, Mr. Perkins, to 1976, Mr. Perkin when those very same people, Mr. Perkins, were victims of invasions where they furnitures, their/ their personal property was destroyed and they were thrown out of doors in 1976, Mr. Perkins.** (*TTR* 35-36)

Here the violence of the 1990s, which is the focus of *Trench Town Rock*, is explicitly linked to the 1970s, the period that informs Brathwaite's

Kingston poetry, signifying a continuation of violence and crime that repeats itself in the burglary of his own home.

Brathwaite emphasizes this notion of continuation by linking the above-mentioned incidents of random harassment and the Marley Manor crimes of the first chapter, which took place in 1990, with a political incident that came to a head in 1992, resulting in street violence: "In 1992 there were gun battles between rival political supporters of the PNP and the Jamaica Labor Party (JLP) after the death in custody of a JLP activist, Lester Coke and the murder of his son that result[ed] in the deaths of 8 people" ("Jamaica"). In *Trench Town Rock*, Brathwaite refers to the death of Lester Coke in detail:

Lester Lloyd Coke, alias Jim Brown (also 'Jim', 'Big Man' [he was], 'Dads', 'Bomber', 'Don') of the gold-coloured Mercedes Benz (*Sun Gleaner*, 15 March 92, p3A) 'identified as a co-leader of [the] notorious [Miami-based] Shower Posse crime gang, has been in custody [in the General Penitentiary] awaiting extradition to the US to face murder charges' (*Ja Record* Sun Feb 9, 1992, p2A) . . .

. . . is apparently the present ruling *The-harder-they-come* Rhygin of the Corporate area, reputed gunman & political activist & 'Don Gorgon' wanted in the US on various charges & ?finally captured (1991) in Kingston in a paramilitary SEARCH+DESTROY ('Rat Patrol') OPERATION & is in police custody (some say 'custardy') here awaiting xtradition... But the word on the street is that **if dem deport Jim Brown to Amerika, Kingston go bun dung flat flat flat like a flat cake inna Bandung** & that a lot of recent voiolence [July-Aug 90], inc that in the Coronation Market (& prob at MM) is connect w/ this

On 2 March 1992, JIM BROWN, about a week after his son Jah T was guNNED down on IM MOTORBIKE ON MAXWELL AVE in broad daylight (1 Feb 92)/d 2 Feb 92 & **400 WAS FE DEAD FE DAT** & the carnAGE had started—some 14 dead or injured—Brown was found 'incinerated' (some reports say 'DEAD FROM SMOKE INHLATION') in IM 'CUSTARDY' (*TTR* 39)[10]

The text links the political nature of the violence on Kingston's streets to a wider global context. Although McKenzie claims that the incidents of police harassment are not of a political nature, Perkins links them to the violence of the 1980 election campaign:

**Now: I remember hearing stories like these, coming, as it happened, from the other side, because in those days in 1980**

................

**as we were coming to the elections and I heard allegation like these**

................

**made on JBC radio & television –**

................

**being told against the soldiers in that year, right? Nothing ever came of it...** (*TTR* 31-32)

The 1980 election campaign is said to have been influenced by the CIA in response to United States opposition to Jamaica's PNP Prime Minister Michael Manley's socialist politics and his close ties with Cuba. The CIA's involvement was actively "fueling the violence of the Jamaica Labour Party" (Wheeler 231). This exposes the region's heavy dependence, both politically and economically, on the west, rendering official independence from colonial rule a farce, which is one of Brathwaite's central points of criticism in *Trench Town Rock*. In this sense, the crime-ridden inferno of Kingston functions as a metaphor for neocolonial dependence at large, and Brathwaite's personal history is tied in with that of the Caribbean region.

## 4.2. "Mi hann come from God": Ananse's Triumph

Like most of Brathwaite's work, *Trench Town Rock*, too, attempts to transcend the duality of colonial oppression and violent resistance via the retrieval of soul or *nam* as utopian moment in the formation of Caribbean selfhood. In *Trench Town Rock*, the desire to reunite with one's *nam* is illustrated in "Kingston in the Kingdoom of this World" (Chapter 3), which incorporates Christian, Rastafarian and voodoo elements and, together with the story of the African trickster Ananse at the end of the book, functions as an alternative, magical, reality to the dismal existence of Sisyphus. "Kingston in the Kingdoom of this World" is a version of Brathwaite's poem "Good Friday 1975: Kingston in the Kingdom of this World" (Wheeler 245).[11] The year 1975 links this poem, and thus the whole of *Trench Town Rock*, to Brathwaite's Kingston poetry. The poem anticipates a utopian state via a liberation from the present alienation of neocolonial dependence. In other words, the poem seeks to reinscribe the original meaning of kingdom into the "doom" of "kingdoom." In connection with Good Friday, this kingdom is the new Jerusalem of Christ's second coming, which, as has been mentioned before, is to be understood as a new form of this-worldly existence rather than life after death. Therefore, Christ's kingdom is a kingdom of *this* world, with Christ himself challenging existing political structures and authorities.

The poem opens with allusions to the Sermon on the Mount, Christ's prophecy of the coming of the new age:

> the wind blows on the hillside
>     and i suffer the little children
> i remember the lilies of the field
>     the fish swim in their shoals of silence
> our flung nets are high wet clouds drifting (*TTR* 47)

But Christ as he appears in the poem is a defeated messiah. He is now imprisoned, awaiting crucifixion. The fact that he "cannot run down the hill-path of faith" (*TTR* 47) also echoes the ghetto dwelling Rastafarians who have been dispersed from their hilltop settlement of Pinnacle. The speaker of the poem is the imprisoned soul or *nam* of the city's zombie body, and by extension the imprisoned selfhood of the region, which the Rastafarians of Pinnacle tried to liberate. The speaker's spiritual qualities are highlighted in words such as "music," "reed," "pen," "word," "lips" in the following passage, suggesting inspiration or contact with the Holy Spirit:

> with this reed i make music
> with this pen i remember the word
> with these lips i can remember the beginning of the
> world (*TTR* 47)

The reference to reed and music harks back to Brathwaite's poem "Flute(s)" (*Middle Passages*), which for him represented the maroon utopia of Irish Town, the beginning of "a new life new words a new world of writing endeav or" (*C* 153). Separated, the body as well as the soul are powerless, "reduced" (*TTR* 47). Unable to connect with each other, both soul and body face death, which is expressed in the inability to produce music. The image of the beaten face in the following quotation recalls the mutilated body of the policeman at the end of Chapter 1:

> he is reduced
>
> > to a bundle of rags/a broken
> > stick
> > that will never whistle through
> > fingerstops into the music
> > of flutes
>
> . . . . . . . . . . . . . . . .
>
> i am reduced
>
> to these black eyes
> this beaten face
> these bleach-
> ing lips blear-
> ing obscenities (*TTR* 47–49)

*Zombies and Messiahs in the Kingdom of this World:* Trench Town Rock

As the imprisoned spirit of Kingston's zombie society, the voice of the poem is not only that of the dispossessed. Elizabeth Wheeler argues that the suburbanite, who at night is imprisoned behind his grilled windows and padlocked doors, also represents Christ:

> ... the Messiah becomes a night-owl suburbanite, preoccupied with his own inability to save other people. The Mount of Olives becomes an uptown neighborhood "where i cannot run down the hill-path of faith ...." Middle-class Kingston may avoid thinking about poverty and violence during the day, but the truth comes out at night. This nighttime vigilance seems almost inevitable in descriptions of Kingston since the late 1960s .... The speaker seems to experience a typical Kingston paradox: because of urban danger, the resident can witness a tropical night but is unable to move freely in it .... Division reduces those on both sides of the grill — rich and poor. (245–47)

The first half of the poem, which refers to the Sermon on the Mount in more traditional images such as the fish and the children, can be ascribed to the voice of the middle class speaker. The second half of the poem creolizes the figure of Christ by associating him with voodoo and Rastafarian beliefs:

> my authority was foot-stamp upon the ground
>     the curves the palms the dancers
> my authority was nyambura inching closer
>     embroideries of fingers. silver earrings balancers (*TTR* 49)

The references to "foot-stamp" and dancing allude to ritual dancing in voodoo culture, performed to invite the *loa* to possess the devotees. Ritual dancing is also part of Rastafarian culture, later secularized in the reggae and rock steady rhythms. The image of the dance, which suggests harmony, represents voodoo and Rasta, in the first instance, as non-aggressive cultures. The other, more veiled, reference to Rastafarian culture, "nyambura inching closer," however, implies a more pro-active revolutionary stance. "Nyambura" is an African name, in this case probably that of an ancestor, but it also evokes "Nyabingi," which Brathwaite in his notes to the first *X/Self* refers to as "a militant Rasta 'nation'" (*X/S* 120). Campbell writes that the Rastafarians "called themselves Nya men — linking their ideas to the anti-colonial movement of Kigezi, Uganda — *Nyabingi* — which called for 'Death to Black and White Oppressors'" (72). In voodoo, too, there exists a more aggressive expression in the form of the Petro cult, which is associated with militant resistance to slavery, such as, for example, the Haitian slave rebellion.[12] The poem thus implies the possibility for utopian change within society via alternative sources of cultural and spiritual identification.

In this context, the poem also invokes the ability of the spirit to transcend the laws of the physical world in an allusion to the Lazarus story:

> my authority was sunlight: the man who arose from
>     the dead called me saviour
>     his eyes had known moons
>     older than jupiters (*TTR* 48)

The passage highlights two aspects that reflect on the importance of the numinous in relation to utopia. One is the revolutionary and subversive understanding of the messiah. The other, linked to the first, is the need for humanity to connect with its own divinity. Bloch argues that religious experience implies an encounter with the uncanny, numinous, or "Utterly Different" (*PH* 3: 1195), which manifests itself in the "inapplicability of immanent-familiar categories" (*PH* 3: 1195). In this sense, an encounter with the numinous always involves a total upsetting of the categories in which we have been brought up to think. The numinous thus always implies a "No to the existing world" (*PH* 3: 1198).

This notion of the "Utterly Different" can be employed as a legitimizing discourse of the authoritarian rule of God the father, a "completely unmediatable despotism, kept remote from human participation" (*PH* 3: 1194). With regard to the contemporary Caribbean, the United States performs such an "unmediatable despotism," alienating the islands from the rest of the Americas by depriving them of the opportunity to be politically, economically and culturally autonomous. However, Bloch points to the possibility of liberating the idea of the "Utterly Different" from authoritarian thinking and to the necessity for it to "be won over for religious or meta-religious humanism" (*PH* 3: 1194), since "[i]t is only the Utterly Different which gives to everything that has been longed for in the deification of man the appropriate dimension of depth" (*PH* 3: 1995). In this aspect of the "humanization of religion" (*PH* 3: 1196),

Bloch's philosophy radically breaks with traditional Christianity and, at the same time, moves beyond western notions of individualism, suggesting that selfhood needs a profound spiritual dimension.

Bloch perceives the central element of Christianity, that which distinguishes Christianity from all other religions, as being the "mediation between the subjective religious world and the taboo of the previous objective religious side — a mediation which is here called kingdom, the kingdom of God" (*PH* 3: 1196). In order to give the idea of kingdom a utopian connotation, Bloch proposes that "God becomes the kingdom of God, and the kingdom of God no longer contains a god" (*PH* 3: 1196). The elimination of God the father gives "the religious kingdom-intention" an "open space before it" (*PH* 3: 1199). In this sense, the openness of the future gives Bloch's notion of utopia a dynamic and flexible element, which prevents it from acquiring a totalitarian structure. Moreover, the elimination of God is "dissolved in the theology of the community but in one which has itself *stepped beyond the threshold of the previously known creature, of its anthropology and sociology*" (*PH* 3: 1196). However, the experience of the "Utterly Different" as numinous or miraculous is retained even then as a reminder of the as yet unrealized kingdom of God within the human community. Bloch argues that what is wished for in religions, "and even more powerfully in those of the messianic invocation of homeland, is that of feeling at home in existence" (*PH* 3: 1196). The messiah leads the human community towards the kingdom of God. He actively challenges God the father and clears the space God occupies for the realization of the kingdom, i.e. utopian potential within the human community.

Both Marcus Garvey and Haile Selassie can be read as messianic figures in the Blochian sense. Both represent the liberation of black people from colonial rule. Garvey in particular aims to prevent the exploitation of natural resources on the African continent by the west. With the west as God the father deprived of hegemonic power, Africa would become a messianic space, a space of freedom and a form of kingdom. In this sense, Africa would be able to function as a manifestation of *Heimat*. For Garveyism and Rastafarianism alike, Africa is both a place of origin, of the origin of the race, and of arrival, a utopian space of the liberation of the race, thus comprising both meanings of *Heimat*.

In Brathwaite's work, the Christian God is often a metaphor for colonial and neocolonial rule. The utopian space of the "creole cosmos," on the other hand, contains elements of a secularized kingdom. Bloch argues that the atheism of messianic religion ("the kingdom ... can only remain ... *without theism*" (*PH* 3: 1200)) does not deprive humanity of the spiritual, but humanity itself acquires divinity. Brathwaite's utopian personae or messiah figures, such as Xango in *X/Self*, Obatala, Legba and Nanny in *The Zea Mexican Diary*, the Rastafarian Early Bird and the voice of the poem in *Trench Town Rock*, and, above all, the figures of Marcus Garvey, Haile Selassie and Bob Marley, embody spiritual aspects of cross-culturality as well as a "No to the existing world order" (*PH* 3: 1198). Contrary to Brathwaite's notion of the Christian God, which is generally negative, Bloch applies to God the term "*ens perfectissimum*" (most perfect being) (*PH* 3: 1199), which in relation to the idea of the secularized kingdom comes to stand for "a place of projection at the head of utopian-radical intention" (*PH* 3: 1199). In Brathwaite's "creole cosmos," the Christian God is dissolved into a plurality of gods from different cultural backgrounds, who in turn represent the *ens perfectissimum* of cross-cultural existence. In this sense, the messiah challenges the position of God and authoritarian rule.

Bloch emphasizes that the Jewish tradition regards the messiah first and foremost as a political liberator who challenges existing social structures. The revolutionary qualities of Jesus lie in the proposal for an equal distribution of wealth without one part of humanity becoming richer by exploiting another. But Jesus also goes beyond the Jewish messiah in that he prophesies a radically different order following the complete destruction of the existing world: "... *the best-attested words of Jesus are eschatological*, he really spoke, as in Mark 13, about the destruction of Jerusalem, of the temple, of the world of the old aeon" (*PH* 3: 1263). The kingdom of God is always a kingdom of this world and not of the world that begins after death, but because of the complete destruction of this world as it now exists, Bloch's idea of the kingdom of God is also radically utopian. In this political immediacy lies Christ's challenge to the ruling powers of his time, and indeed of any time.

In the New World, the apocalyptic element of messianic religion occurs most prominently in the Rastafarian movement. In Brathwaite's poem "Starvation" (*Black + Blues*), a Rastafarian prophesies the downfall of Babylon represented in the poem by the American tourist industry and the presence of consumer goods. The speaker considers himself a "sufferer." Wheeler points out that "'sufferer' is the standard Rasta term for oppressed blacks, trapped in Babylonian captivity far from Africa" (249).[13] Christ himself is a sufferer, though in a more general sense, as are his counterparts in *Trench Town Rock*, *Shar* and *The Zea Mexican Diary*. The appearance of Rastafarian culture in the dystopian cityscape of *Trench Town Rock* is crucial as it has the potential to convert its hopelessness into the possibility of a new beginning: "The cosmos, not as worshipped . . . but as collapsing, becomes the instrument, indeed the location of the kingdom . . ." (*PH* 3: 1265). In this sense, the dystopian element in Brathwaite's writing is less an expression of despair than of anticipation. The miracle of the resurrection of Lazarus alluded to in "Kingston in the Kingdoom of this World" points towards the possibility of a new world order. Miracles exist according to different laws, are expressions of a world that has not yet been, in which the laws of this world do not apply anymore. Jesus himself regarded his miracles as signs, and in connection with the eschatological nature of his role as messiah, his miracles become "*signs* of the coming end" (*PH* 3: 1305).

The society described in *Trench Town Rock* is profoundly deprived of the miraculous or numinous. Consequently, there exists no sense of reverence among its members. Instead, people prey or scavenge on each other. Brathwaite illustrates his perception of "human scavenging" in Chapter 5 of *Trench Town Rock*, "Short History of Dis or Middle Passages Today." The *Città di Ditte*, the "City of Dis," is the entrance to the lower circles of Dante's hell, the abode of those souls who deliberately sinned during their lifetimes (as opposed to the souls in the upper circles, who are guilty of sins of neglect and indifference).[14] In his mind's journey, Brathwaite has arrived in the lower regions of his society's hell, although the quest image can also be applied to society itself, which, severed from its imprisoned spirit of independence, sinks deeper and deeper into its own inferno. Consequently, whereas Brathwaite refers to society's indifference to victims of crime at the beginning of *Trench Town Rock* ("no one say a prayer" (*TTR* 16)), he now concentrates on criminal activity itself, which enters the public consciousness via the newspapers:

# Chopping off Peoples Dreams

> . . . The *TUESDAY STAR* has learned that the woman who was wearing a thick bracelet stepped off the bus and into the path of a man armed with a meat chopper. Poised with the sharp weapon, the man inflicted a single blow which severed the woman's arm. When the arm fell to the ground, the man

took it up, and while running, he removed the bracelet and threw away the arm. Eyewitnesses told the *TUESDAY STAR* that the woman fainted and was immediately removed from the scene by a passing motorist.... (*TTR* 71–72)

Another article refers to the act of human scavenging directly:

## Human scavengers loot death car

By Claire Clarke
*S Gleaner*, 31 Mar 1991
With tracks of blood and brain marrow trailed around the site, a woman in the crowd excitedly captured a tube of lipstick from the wreckage. This young woman had also located a shoe saying, "Mi like it, but mi nuh know whey de nex one dey." Scanning the scene, she realized that the other foot was still inside the contorted machine of death; she attempted to close in and capture her prize, but the police intercepted, so for the time being she let it be. (*TTR* 69)

Other newspaper clips Brathwaite employs in this chapter illustrate society's unconcern for newborn life:

# Bad Memories of
or the half-
                hazard birthing of Caliban

# Jubilee

Tonia Byfield [herself an 'inmate' of the Jubilee Maternity Hospital]...said she witnessed some mothers undergoing painful experiences. One mother was ordered to go into the waiting room and sit there until the nurse attended to her. The baby's head appeared as the mother moaned. The nurses ignored her and she had to run to the delivery room with the baby head between her legs. Another mother, who had been in labour, said she went for a nurse on hearing the cry of [another] mother that [her] baby was on the way. She said the nurse merely said **'mek she stay down there an bawl.'** *SG* Nov 3, 1991 (*TTR* 69)

The reference to the birth of Caliban, which appears to be Brathwaite's own subtitle to the article, gives this apparently random event a particular significance in relation to the birth of Caribbean selfhood. For Brathwaite, the figure of Caliban represents both an awareness of ancestral heritage and a forward-intention in the creation of a uniquely Caribbean self. The disrespect for newborn life exhibited in the above *Gleaner* article reflects Caribbean society's disregard in relation its own future. Thus the birth of Caliban/Caribbean man is hazardous and risky.

Likewise, society's disrespect for the dead has, in Brathwaite's eyes, a deeper implication than the following lines from the *Sunday Gleaner* suggest:

# Shame of May Pen Cemetery
*'Gone to the bones'*

On Wednesday, on the second visit in a few days, a *Sunday Gleaner* team found the skeleton of a man who seemed to have been buried years ago. The skeletal remains were dressed in a pair of socks and blue pants. All that remained of him were the bones scattered on the ground nearby and the bones which remained inside the socks. The casket in which he was laid to rest was nowhere to be seen...

## A Creole Experiment

> One mausoleum belonging to the late Bishop Mary Louise Coore stood as an old derelict structure. The concrete pillars supporting the roof had been crudely chopped into, the grilles dug out and the steel stolen leaving a mass of rubble and garbage on top of the grave... (*TTR* 70–71)

The dead, the living and the unborn are connected through the world axis. In its disrespect for all of these spheres of existence, the society of *Trench Town Rock* breaks the communion symbolized by the tree of life. In their disregard for past and future, the members of this society also sever themselves from their dreams, which is what the texts suggests with the headline "Chopping off Peoples Dreams." The city or society as body also reappears here. The zombie body of Kingston, and of the Caribbean as a whole, is deprived of its soul and thus of its ability for creative dreaming. What Brathwaite calls "human scavenging" thus stands for Caribbean society's most extreme form of spiritual and cultural uprooting and dehumanization. Consequently, the second half of the chapter title, "Middle Passages Today," is an apt one, connecting the fragmentation of bodies to the violent uprooting caused by the slave trade and establishing a continuity between past and present trauma. Brathwaite observes the prevalence of the Middle Passage experience in the contemporary Caribbean as the "Age of Dis," which he describes in terms of rupture: "Distress Dispair & Disrespect. Distrust Disrupt Distruction" (*TTR* 73). The "Age of Dis" is an age of *dis*topia and Kingston itself its focal point, the City of Dis.

The alienation implied in Bloch's notion of anti-utopia is that of society from itself and from its natural environment. The miraculous or numinous as it breaks into the "darkness of the lived moment" can, consequently, be regarded as an anticipation of utopia: "The miraculous is the flash of light of the subject and of the object, beside which nothing alienated exists any more and in which subject and object have simultaneously ceased to be separate" (*PH* 3: 1311). Utopia as an instance of communion represents the end of desire, an instance of arrival. In *Trench Town Rock*, desire appears as excessive greed, resulting in the death of what is desired in a similar way as the greed of Europe's colonial powers resulted in the exploitation and exhaustion of natural and human resources in the New World and elsewhere. The image of the dog and its master at the end of "Short History of Dis" illustrates this:

Near where I write this now a man is training dogs to guard you or to kill you.

. . . he grieves the dog an order & it dis/obeys. he hits it wham wham wham. the grey hound howls. the others writhe & crash against their cages in dis/pair.

. . . **command**. the salivating canine howls & leaps & tries to break away. the black whip turns it back & almost breaks its back.

. . . the Man commands. until the thin bitch whimpers. tail comes down. & falls. till in that silent yard. only the fire burns (*TTR* 73–74)

Echoing the historical continuity signified by the image of the Middle Passage, Brathwaite stresses that Caribbean societies have internalized the power relations of master and slave (which appears here as master and dog — a graphic reminder of the dehumanized self of the slave), so that they are not only victims of new colonial powers such as the Unites States but also of their own aggression and greed. Moreover, the death of what is desired is not confined to human society but includes the natural environment. Social catastrophe is again mirrored in natural catastrophe:

**The grills go up. the old nightwatchmen disappear. Welcome the red-tooth dog. the squat-face bodyguard. Those with good sense walk with their sawn-off shotguns. M16s & AK48s enter the rapidly declining currency of grace & courtesy. No Natty Dread but Nutty Morgan hero of the nineteen-ninety-ninety-ones. Orlando Patto's Dungle of the 60s Sisyphus become the Riverton City (Kingston) Dump of 1992: an image of a city smouldering in garbage. & men & woman plundering that monstrous HELL of stench & detritus & death. dead rat. live rat. for bread. dead rotting flesh. dead rotting fish. the decomposing contexts of yr kitchen sink & toilet bowl & latrine. . .**

## A Creole Experiment

into that Dump goes the dead body of one University lecture & his woman frenn. profane cremation of the silence that surrounds that loss that no one hardly notices. (*TTR* 68)[15]

The messiah figures of *Trench Town Rock* point beyond this dystopian rubbish dump of human life. They represent instances of the miraculous and appear as the possibility of mediation between estranged subject and object. The most striking example of such mediation, however, does not appear in *Trench Town Rock*, but in *The Zea Mexican Diary* in the incarnation of Legba in Mr Reid. Legba/Mr Reid is one of the most profound expressions of "arrived-at Being" in Brathwaite's work. In Mr Reid's all-inclusive gesture of the tree planting, Caribbean humanity (the unborn, the living, and the dead) finds a home in the Caribbean soil. In their sustainable mode of farming, the Rastafarians of Pinnacle, too, express such a sense of being rooted in the Caribbean soil. Like the maroon communities of past centuries, Pinnacle can be regarded as an instance of kingdom, as a messianic space, and the inclusion of nature into the human community is of vital importance in the realization of kingdom. In this sense, the Caribbean emerges as a focal point of utopian thinking in Brathwaite's work.

In Chapter 4 of *Trench Town Rock*, which describes the burglary of his Marley Manor apartment, Brathwaite himself becomes a suffering messiah figure. He also identifies with the murdered Early Bird. In this sense, Chapter 4 mirrors Chapter 1. Like Bird, Brathwaite has his hands tied, and like Bird, he experiences death: "*. . . and all this time my bright ears hearing like the rape of what was once my room: swishes & billows & clatterings down & then again & again somebody wd sit on the bed near my head with the hard & hot & cold of the gun at the back of my neck the other hand drowning me into the blackwater dark of the mattress...*" (*TTR* 59). Brathwaite undergoes a metaphorical death in that the bullet never physically enters his head. Rather, it leaves his psyche maimed as he explains in *ConVERSations with Nathaniel Mackey*:

```
    — he finally pushes the hard bone of his gun into the
  black of my skull — at the back there into the cleft just
       above the nick and press or whatever the trigger
           and it goes click, see? there's this click
      — I could hear it for the forever of nothing happening
```

*Zombies and Messiahs in the Kingdom of this World:* Trench Town Rock

> In other words, the bullet — if there *is* a bullet
> — pass through my brain without physical contact, or I no
> longer have the physical contact to receive the bullet
> But I *feel* it go through my mind, right? all its detail of
> rushing gold and shatter and catastrophe and silence
>
> . . . I mean — and I know this — that I'm not the same
> person after this experience and that either I'm dead
> — lookin and talkin to you the living; or I'm talking
> to what my sister call 'a cloud of witnesses'. . . .
>
> (*C* 246–47)[16]

Brathwaite has internalized the suffering he witnessed at the beginning of *Trench Town Rock*. Consequently, the crime scene shifts from outside of the Marley Manor apartment complex to the inside. The burglary and ransacking of the apartment is described in terms of natural catastrophe, of a hurricane breaking into Brathwaite's life, which links the experience of *Trench Town Rock* to *Shar* and *The Zea Mexican Diary*. Again, environmental devastation mirrors psychic devastation:

> *...my room like thesea—thedebris&litteralloverthebeaches—bibliography files & my poetry manuscript folders all trampled & curled by the breakers—books hit by like a hurricane—what more can I tell you?—clothes torn from their hooks & their shoulders—my life like torn from its moorings&somethinglikespiderscrawlingovermyfaces...*
> (*TTR* 59)

Despite this, the apocalyptic destruction of his creative life, which he mourns and which is an echo of the death of the "creative EKB" in *The Zea Mexican Diary*, gives way to new creativity in *DreamStories*, where a form of psychic healing begins. In *Trench Town Rock*, however, death overshadows hope, "my death and the death, as I experience it, of my loved — o loved society and culture" (*C* 278).

Contrary to the teachings of the church, Bloch considers death as the ultimate anti-utopia of messianic religion, as that which essentially does not belong to the fulfillment of kingdom. Christ's death was not a voluntary sacrifice to redeem the world's sins. He died because he was a "rebel against custom and the power of rulers..., a trouble-maker and loosener of all family bonds" (*PH* 3: 1262). Thus "the death on the cross came from without, not from within" (*PH* 3: 1262). Death was a sign that the messiah had failed. Likewise, to Brathwaite death comes from without, not from within. His suffering does not redeem the society that makes him suffer. Instead, society and its existing structures render his vision of a "creole cosmos" a failure. Society has, indeed, thrown him, "one University lecture," and his vision on the rubbish dump.

Despite this, utopian anticipation has the last word. The Ananse story, "Anansese," taken from Neville Dawes's *The Last Enchantment* (1960), concludes *Trench Town Rock*. "Anansese" contains elements of the miraculous and points towards the possibility of a different world order. Ananse is an African trickster who has been transported to the New World via the Middle Passage. In *Trench Town Rock*, the Ananse story is presented in a West Indian idiom, illustrating the sea change Ananse has undergone. The trickster is generally a "transformer, or culture hero, who in a mythic age at the beginning of the world helps shape human culture into its familiar form" ("Tricksters: An Overview" 45). He combines "three modes of sacrality: the divine, the animal, and the human" (45). Especially the African trickster "yokes together bodiliness and transcendence, society and individuality" ("African Tricksters" 47). His creative energy and his capacity for appropriation and change are reflected in his "crav[ing] modes of being other than his own" ("Tricksters" 45). The Ananse story recorded in *Trench Town Rock* represents precisely this capacity:

> *Ananse go until im see a woman givin er baby black tea. Him seh, 'Ow yu givin yu baby black tea an I have milk'*
>
> *The Woman tek de milk give it to er baby, baby drink it off*
>
> *Ananse se, 'Come come Woman gi me mi milk mi milk*

> *come from Cow Cow eat mi grass mi grass come from*
> *Man Man bruk mi knife mi knife come from Granny*
> *Granny eat mi rat mi rat come from PingWing*
> *PingWing juk mi hann*
> *mi hann come from God'*
>
> *The woman seh 'A cyaan gi yu milk cause*
> *Baby drink it off, but tek dis blue...'*
>                                     (TTR 78)

In tracing his possessions back to God, Ananse reveals his divine aspect, but he does not insist on keeping what is rightfully his. He instead puts it to the service of the human community, thus helping to shape human culture. His exchange of gifts with humans and animals, moreover, links this world to its transcendent origin and constantly infuses it with creative energy. Ananse's refusal to insist on a superiority derived from his divinity also functions as an antidote to the struggle between oppression and resistance. He anticipates the kingdom of God and so becomes a messiah figure. In Ananse, the "humanization of religion" is not only a humanization of God, but also a humanization of the dehumanized dispossessed. Like Christ, Ananse raises the despised and dehumanized into divinity while, at the same time, abandoning his God-aspect to enter into communion with the human.

In Akan mythology, Ananse desires and obtains, after a period of trial, the stories of the sky-god Nyame and becomes "the treasurer of all the stories that have ever been told," so that "whenever a man wishes to tell a story for the entertainment of his people, he must acknowledge first of all that the tale is a great gift, given to him by Anansi, the spider" (Duane 53).[17] Thus Ananse is similar to Legba, interpreter of the divine word. Through Ananse's, and indirectly through Legba's, access to the divine word Brathwaite reopens the gate between the physical and the metaphysical world. In this way, he reinfuses the zombie bodies of *Trench Town Rock* with a soul.

In his emphasis on the need for communal support and the latent possibility of its realization "in the kingdom of this world," Brathwaite's primarily dystopian vision of Kingston contains a strongly utopian element. This communal consciousness is akin to Ananse's web that connects the physical to the metaphysical world. In this magical space, "creole" acquires a new dimension, referring to the interpenetration not only of cultures but of modes of existence. In this sense, Ananse's web gathers together the different spheres of existence (the dead, the human, and the divine) into the utopian space of *Heimat*.

That *Trench Town Rock* should end with Ananse's triumph when most of the book celebrates Rastafarian culture seems somewhat contradictory. However, it explains itself in the symbolism of the lion and the spider, which represent two different personality types of the African diaspora. The Rastafarians identified with the lion as a symbol of black pride and as a reaction against the apparently docile Quashie or cunning Ananse personality of the slave (Campbell 99). Ananse in particular can be associated with New World African tradition of "Signifyin(g)," in which meaning is constantly deferred as the speaker engages in rhetorical games such as punning or parodying. Henry Louis Gates defines "Signifyin(g)" as "black double-voicedness," which entails an attempt "to disrupt the signifier by displacing its signified in an intentional act of will" (Gates 51).[18] The Rastafarians, however, "believed that . . . black people should drop these character traits of the adaptable hustler and be straightforward with their fellow men and women" (Campbell 99). The triumph of Ananse suggests that for Brathwaite, despite his admiration for Rastafarian culture, the personality of the spider is more adaptable and resilient in the face of suffering and trauma than the kingly lion and thus a more fitting personality to sustain him through the devastation he encounters in his own personal life.[19] Moreover, Haile Selassie, the "Lion of Judah," is ultimately, despite his messianic aspects, a God-as-father figure and occupies the messianic space of kingdom alone. Ananse, on the other hand, challenges the rule of the father, the sky-god Nyame, by obtaining his stories and renounces his own divinity by becoming human and animal. Therefore, *Trench Town Rock* celebrates the triumph of humility over pride and of the "humanization of religion" over the apotheosis of earthly rulers.

# Chapter 5

# *DreamStories:* The Far Side of the Mirror

⸻ ◇◆◇ ⸻

## 5.1. "A Most Ancient Place": Rift Valleys of the Psyche

*DreamStories* (*DS*) (1994) is a reworking of the traumatic events of *The Zea Mexican Diary, Shar,* and *Trench Town Rock,* and the encoding of these events in dream sequences. Brathwaite's own perception of dreaming and writing *DreamStories* is that it functioned as a process of healing and a doorway into a new phase of creativity leading on from his death by the "ghost bullet" recorded in *Trench Town Rock*:

. . . But since I'm died, a strange set of circumstances begin to make themselves shall we say 'possible' And I begin to dream, stepping on these stones of pearl and peril, back into each early morning, re/living, re/learning . . . is where and how, I suppose, I begin to restore the *fragments* . . . of my infernal psyche. These constant ?curative haunts that—

## A Creole Experiment

```
for some reason — a kind of like compulsion, as if I . .
.blind, am following the shadow of i/self. (C 164-65)
```

In a letter to Gordon Rohlehr, Brathwaite describes *DreamStories* as "a kind of RIFT VALLEY in my senscape after the psychic disaster slippages of Mexican (86) Shar (88) TTR (90)" (qtd. in "Dream Journeys," *DreamStories* iii). Although the geological phenomenon known as "rift valley" can be found all over the globe, Brathwaite is most likely to derive his metaphor from the Great Rift Valley of eastern Africa, as he once again returns to his African heritage for spiritual sustenance. Due to the violent history of its formation, the Great Rift Valley is an apt metaphor for Brathwaite's own traumatic experiences.[1]

In *Feeling the Spirit: Searching the World for the People of Africa* (1994), African-American photographer Chester Higgins documents his journey in search of African heritage throughout the world. He begins his search in the highlands of north-central Ethiopia, overlooking the Great Rift Valley, where the world's oldest human remains have been found. As a response to these finds, Higgins calls the Great Rift Valley "a most ancient place" (10).[2] In *DreamStories*, Brathwaite undertakes an inner journey to the "most ancient place" or root of his trauma, where he relives Mexican's death and the destruction of his house but also finds spiritual sustenance as Mexican and his then new muse and wife-to-be Dream Chad (Beverly) merge with Sycorax, the guardian of *nam*, who possesses the power of healing. Brathwaite's "most ancient place" is a place of healing precisely because it exposes him to trauma. The act of dreaming is also the poet's retreat into the most remote, unconscious parts of his psyche.

In *DreamsStories*, as in much of his "video-style" work, Brathwaite links his own personal anguish to the wider Caribbean context, in particular the history of his slave ancestors, thus establishing a continuity between past and present, between colonial and neocolonial dependence. In this sense, *DreamStories* reiterates the concerns voiced in *X/Self* and *Ancestors* by showing how past and present are inseparably linked. *DreamStories* also refers back to the autobiographical trilogy in that it employs the Middle Passage as a metaphor of individual suffering in a contemporary Caribbean setting. In *DreamStories*, therefore, Brathwaite journeys back not only to the "most ancient place" of his psyche but also to that of Caribbean history.

Despite their dreamlike quality and relative opacity, the individual dreamstories are not mere recordings of dreams, as Brathwaite himself indicates in *ConVERSations*. Instead the dreams serve as "stepping stones." Dreaming becomes a preliminary activity to the production of literature. In the "silence of dreams" (Badejo ix), the silence before words, Brathwaite's *DreamStories* performs a journey into the unconscious to release the pain caused by his loss and to rework the traumatic experiences of his life into a story. Thus, as stories, the pieces collected here are the product of a deliberate act of artistic creation, and as such they are transported away from the realm of the imaginary into the symbolic.

As outlined in the introductory chapter, the Caribbean unconscious or imaginary is synonymous with black folk culture. The memory of Africa in all its forms is the "dream book" (Bundy 13) of the Caribbean.[3] For Lacan, the dividing line between imaginary and symbolic is the mirror. Brathwaite's journey into the dream book is a journey to the far side of that mirror. In a Caribbean context, the mirror also triggers other, more local associations. In voodoo cosmology, which echoes throughout *DreamStories*, the mirror is a dividing sphere between the world of the living and the world of the dead and the *loa*. Traveling to the other side of the mirror, Brathwaite is "following the shadow of i/self," the victim of the ghost bullet, into the afterworld. In this sense, *DreamStories* is an account of how Brathwaite sees himself and the Caribbean from the vantage point of death.

## 5.2. "The Black Angel"

In "The Black Angel," the first story, the journey to the other side becomes a process of initiation. "The Black Angel" is the only text in *DreamStories* that does not directly refer to the events of *The Zea Mexican Diary*, *Shar* and *Trench Town Rock*. (The story was first written and published long before these events in the 1950s).[4] Its central image is a spiritual battle in the guise of a boxing match that involves a loss of innocence and marks the beginning of independent selfhood in the narrating subject.

The story is set in a labor camp surrounded by a forest that separates its inhabitants from the outside world:

> . . . We were the downspring of lovers, convicts, the poor; and had been brought to this forest by the Factory Committee from we were born or, in some cases, from infancy

Many of us were mad, some were idiots, and a few suffered from enhystamins, hysterias, defi ciencies & allergies that behaved like liars, tu bers & blood diseases: result of the vicious in-

ternal bleeding of our impenitential ancestors And the women in the camp, immune themsel ves, transported these viruses/diseases to the ducks & hearts, the kidneys & the livids, the axons & the lymph tracts of the others of us

Sometimes our doctors switched us on so that we cd watch our cells divide & multiply on tele vision/ though of course I didn't come to learn about this prodigal technology until the day af ter my birthday on 11 Mayhem 2004

but despite all this (perhaps because of it?) — we po ssessed — I know this now — an xtraordinary in nocence of soul; and though we were neurotic- cally sensitive and abject to depressions & pr ofound hallucinations, we possessed a moral integrity and equilibrium which was quite as- tonishing; though I wonder still if 'equilibrium' is the world I want, since in our 'unspoiled sou ls', there seldom was the need for balance, sin ce the antagonism of temptations, the wings < & leers of evil, were unknown to us. (*DS* 8-9)

Unlike in the other dreamstories, the narrator of "The Black Angel" is not as easily identifiable with Brathwaite himself. However, there are some instances where the narrator has certain similarities with Brathwaite and can be regarded as the author's double or dreaming self. 11 May is Brathwaite's own birthday. It becomes "Mayhem" in the story to highlight the disaster of his birth, producing a social "misfit" without hope of living anywhere else except on the margins of society. After his own experience of society's indifference, Brathwaite, too, sees himself in that position. The similarity between author and narrator and the reference to Columbus and Dream Chad later in the story ("by the time Dream Chad arrive in the late fifteenth century, about the time of the discovery of Christofere Columbus" (*DS* 13)) anchor the otherwise unspecific story both in an autobiographical as well as in the wider Caribbean context.

The camp represents, and at the same time inverts, the Caribbean plantation that echoes in the structure of the labor camp, where people mainly live to work and do little else outside their working hours. Inversion is used as an alienation effect and is achieved by a reversion of time, situating the plantation in the twenty-first century (2004) and letting time move backwards, so that the reference to Columbus's arrival in the Americas in the fifteenth century is referred to as the future. As I have argued in my reading of *Trench Town Rock*, the alienation that accompanies ghetto existence and most other forms of modern Caribbean life is the result of an inability to regard the Caribbean as *Heimat*. In "The Black Angel," Brathwaite traces this alienation back to the days of slavery and links it to the erasure of the slaves' African names and languages and the enforced use of the master's tongue, resulting in the loss of a vital form of cultural identification. The narrator seems uncomfortable in his use of terms such as "xtraordinary innocence of soul" and "unspoiled souls" above and "silent ruminations" and "watchful anticipation" elsewhere in the story (*DS* 18), the gloss showing that they are quotations:

> that's the way we used to talk in those days >
> in that place > formal-like like that
>
> from reaping cheap-edition 19th century
> 'Victorian' proseworks
>
> (*DS* 18-19)

Through this adopted language, the narrator is forced to take on the alienating gaze of a Victorian Englishman, which prevents him from creating an unmediated relationship with his social and natural environment. His use of a borrowed language also prevents him from understanding his surroundings. In this context, "innocence of soul" echoes the notion of the Caribbean as paradise on earth and its inhabitants as "noble savages," myths to which Columbus and his successors contributed. In "The Black Angel," however, innocence is not incorruptibility but ignorance of how the outside world exploits the laborers, keeping them like slaves. Innocence here is ignorance of cultural heritage and apathy brought about by engineered hallucinations. In this respect, the story criticizes the Caribbean's own inertia in the face of exploitation and dependence.

The spiritual struggle around which the story centers moves the narrator's "innocence of soul" towards spiritual awareness by connecting him with his *nam*. *Nam*, the submerged African psyche of the Caribbean, its "most ancient place," is the place where the individual connects with ancestral memory. The agents of the narrator's initiation are Ta Mega and Kappo (who is identical with the Black Angel, although the narrator fails to realize this). Ta Mega is described as "pure gypsy, the only person not connected w/ the factory" and also as "what our cheap editions called 'an ancient hag'" (*DS* 22). In her role as spiritual guardian of the narrator's family and through her power to cast and exorcise spells — her "myalistic powve rs" (*DS* 22) — she is a Sycorax figure.[5] The narrator's use of Prospero's language ("ancient hag") accounts for his disrespect for Ta Mega's powers, which he regards as "unfocussed hocuspocusses" (*DS* 23).

Kappo, too, is an outsider to the camp: "As I have said before, we are native here: either brought in in early childhood, or *barn ya*. Yet only three months ago a grown man, with a strange outstanding jacket, had appeared among us" (*DS* 11). Kappo's jacket acquires the name Black Angel because "he kept the high collar sticking up like little ears or wings around his head" (*DS* 8). At first the term "Black Angel" evokes associations with Lucifer, the fallen angel in Christian mythology. This, as we shall see, is due to the Victorian diction the narrator uses, whose rigid classification of the world into black and white or good and evil will, in the course of the story, be deconstructed.

The boxing bout between Kappo and the narrator is an unofficial event with no spectators. It happens on their way home from work and in the wider context of the "more > public spectacle in the form of Championship (s)" (*DS* 10), boxing being "our only recreation at the camp ... after work" (*DS* 10). These championships are also referred to as "'Charlemagneships' after an ancient disused foundry on the premises" (*DS* 10). The mentioning of Charlemagne connects *DreamStories* to *X/Self*, where the emperor appears as one of the first imperialists. Here his name occurs as a reminder of how closely Caribbean and European histories are intertwined. The mentioning of Charlemagne also introduces an overlap of different geographical sites that is characteristic of many of the other dreamstories.[6]

Unlike the recreational boxing of the camp championships, the scuffle started by Kappo has its major impact not in the physical but the metaphysical realm:

> Kappo hit me, he didn't actually hit my chin or my face, but he hit something bright like **nam** or a star or a far like a jewel inside me – my **inn**o cence, it seems – my spirit or my soul – and it < was this xistence – inside – within me, which involuntary groaned & cried out every time
>
> I can't say how long it went on like this. I remember struggling back against him with all m/y will It was my *will*, not my physical strength, I discovered, I had to call upon, to use. I remember suddenly struggling against him w/this inner force & was then I saw my blows hit not
>
> Kappo
>
> but like the Black Angel. It had assumed like an entity all its own.
> 
>             . . . &
> I felt, too, that this Other, opposing me, was in tent on hurting . trying to break . to conk . even to *conquer* me; and that if he continued to hit me as he was doing, that this Black Angel . . .
>
> wd wrench me out from the ital consciousness of my body. (*DS* 16-17)

## A Creole Experiment

The destruction of a person's *nam* implies the total obliteration of one's being, and the Black Angel seems intent on achieving that.

The image of *nam* as jewel undermines the Christian assumption of the opposition of good and evil. African-American science-fiction author Samuel R. Delany argues that the fracturing qualities of jewels break up the seemingly monolithic structure of reality:

> The thing about jewels is that they have many bright and sharp-edged faces. They're signs of wealth, adventure, and power. . . . They reflect and refract the light that passes through them. In so doing, they shatter unitary images. Look through them and things become at once fragmented and multiple. The refractive quality of cut gems is a metaphor for analysis, brilliance, and pluralism. (Tatsumi 37)[7]

In "Images of Creativity and the Art of Writing in *The Arrivants*," Pamela Mordecai refers to the refractive quality of Brathwaite's images as "prismatic vision" (21), which she defines as "a non-linear style of cognition" (21) and which resonates with Brathwaite's own notion of magical realism. Mordecai argues that "prismatic vision" is "induced in creole-speaking communities by the conjunction of cultures" (21). Seen through the jewel of *nam*, the unitary image of the Black Angel as evil becomes shattered and opens up to embrace other identifications. In order to see through the jewel of *nam*, the protagonist of "The Black Angel" has to retrieve it from the "underwaters" (*DS* 28) of his soul. It is Ta Mega who sends him on this journey.

Ta Mega and the women of the camp are reminiscent of those in Brathwaite's other books, such as *Mother Poem* and *The Zea Mexican Diary*, exhibiting a closer connection to the Caribbean imaginary than men. Ta Mega's myalistic powers enable her to commune with the *loa* and, through this communication, to achieve profound vision. The drug-induced hallucinations of the men, on the other hand, are false visions and represent a form of escapism. As someone who stands between this world and that of the *loa* on the space where the mirror divides the two, Ta Mega can also be regarded as an incarnation of Legba. The narrator describes her as looking "more like an old man than a woman" (*DS* 22), and Legba himself is both male and female.[8]

After the narrator's fight with the Black Angel, Ta Mega draws an astrological chart on the young man's chest to determine what has suddenly caused her to fear for his welfare, "like if I had killed somebody or was myself threatened" (*DS* 25). During this procedure the narrator undergoes the necessary journey into the self:

> **deep in the very underwaters of myself I trembled**
> **it was as if my spirit was waking up in the middle of**
> **a very dark night**
> **as if I was alone in a wood of presences & powers**
> **vague enraged potentialities I could not see or name**
>
> **and beyond this wood**
> **moving somewhere out beyond. a moving**
> **gentleness like the leaves of trees. Their veins**
> **against the blue of space becoming wind of space.**
> **And between this wind. this light of outer efflurage**
> **were these dark forms**
>
> **and when they seemed to move. they threw a**
> **shadow on my spirit. as a shadow passing over a**
> **dark wood indarkens the faint trail**
> (*DS* 28)

The "underwaters" of the self are synonymous with the unconscious or imaginary. The narrator of the dreamstory echoes Brathwaite's "straitened subject" in *The Zea Mexican Diary*, trapped in a forest that, like Dante's forest at the beginning of *The Divine Comedy*, symbolizes loss of direction. The light beyond the forest in the above passage indicates an awakening of the spirit, a light of hope beyond the "darkness of the lived moment." The "underwaters" also function on a cultural level as the location of *nam*, the point where personal selfhood intersects with that of one's ancestors and that of the *loa*, the ancestors of humanity. In voodoo belief, a similar underwater forest is situated in Guinée, the island below the waters, which is regarded as the dwelling place of the *loa* and the dead. The forest itself is guarded by the *loa* Gran Bois. Thus the powers, presences and potentialities the narrator encounters on his inward journey could be read as the dead and the *loa*, who are "enraged" at his disregard for them, mirrored in his disrespect for Ta Mega.

 The awakening of the narrator's spirit is accompanied by instructions given by Eshu, the divine interpreter of the Yoruba Ifa oracle:

*A Creole Experiment*

> . . . I heard a dream or scream or voice that spoke to me
>
> of Eye and Eyevil = **Eshu** = singing in my distant ear like a mosquito & what seemed like Mephistopheles where there was no sun or struggle. only this eclipse : Ta Mega and my mother fighting for my light. (*DS* 30)

Eshu is the Yoruba equivalent to Dahomean Legba and, like the latter, a trickster. As pointed out previously, tricksters do mischief in order to teach. They bring death in order to create new life: hence the fusion of "eye" (enlightenment) and "evil" (mischief, death). Here Eshu/Legba/Ta Mega teaches that spiritual growth can only be achieved when one's inner "evils" or shadows are overcome. The battle in the narrator's soul mirrors his earlier battle with the Black Angel, only that the guardians of his *nam* fight in his stead. The Black Angel is the narrator's own shadow (in the Jungian sense), an internalized Prospero, present in the language he uses, which alienates him from the tradition that Ta Mega and his mother embody. The Black Angel is also an aspect of Eshu, as he connects the narrator to his *nam*, and is destructive only to those who fail to follow suit, such as other camp members who engage in a fight with Kappo. The refractive jewel of *nam* thus has the power to break up the binary — Sisyphean — opposition of good and evil, self and other, and opens it to the cross-culturality of the "creole cosmos."

At the end of the story, the narrator has gained spiritual power. As Delta, a newcomer to the camp, engages in a fight with Kappo, the narrator is able to witness Delta's spiritual pain:

> and so it was that the memory of my own xperience, that pressure, these same presentiments & groans, came back to me
>
> Δelta's psychic pain within me reawakening some deeper sound within me like an echo
>
> . . .
>
> **'mwe do not want to die,'**
> I heard like in the marrow of a dream my own voice

>           saying
>            ...
>
> # 'mwe na want a die'
>
> and like Ta Mega and my mother were telling me these
> words & listening to them at the same said time, though it
> was
> Δelta somehow I was hearing speaking
> (*DS* 34)

However, despite reliving his own experience, he fails to become a guide or guardian himself, to support the community from within (Ta Mega and the Black Angel come from outside) and convert their drugged hallucinations into visions that could change the plantation-like conditions under which they live. He seems afraid to communicate his knowledge and thus remains powerless:

> I wanted to shout out to him something like
>
> 'Remember not force, man, not force but will! Δelta will!'
>
> But like he couldn't hear because I couldn't sp eak & in any case my words, as *wrods*, felt foo lish on my tongue & I knew or thought I knew that neither
>
> Δelta nor the men who watched the fight wd > understand. Sun went black out & my head hurt worse. (*DS* 37)

The failure to communicate his knowledge ultimately prevents his spiritual growth. This is reflected at the very end of the story in his inability to see that Kappo and the Black Angel are one and the same, although he succeeds in overcoming the Black Angel by throwing the jacket into the fire and the light from beyond the forest reaches him:

*A Creole Experiment*

***B****ut when I throw away the jacket the stone was roll away & the great sun come shining in/to my now known darkened wood like a great gong*

(*DS* 43)

In other words, the narrator achieves a subliminal reawakening for himself, but fails to communicate his knowledge in a language that is authentic and not derivative. In this context it is interesting to note that the first version of the story was written two years before Brathwaite went to live in Ghana. First composed in 1953, "The Black Angel" dates back to a time before the author achieved a full reconnection with his own ancestral heritage, his *nam*.

In relation to the imaginary and symbolic dimensions of *DreamStories*, one could argue that the birth chart Ta Mega draws on the narrator's chest becomes an opening to the unconscious. It functions as a mirror surface. By crossing over to the other side the narrator inadvertently realigns himself with his true purpose in life, but he is responsible for interpreting that chart and for making it accessible in symbolic form. This he fails to do. He remains on the far side of the mirror, as yet unable to translate his experience. In this sense, it seems a very apt first story as it shows the personal as well as creative struggle Brathwaite himself was undergoing when he was writing *DreamStories*.

## 5.3. "Dream Chad"

Whereas "The Black Angel" reaches back to a period preceding the "psychic disaster slippages of Mexican (86) Shar (88) TTR (90)," the second story, "Dream Chad," begins the creative reworking of the actual events described in *The Zea Mexican Diary*, *Shar*, and *Trench Town Rock*. "Dream Chad" is preceded by an introductory note in which Brathwaite relates the writing of the story on a rented computer at Harvard University, where he was based in the summer of 1988. The crucial point of Brathwaite's explanatory introduction is that the computer keeps destroying the text, obliterating it from its memory every time the author comes to the end of its composition. This instance of cyber-obliteration becomes a premonition of the destruction of his house by Hurricane Gilbert later that same summer. With hindsight the poet sees himself as writing about "event(s) that had in fact not yet taken place" (*DS* 48):

> But as I was finishing this story – before, in fact, I cd print it o-ut – the machine shall we say *malfunctioned* and I lost nearly a-ll its oratory & I had to reconstruct it all again from scratch & each time I came to the end & was about to run it off, the sa-
>
> me strange **deconstruction** occurred...
>
> ...but in my persistent HEAT + HEART went out &
>
> ## rented another computer
>
> & ran the story in & off before the spirit cd re/ programme it-self into the new cinnamon instrument...
>
> But a few days after the printout, I watched Hurricane Gilbert rise up out of the sea...
> ...towards Jamaica. And as soon as I saw it I kn-ew that this was Io & that that was why Sycorax or the Spirit of the Machination had perhaps tried to stop me writing 'it'. (*DS* 48–49)

Here writing is very literally associated with creating and shaping the world, for better or worse. In "The African Presence in Caribbean Literature," Brathwaite argues that this perception of the word is common throughout Africa and the diaspora: language has "the power to affect life" (241). The loss of the story becomes synonymous with Brathwaite's own "memory loss" when his archive is destroyed. However, the destructive "Spirit of the Machination" is also Sycorax, the muse in the machine, who is largely responsible for Brathwaite's numerous rewritings of poems published before the obliteration of his archive, obliteration giving a new creative impulse, as the end of *Shar* already indicated. In this context, the "Eagle" computer, which belonged to Mexican, contains not only *his* memory in the form of his poems but also *her* memory in that she typed all his work into the machine. Despite the impression one gets in *Shar* and later in *ConVER-*

*Sations*, Brathwaite's archive, "the bulk of my life's work though very much in disarray & hurt & hurl & ruin, had not (?yet) been (totally) destroyed" and "that part of the houm that had housed the Eagle & the archives etc had somehow miraculously survived the storm" (*DS* 49). Brathwaite's inconclusive statements about the extent of the destruction can perhaps best be understood when, as pointed out previously, all three traumatic events are read together, with Mexican's death equaling the death of his poetic inspiration, and with his written life becoming identical with his whole self, so that his whole self dies or is destroyed along with Mexican. This sense of total obliteration is illuminated in "Dream Chad."

The story begins with Brathwaite's dreaming self walking across Harvard campus with a friend, Randy Birkenhead, who is described as a descendent of the Pilgrim Fathers ("he had come over w/ his hungry Pilgrim Father" (*DS* 52)). In the course of the dream, Birkenhead becomes an "Ole . Summer Bajan Man" (*DS* 51) wearing the Black Angel, "this musty ole black jack/et" (*DS* 51–52) from the previous story, connecting the seemingly separate dreamstories through recurring images. Noticeably, the Black Angel has converted from an other to a familiar with whom Brathwaite's dreaming self is engaged in dialogue (also of a cross-cultural nature, considering the European origin of Randy Birkenhead).

The walk across campus becomes a journey towards Dream Chad, whom the author's dream self sees "stand/in beyo nd the stalks of the railings on the other side of the ocean" (*DS* 59). The "other side of the ocean" is both Jamaica, where Chad is looking after Brathwaite's house in Irish Town, and the afterworld, where Mexican now is. Within Brathwaite's traumatized psyche, the afterworld is another version of the "most ancient place," of his sorrow (Mexican) as well as of his healing (Chad). In *Masks* (1968), Lake Chad is depicted as the center and soul of Africa, it being the "most ancient place" of humanity. Therefore, Chad becomes "the soul / of the world" (*Arrivants* 105).[9] By referring to his new partner as Chad, Brathwaite regards her as his guide on his journey into his own soul, which in the dreamstory begins on a lawn at Harvard, and which, like *nam*, connects him to the soul of Africa (just as Mexican has connected him to the idea of the "creole cosmos"). Both women, in fact, stand at the beginning and at the end of the journey. Therefore, in the course of the dreamstory, they merge into one persona, and the journey becomes the act of writing the story itself. However, the "Path of Words" (Benítez-Rojo 184) that Brathwaite creates between Africa and the Caribbean, between Chad and Mexican, turns in upon itself and becomes a labyrinth, a Dantean forest, where the poet temporarily loses direction.[10] The labyrinth, which is to occur again in subsequent stories, represents the loss of direction that Brathwaite experiences after Mexican's death. When he finally reunites with her, she has become Chad:

> **& it tek im so long to write
> this all down that e loss like
> im wife & him way & e hard
> was to go back & check
> where she was on that
> crescent & curvin sidewalk or
> wharf of arrival beyond the
> railings off Harvard Yard
> an by th time e fine where she was in the dream she wasnt
> lookin at him anymore but at like a fly on fire alight/ in a
> darken room**
>
> (*DS* 61)

The guide or muse directs the poet's gaze away from her as source of inspiration towards a force that embodies "the end of all we knew. we had known. of certainly all I had owned. of all I had earned" (*DS* 63). The fire that destroys his house (the mirror inverts, and water becomes fire) destroys the work of the poet and his muse, the "experiment of communion" within the utopian space of marriage. The fire also destroys the utopian space of the house itself, the elemental cell of the "creole cosmos," from which should have developed the global "experiment of communion." Moreover, the house contains the work of his life and thus becomes synonymous with his head in the dream: "how there was like this great leap of flame like the pain in my head coming out of the far side of the roof of my skull like the future of flame" (*DS* 62).

This failure to sustain his vision is illuminated in the association of the destroyed house at Irish Town with the burning houses in Jean Rhys's *Wide Sargasso Sea* (1966):

**this great leap of flame like the pain . . . .
in my head coming out of the side of my skull.**

> ... where I had from time to time felt it fl
> ack/ing & flar/ing so that here I am now w/ thes
> (e) ants in my irises. spindels of orch-
> ids dancehalling the walls of my horror – another
> inadequate word for the flame in my head like in the
> Jean Rhys **Sargasso Sea** story – the thick red
>
> crackling strands of her hair leaping up from
> the floor of the navel & crying out
> *Tina Tina Tina Tina*
> as if she was trying to jump from the
> Harvard Yaad
> w/ its woden bucket stood at that step-up well
> to reach Bougainvillea/Coulibri
>
> (*DS* 70–71)

Brathwaite refers here to the very end of *Wide Sargasso Sea*, after Antoinette in her dream has set fire to Thornfield Hall and, looking down from the roof, sees Coulibri, her childhood home:

> The wind caught my hair and it streamed out like wings. It might bear me up, I thought, if I jumped to those hard stones. But when I looked over the edge I saw the pool at Coulibri. Tia was there. She beckoned to me and when I hesitated, she laughed. I heard her say, You frightened? And I heard the man's voice, Bertha! Bertha! All this I saw and heard in a fraction of a second. And the sky so red. Someone screamed and I thought, *Why did I scream?* I called 'Tia!' and jumped and woke. (152)

At the beginning of Rhys's novel, Coulibri itself, which in "Dream Chad" becomes synonymous with Brathwaite's house in Irish Town, burns down and afterwards exists only in Antoinette's memory. Coulibri becomes at once mythic and utopian. For Antoinette, her childhood home is a mythic place, synonymous with the garden of Eden, where the tree of life and "all the flowers in the world" (102) grow and which, because it is situated in the past, becomes inaccessible. That the Edenic image of Coulibri should return at the end of the novel, however, suggests that it is not imprisoned in the past. The Coulibri at the end of Rhys's novel becomes a utopian space, situated in the future, which, at least in Antoinette's dream, begins after Thornfield Hall, her "darkness of the lived moment," is burnt down. In its utopian version, Coulibri represents an aspect of the "creole cosmos" as it envisions the Caribbean as *Heimat* and, above all, as a place without racial divides. The notion of apocalypse that accompanies Antoinette's dream of fire embodies Bloch's idea of messianic faith discussed in chapter four, in that total destruction of the present moment or the world as it now exists opens the door to the kingdom, which is the utopian dimension of Eden.

Brathwaite's reference to Coulibri in "Dream Chad," however, does not point to any utopian qualities, as if in its passage through the mirror it had been turned upside down, revealing only the dystopian reality of Sisyphus. Brathwaite's Coulibri burns down *at the end* of the story, Rhys's *at the beginning* of *Wide Sargasso Sea*. Brathwaite's Coulibri has thus no opportunity to unlock its utopian qualities. The story collapses into the "darkness of the lived moment." Brathwaite's darkening vision is depicted as a rupture in the dialogue between poet and muse. The muse complains that his vision, the utopian space of "her house," is "made of cardboar(d)" (*DS* 65). The cardboard house is, of course, also a reference to the end of *Wide Sargasso Sea* when Antoinette has become Bertha, who is trapped between the cardboard covers of Charlotte Brontë's novel. The burning down of Thornfield Hall is in this sense a burning of the English book, Bertha's liberation from the prison of Brontë's text. Dream Chad's complaint that her house is also a cardboard world suggests that the poet does not use his words to shape a different reality, which is what Rhys does in her rewriting of *Jane Eyre*. Chad intimates that the poet fails to fulfill his own dream. In this dark time of creative death the muse reminds him of his responsibility towards his vision.

## 5.4. "Dream Crabs"

In sharp contrast to the agony of destruction and separation in "Dream Chad," "Dream Crabs," the third dreamstory, begins with a sense of "arrived-at Being":

## A Creole Experiment

> And so at last we went down into this deep bay like it was River Bay only the slides of the cliffs were higher and it was dark like at River Bay & there was this eternal sound of the snake of the sea for the three of us – & you I kno-w) were happy to be there as if you had at last found a home somewhere where y-ou were so glad to come to
> (*DS* 74)

Bearing in mind that Brathwaite regards *DreamStories* as a journey into death, the island is reminiscent of the Elysian Fields, the resting place of the blessed dead in classical mythology. The dream island also echoes the "island below the waters," the abode of the *loa*. Here Brathwaite follows his wife into death via his dreams to guide her to a place where she can spend the afterlife in happiness.

In the wider context of Brathwaite's life, the island is Barbados (River Bay being in Barbados), but also St Lucia, where Brathwaite and Mexican lived in 1962 after their return from Ghana, "among the gushin(g) Pitons of that vulcan island drowsed in trees" (*DS* 75), and where Brathwaite worked in the extramural department of the University of the West Indies. On the whole, the island reflects the poet's vision of the Caribbean as *Heimat*, as a place of "arrived-at Being" after the journey into the African past (which is the subject of *Masks*). As his first home in the Caribbean after his stay in Ghana, St Lucia is therefore also his "first tropical oceanic landfall since Gorée" (*DS* 75), Gorée being an island off the coast of Senegal, famous for its slave castle. In creating a link between the Middle Passage and his own crossing of the Atlantic in both directions (a "tidalectic" Middle Passage), Brathwaite fuses personal and communal memory, implying that the Caribbean can become a place of "arrived-at Being" not just for himself but for the Caribbean population as a whole.

As a potentially utopian community, the Caribbean becomes linked to another utopia, Atlantis:

> . . . the concorde flies in w/
> that same simple brightened

> edge of early morning . com
> ing in like pale heron or a fly
> ing snake out of Atlantis . its
> lean *mkonde* neck already >
> leaning down towards the ai
> rport . the tide low & the fish
> erman up to his knees . in
> both continents of firefly wa-
> ter . looking up sometimes >
> shading his invisible eyes fr-
> om the blue or gold or grey
> breaking of the sound barri-
> er . depending on the stare .
> of sky over the flickering ree
> (f) (*DS* 75–76)

In "History, the Caribbean Writer and *X/Self*" (1990), Brathwaite describes Atlantis, situated halfway between the Caribbean and Africa, as belonging to the Caribbean archipelago but having become submerged in the ocean as well as in the collective memory of the region:

> We in the Caribbean had this strange memory, it seems, of an Atlantis which had disappeared, and the waves that washed upon the shores whispered words like "Atlantis" which we heard but couldn't understand. And then there was the memory of that tremendous catastrophe that had created the island: how the mountain range that had run at right angles to the great Andean-Rockies chain along the Western continent, that ran through Mexico and through Yucatan into the Atlantic and perhaps ended in Atlantis, had cataclysmically disappeared. The islands that we inhabit are in fact the sunken tops of a mountain chain and the people who inhabit them have an echo of that catastrophe in their memory. It is part of our psyche. (26)

In imagining the Caribbean as having undergone a similar trauma as the landscape of Africa during the formation of the Great Rift Valley, Brathwaite presents the New World as a mirror image of the Old, with Atlantis as the virtual point, the mirror surface, where both converge.

## A Creole Experiment

Atlantis is both a mythic place, situated in the inaccessible space of the past, here symbolized by its submergence in the Atlantic Ocean, and a place that represents the utopian possibility of the Atlantic world.[11] In this sense, the image of Atlantis incorporates the longing for *Heimat* on both sides of the Atlantic.

The serpents mentioned in the dreamstory originate in Atlantis. They echo the union of the *loa* Damballah and Ayida: "[Damballah] is shown as a snake, arched in the path that the sun travels across the sky; sometimes half the arch is composed of his female counterpart, Ayida, the rainbow.... Damballah and Ayida, who together represent the sexual totality, encompass the cosmos as a serpent coiled about the world" (Deren 115–16). The union of the serpents is the divine answer to human questing and represents an instance of "arrived-at Being" or communion. In *Gods of the Middle Passage*, Brathwaite describes their union as a form of creolization in which the sky serpent Damballah becomes interchangeable with the rainbow Ayida:

> Damballa Wèdo . . . is generally recognized as the husband of Ayida Wèdo (=Dahomey), though occasionally — and this <u>occasion</u> is part of the New World process of <u>re/foundation</u> <u>trans/formation</u> — the two — divine androgyny — are merged into Damballa-Ayida. In both Haiti and Wèdo, Damballa (Da/mballa) is 'identified with the rainbow and is symbolized as a snake'. (6)[12]

As rainbow, Damballah becomes a symbol of the African migration across the "parent continent" to the New World (*Gods of the Middle Passage* 6). The fisherman in the above passage from "Dream Crabs," who stands with one foot in each continent, is a mirror image of the Concorde that is Damballah, the flying snake or sky serpent. Damballah comes directly "out of Atlantis," which makes the mythic island overlap with Guinée, the abode of the *loa*. The Concorde's "*mkonde* neck" echoes the Mkonde Plateau, which is part of the East African Rift System. The Concorde travels from this "most ancient place" of the African people, to their new home in the Americas, thus spanning the history of African migration that Brathwaite describes in *Masks* as beginning long before the Middle Passage in Egypt, situated in the vicinity of the Great Rift Valley. In the image of Damballah, Brathwaite links Europe, Africa, and the Caribbean in the virtual space of Atlantis. He becomes the *Grand Chemin* of cultural traffic from the Old World to the New and from the past into the future. In this sense, he functions as an equivalent to *nam*. Damballah is thus a *loa* who embodies utopian possibility. Moreover, in employing Damballah as a geographical bridge between Africa and the Caribbean, Brathwaite introduces the *Grand Chemin* as a horizontal axis, which connects the notion of a horizontal and "tidalectic" connection with that of the world axis or tree.

The union of Damballah and Ayida mirrors the union of Mexican and Brathwaite on the dream island and is depicted in the communion of eating a meal of crabs "to celebrate that you at last seemed happy and at home" (*DS* 77). However, the vision of a utopian place established in the story is interspersed with a sense of foreboding signaling the end of happiness and communion:

> . . . w-
> (e) live for one full happy pa-
> ssion-fruit & pomme cythère
> year until our ti-noir puppy
> brake it leg & die of the most
> brilliant colours I have ever .
> seen . . . (*DS* 75)

The death of the puppy destroys the Edenic peace of the dream, as does the eating of the crabs, "our assassin fin gers enjoying them" (*DS* 77). In *ConVERSations*, Brathwaite refers to the crab image in *DreamStories* as a "tumou(r)" (*C* 159). The crabs, therefore, also encode Mexican's death from cancer ("cancer" being Latin for "crab"), which would explain why the eating of the crabs is ultimately connected to the death or sacrifice of their union (whereas before the crabs were the sacrifice that led to the lovers' communion). The pun of "crabs" and "carabs" (*DS* 74) in the story associates the crab with the Egyptian scarab, symbol of death but also of rebirth that concludes *Ancestors*.

In voodoo, the cosmic totality is also, and chiefly, represented by the divine twins, the Marassa, who are always accompanied by a third principle, which represents the union of the two: "The Twins are not to be separated into competitive, conflicting dualism. In Voudoun one *and* one make three . . . ; for the *and* of the equation is the third . . . part . . . , the relationship which makes all the parts meaningful" (Deren 41). The couple in "Dream Crabs" thus also echo the Marassa. Mexican's death from cancer obliterates the third principle, representing the severance of the twins' union.

In the context of the disruption of peace on the Edenic island, the sea snake and the sky serpent echo the biblical serpent associated with the fall, and the crabs can be read as the forbidden fruit. Thus, in the light of Christianity, the snake symbol becomes ambivalent, and the moment of "arrived-at Being," seemingly achieved in "Dream Crabs," is reverted in "4th Traveller," where the journey into the labyrinth of dream, into the afterworld of trauma, begins anew.

## 5.5. "4th Traveller"

In "4th Traveller," Brathwaite again reworks the classical theme of the underworld journey. Set "four weeks after Mexican died" (*DS* 80), the story focuses on Brathwaite's dreaming self, his father, a woman, and an unnamed fourth traveler "delivering canes in a cart into the depths of the black country" (*DS* 80). The journey's destination is Zion, "the village our burden sought" (*DS* 80), "where we wd sell the day's load & so be able to begin again like fresh moorings begin again light light light w/ out burden" (*DS* 81–82). This passage echoes Brathwaite's lament in *The Zea Mexican Diary* that Mexican had died prematurely without completing the full cycle of her life. Moreover, his own vision of a "creole cosmos" comes to an abrupt, if temporary, standstill with Mexican's death. In the *Diary*, Brathwaite describes the creative process as molding flesh into light (see *ZMD* 130), the light metaphor designating the utopian qualities of the creative imagination that is able to transcend the "darkness of the lived moment." His wife's death traps his poetic vision in this darkness, which in "4th Traveller" becomes "the depths of the black country." Reaching the village of Zion is thus essential and becomes symbolic of the re-emergence of this vision into new light and purpose. In this context, the canes that are to be delivered signify the labor involved in creative work, which Brathwaite refers to as "the 40 days in the wilderness" in *The Zea Mexican Diary* (*ZMD* 151).

However, the travelers in the story do not reach the "light w/ out burden"; nor do they find their way to Zion. Instead, they arrive in the "village of the dead" (*DS* 80) or "that village of it seemed the damned" (*DS* 82). The travelers' seemingly inevitable arrival at this place is intimated already at the end of "Dream Crabs," where the crab flesh is referred to as "that white 'circle of concentration' . . . as I was to see later in that village or rather camp of the damned in the Cockpits of Jamaica" (*DS* 77). The crabs themselves reappear in "4th Traveller" in the form of the village inhabitants, who confront the travelers "like crabs playing dismal cards . squat . enclose (d) within their crustacean boundaries of petties pincers claw (s) of silence, *yes*. And we wd need help ... to get up there" (*DS* 81). This help, however, is not given by the crab-people the travelers encounter. Whereas in "Dream Crabs" the crabs appear deprived of their protective shells, thus becoming, at least initially, the medium of communion, the emphasis here is on their "crustacean boundaries," which at once protect and isolate, making communication or communion impossible.

In connection with the crabs, the story also plays on the concept of *maronage*. Cockpit Country is Jamaican maroon country, and in the course of the story the travelers become maroons themselves. Therefore, the burden of canes also represents the burden of the region's plantation past. The theme of *maronage*, which usually has a positive connotation in Brathwaite's work, here becomes ambivalent in that *maronage* involves isolation. The maroon state is separate from colonial society but also, in a sense, part of it as it defines itself against the plantation. Through this ideological dependence, the maroon state is also, in a mild sense, a "scavenge John Crow culture" (*Shar*), and this act of scavenging takes on extreme proportions in the last of the dreamstories, "Salvages." Thus Brathwaite depicts the downside of the otherwise utopian concept of *maronage*, viewing it through the prism of his own isolation and loss. In "Caliban's Guarden," Brathwaite argues that this double meaning of *maronage* is part of what constitutes Caribbean experience. By choosing "to opt out of the plantation," the maroons "were in danger of becoming marooned in addition to being maroons — a paradox and a contradiction but still a very real part of our collective psyche" (3). Due to the prevalence of this second meaning of *maronage* as introversion, the travelers fail to reach Zion, the utopian side/site of maroon existence (the "Zionism" of a "NewAfrican heaven & haven"). Instead they become "marooned out here in the tired shoes of discouragement & the dust of fatigue" (*DS* 82).

However, towards the end of the story, Brathwaite states that "there was always hope in this dream" (*DS* 88), and this hope is contained in the prospect of a connection with *nam*. This hope for a connection with *nam* is expressed in the travelers' courage to challenge the villagers' indifference, and their at times even outright hostility, with regard to their task of delivering the burden of canes. The travelers' desire to gain access to their *nam* is also expressed in their refusal to stay in the village of the dead, pleading for guidance. They decide to find their own way to Zion, which in the logic of the dream makes them runaway slaves, maroons. In the fourth part of the story, Brathwaite explains the villagers' hostility with his rejection as poet and person by a society that does not acknowledge his real effort to create a "creole cosmos" in the form of the Irish Town maroon project. The poet's move towards psychological *maronage* is a protection against his pain of isolation (echoing the pain caused by his wife's death). At the same time, it is an effort to recapture his original vision.

The subsequent journey or flight is a journey towards *nam*, where the travelers seek protection and spiritual sustenance. However, in order to retrieve it, the travelers, and Brathwaite through them, have to descend into the "darkness of the lived moment," which is realized within the story in the retrieval of a tea pot from the mud where it has been lost:

> ... we put a brave face of warrior against them like when a worn enamel tea-pot has fallen into the dirt into soft mud & its treasured though ignored & thoughtless face is obscured for a moment but you sink back down behind it in the dark world w / its so little water & bring
>
> it back up bring it back out & begin cleaning its face slowly slowly softly w/the so little water. the palm of yr hand caressing its perhaps very ordinary features....
> ... finding & following the familiar & domestic grooved features of the fallen but retrievable item & object. putting a brave face back upon it. (*DS* 82)

The movement sketched in the retrieval of the tea pot is in part repeated in the journey that follows, which is at first led by the father bearing a torchlight. Soon, however, he lags behind "since he was sick & you cd see & feel how grey & broken down his brown skin had become & how he breathin hard & tryin not to cough w/ that dry gravel soughing of the middle passage" (*DS* 84). Due to the cultural uprooting of the Middle Passage and the suppression of the memory of all things African, the father cannot function as ancestor and guide. The father's sickness is a metaphor for his inability to reconnect his son to the mother culture of Africa and thus he cannot give his son's search a sense of direction.

The journey towards *nam* is, of course, also a journey back into the history of the Caribbean and into the history of maroon resistance. During colonial rule, Jamaica was only settled on the coast, making the labyrinth, an echo of the dream space itself, is described as a safe place, as "a good careful spot to enjoy safe ty in" (*DS* 88–89). It is a psychic or mental space where Brathwaite temporarily seeks refuge but from where he later emerges to create his second maroon project in CowPastor. On one level, Brathwaite's desire for retreat is a reaction against the pain caused by Mexican's death and the subsequent wish to "escape into the minefield of unmemory" (*DS* 90).

The more social dimension of this retreat becomes evident in the fourth section of "4th Traveller." Here the crab-creatures of the village of the damned appear as "visitors. led by a tall bespe ctacled deconstructionist critic. . . . their eyes . . . like crabs or carabs > on poles advancing behind their self-contained & scurrying le ader" (*DS* 91). Being in a sense an heir of New Criticism, Deconstruction reads nothing but the text. Brathwaite's creative vision, on the other hand, is an all-inclusive project that makes no distinction between "literary" and word. The presence of the "deconstructionist critic" suggests that Brathwaite's project, and his perception that literature can change the world, is being challenged. The poet's reaction is to recoil from the critic's momentary triumph, from "his smirk. the smock of his body coming to see me. his head held high" (*DS* 91). Together with his female companion, he returns to the dream landscape:

> . . . two of us went back out & up back up that slippering hillside where we found our father, wounded *yes*, & slow . . . & we carried him the next day on to the next village further along the ridge of despair . . . they . were saying that the 4th Traveller had not survived . . . perishing alone out there on the > night of the hillside . . . in this dark village of the dead where I now sit as foreman . digging yr gra ves in the game of yr luck or yr **warri**. dealing my cards in th (e) i/sol ence < (*DS* 92)

In the introduction to *DreamStories*, Gordon Rohlehr suggests that the fourth traveler is Brathwaite's Edward persona, "the author's earlier self/identity/persona, who perishes during the night journey of the straitened subject in order that a tougher, more severe *Kamau* persona might emerge" (xiv). The Kamau persona, as has been pointed out in the chapter on *The Zea Mexican Diary*, is the poet in resistance, the maroon existence of his creativity. In this sense, the dream is a space where *maronage* can be reimagined. The retreat into the maroon shell of the dream is also a retreat into the womb of *nam*, where the self in resistance is conceived and born. As Brathwaite emphasizes hull" (*DS* 87). This movement of landslide echoes the mudslide of *Shar* as well as the mother's vision in "Fever" (*Mother Poem*):

and there was a landslide of memories

i grew softer and softer
until i could no longer remain still in that place
root upon wheels, i began my soft seam of descent
fold upon fold of cloth, strip upon strip of rumble

i moved downwards into that valley:
outhouse, train line, battlement of bridge i rolled away

. . . . . . . . . . . . . . . . . . . . . . . . .

so i moved down into the old watercourses

echo pebble trickle of worn stone
shaken voice of coral curling its own pattern to the sea

(*MP* 16–17)

The "landslide of memories" again suggests the movement into the "most ancient place" of pain, which is also the location of *nam*, as are the "old watercourses" in *Mother Poem*. In moments of crisis, the mother "discovers her underground resources (her *nam*)" (*MP* Preface), as does Brathwaite himself in the dreamstory. The travelers in "4th Traveller" come upon a similar form of underground resource at the bottom of the hill, the seeming end of their descent: ". . . there were steps of stone now ruins. as if we had. as chilldren found some old reservoir where the island stored its valour > though these stone steps seemed larger, somehow, & older & like more ruined . . ." (*DS* 87). The stone steps echo the "carved footsteps" of the initial stanzas of *Mother Poem*, which Brathwaite identifies as the Amerindian presence, the "most ancient place" in the Caribbean landscape and psyche.[15]

The reservoir is, however, not the end of the journey. The steps lead the travelers further, into the subterranean ruins of a plantation Great House, which subsequently shapeshifts into a labyrinthine dungeon and a prehistoric cave. The second traveler to arrive at the labyrinth together with the poet's dreaming self is the unnamed woman, possibly either Dream Chad or a memory of Mexican. The subterranean the serpent becomes associated with the messiah because it imparts knowledge. The messiah, in turn, ultimately brings about the end of the rule of God the father and paves the way for the kingdom, where the divine manifests in the human.[14] The act of possession in voodoo, when the *loa* enters the human servitor, is also a form of the divine finding expression in and through the human. The serpent in the canefield is an aspect of Damballah, as Brathwaite himself states in *ConVERSations with Nathaniel Mackey*, "a totem reptile" (*C* 266), and the note of hope that, as he claims, pervades the story originates from the presence of Damballah. In *ConVERSations*, Brathwaite claims that he himself becomes Damballah (*C* 266), but the *loa* is present both in the snake mutation of the travelers and as an entity outside, somewhere in the canefield that has become a primeval swamp. The presence of the serpent functions as a substitute for the lost torchlight:

> ... still we hope
>
> (d) that like dolphones, there wd be some compass, some blind gravitational astrolabe of sound finding our way, stripped stripped, flowing w / *macca* following a leader along the dark of our bellies. writhing away into night, circling over & over into the right / hand side of the god, like when we picked up . the teapot & polished it ... (*DS* 85)

The compass-like entity of Damballah is here merely referred to as "the god." The travelers imagine him, dream him into existence, but have as yet no clear picture of him, not even a name. He is obscured within the "darkness of the lived moment" and finds expression merely in the vague hope of their survival "before they begin burning down the canes when they cdnt find < us" (*DS* 85).

Damballah embodies the process of creolization. Although he already exists as an African deity, he is reborn as something new in the New World, adjusting to the changing needs of the African diaspora. In the story, the conception of Damballah as a utopian image is juxtaposed with a movement back in historical time. This "journey into the past and hinterland" is, as Brathwaite states in "Timehri," "a movement of possession into present and future" (42). The journey backwards in time and downwards towards *nam* is described in the dreamstory as "sailing back ... to the genesis of the world" in a downward movement "towards what seemed to be the bottom of the hill or inaccessible interior an ideal hideout for runaway slaves. In this sense, the travelers' movement away from the village becomes a movement towards personal and cultural independence. As the travelers become runaway slaves themselves, so the villagers, who pursue them, lose their maroon qualities and become plantation owners trying to recapture their human property: "... we cd feel < our hair like moving stupid helpless headless above the leaf & heat our bodies mate, waiting the crack or cutlass or howe ver they had plan to cut us up or down near that caul canefield of the village when we had heard ourselves say *quick* & we < were quickly down & entered in that pain in/ to this canefield ..." (*DS* 84). The travelers enter the "sheer of future darkness" (*DS* 84), which the canefield represents. They have to adapt to new conditions of life, just as the maroons before them had to adapt to living in the alien environment of the New World. The darkness of the canefield, into which they enter without guidance ("our torchlight had been lost or gone < out" (*DS* 84)), becomes the "darkness of the lived moment." In this sense, the travelers are walking in the dark, with the utopian moment of their liberation, here symbolized by the guiding torchlight, remaining out of sight. In other words, the travelers have to be their own light; they have to create themselves as something totally new, have to become their own "horizon of utopia" (*PH* 1: 202), in a confrontation of the African spirit with the American place.

This creation of a completely new way of being is rendered here in the mutation of the travelers into serpents:

> ... we <
> were quickly down & entered in that pain in / to this canefield
> w / its dark murmur-water whisper secrets & abysses that wer
> (e) close & birdless & took away the breath our bodies made,
> crawling, flung flat down & quickly on our bellies into a new
> form of species, as it were, into the ancient coil & lash of the >
>
> serpent born before Adam, as old as the tree & the writhe of
> wind in the eden & vegetable green veridian eye / vening of cl
> ingers & maroons. like all those who tried escape into swamp
> (s). out of the huts of their hearts. into the dreams of their chi-
> lldren, steel & unmanacled ... (*DS* 84–85)

The biblical serpent alluded to here opposes the rule of God. As we have seen, in Brathwaite's work the rule of the Christian God is often synonymous with colonial rule.[13] In Gnostic belief, on the other hand, in *ConVERSations*, *DreamStories* is about death as well as rebirth. In this sense, the labyrinth of dreams, into which the poet retreats, echoes the womb/tomb myths of many different cultures. The movement from the death of the Edward persona towards the conception of the Kamau persona, indicated in the fetal position the dream self assumes ("tuckin my head down into my belly closing my eyes" (*DS* 91)), acquires the characteristics of an initiation ritual.

In this context, the circumstances that led to Brathwaite's renaming are interesting to consider. He received the name Kamau from Ngũgĩ's grandmother on a visit to Gikuyuland in Kenya. Gikuyuland is part of the East African Rift System. Thus the Kamau persona of the story can be said to emerge from the "most ancient place" both of the poet's psyche and the collective psyche of the African diaspora. The remaining texts of *DreamStories* focus on the poet's return from the womb/tomb of dream.

## 5.6. "Dream Haiti"

"Dream Haiti" thematizes the drowning of Haitian refugees as they try to reach the United States in search of a life without poverty. Their overcrowded boat, in which they attempt to enter North America illegally, capsizes. Brathwaite refers to an event of the late 1980s that was well documented on television, a fact the poet frequently draws attention to. The coast guards make no effort to pull the drowning out of the water, and neither do the African-American poets, Brathwaite's dreaming self among them, who are also on "the US Coast Guard cutter" (*DS* 95) of the dream. The artists are described as isolated from the concerns of the poor of the region. Consequently, they become "strangers to / each other" (*DS* 101). They throw no lifelines to the drowning, "life-line" also being the title of an anthology within the story (*DS* 97). In other words, the poets refuse to speak on behalf of those who have no voice, which in Brathwaite's view makes the words they do write and speak ineffectual and empty.

The exodus of the Caribbean poor to the rich United States is presented as a Middle Passage in the sense of the poor selling themselves to the rich and thus giving themselves willfully — or blindly — into a new form of enslavement. The drowning, moreover, echo the numerous slaves thrown overboard during the original Atlantic crossing. The poets watching from the ship, therefore, become conspirators in the modern-day slave trade and Middle Passage. Brathwaite, however, does point to a way out of this isolation in that his own perspective on the ship alternates with that of a drowning refugee, thus establishing a dialogue within the writing self. The poet himself becomes one of the drowning. There is then, after all, a reaching out, a throwing of lifelines in the form of compassion as a "suffering with" the dispossessed.

Parts of "Dream Haiti" also appear in *ConVERSations* and in Brathwaite's 1995 Sir Philip Sherlock Celebration Lecture, "New Gods of the Middle Passage."[16] In "New Gods" Brathwaite quotes extensively from his early poetry, such as "Negus" and "Caliban," the latter in response to "an antiseptic critic in london" who accuses the poet of celebrating "the seemingly endless / purgatorial experience / of black people" (23). The extract of "Dream Haiti" that follows "Caliban" in the lecture continues the theme of the earlier poem and serves as an example of why it is necessary to focus on said purgatorial experience. Brathwaite creates a link between the television image of a drowned Haitian boy, "in my hand / like a dolphin but dead," and the events of Rwanda of the mid-1990s, to which Brathwaite has dedicated a whole cycle of poems ("New Gods" 32). Brathwaite says that Rwanda is, in fact, "the middlepassage of another xperience" (52), which echoes his statement in McSweeney's *Raintaxi* interview that the Middle Passage is an "ongoing catastrophe." As in the *DreamStories* version, the poet in "New Gods" appears as one of the drowning. The use of television imagery has the effect that the readers become the spectators, the ones who just look on but do nothing. Brathwaite might also be intimating that television culture has made people in the west insensitive to the human catastrophe happening under their very noses but too far away to affect them directly.

"Dream Haiti" shows the poet confronted with a choice: he can either stay on the boat looking on or he can become one of the drowning. This choice has not only moral consequences but also artistic ones. It represents two different worlds of writing, one situated within the west and one outside of it. By leaping off the boat (something we do not actually witness but can infer), Brathwaite opts out of the western literary market, and his "video style," which does not "sell," embodies this choice. In this sense, as I have stated in the introduction to this study, his works increasingly challenge western paradigms and the very idea of the book, creating "a testament of dissidence with respect to the West" (Torres-Saillant, *Caribbean Poetics* 143). Brathwaite also appeals to the transformative power of language and enacts his conviction that life and art are in fact inseparable. By picturing the poet both on the boat and in the water, the perspective of the story bridges or blurs the divide between life and art. The context in which "Dream Haiti" is situated in *ConVERSations* is Brathwaite's discussion of the dreamstory as a new form of poetry. He argues that conventional poetry does not offer the range of expression he desires. He, therefore, proposes a fusion of poetry and forms of prose, such as "clippings, quotations, contextual information, footnotes, video" (*C* 231), which give the dreamstory a montage quality. This echoes the poet's transition from onlooker to participant. As he bridges the gap between art and life, he also bridges the divide between genres.

## 5.7. "Grease"

"Grease" explores the interrelationship of environmental pollution and human catastrophe addressed in *Trench Town Rock* and "Pixie" but also in his earlier works, such as "Francina" in *Islands*, and again later in *Words Need Love Too*. "Grease" illustrates both catastrophes in the loveless relationship between a Kingston plumber and his wife. Aggression towards the environment due to the lack of a sense of rootedness and *Heimat* mirrors the corruption and aggressive behavior of people towards each other. Again, alienation from the land and from each other is regarded as a result of neocolonial exploitation, represented in the following passage by the presumably foreign ships and factories:

> but there was so much punk
> & pollution now in his heart. those
> darkening frills of water turning the
> shoreline to mangroves with the slow
> black lips of what all those
>
> ships & fats & fact-
> ories had voided onto the shore of
> what shd have been white sand

(*DS* 121)

The rootlessness and the subsequent violence of the plumber towards his wife are explained by the fact that the couple moved "away from her mother into / this ungovernmental / yard" (*DS* 124).

This, of course, echoes the government yards of Trench Town, which many perceived were neglected by the very government that had them built, hence Brathwaite's use of "ungovernmental." Although she is not explicitly named, the mother is most likely to be Sycorax, guardian of *nam*, and moving away from the mother is a moving into the Dungle of human existence, away from the possibility of living in human dignity and independence. However, the woman finds liberation in an adulterous affair with a locksmith, who is a Legba figure. As Legba is the guardian of the door between the worlds, the locksmith embodies the promise of unlocking the door to a new "experiment of communion."

The story is pervaded by a general sense of loss, abandonment and despair. The environmental devastation of "Grease" mirrors not only the human tragedy but also the loss of dignity of a Caribbean increasingly dependent on tourism and foreign investment, which has proved to be detrimental to the local ecology. These are ongoing concerns in Brathwaite's work and will emerge again in *Words Need Love Too* and other works written during the CowPastor period.

### 5.8. "Salvages"

In "Salvages," the last of the dreamstories, Brathwaite voices his rejection of "i/sol ence," of hiding within the "crustacean boundaries" mentioned in "4th Traveller," by inventing a double or shadow, Gareth:

> ... And I never know
> that he/who sometimes seemed to be me,
> sometimes even me, was in anyway ill or feeling
> ill or having problems of any kind
>
> or anything like that. that in other words he was
> like me. with nothing wrong that I was aware of
> (*DS* 138)

Despite the distance he tries to create between Gareth and his dream self, he feels they share a form of mental or spiritual illness as "Garath & me had / become mwe or something dream siam- / mese like that" (*DS* 143):

> ... though sometimes there was this sensation

> behind my eyes like a kind of hand/clap or mist
> & a slow
> soft steady fever in the bones of my hands ...
> (*DS* 138–39)

In the context of the previous stories, the mist behind the eyes of the protagonists is a social illness, a "deregulation" (*DS* 150) as it is referred to, recalling the social "misfits" of "The Black Angel." The clouding of the eyes can be read as short-sightedness regarding the possibility of social change, which links Gareth of "Salvages" to the camp workers in the first dreamstory and to the youths of Brathwaite's Kingston poetry, whose escape into drugged hallucination prevents them from real creative vision.

"Salvages" takes place entirely on or in the sea surrounding Barbados. Brathwaite's dreaming self and his twin Gareth are pursued by United States coast guards who appear as

> sea-
> doctors or pharmacists or something like that -
> some serious or at least serious-looking white
> guys like from the CIA one of whom seemed to be
> like my old friend Randy Burkenheit from
>
> # Dream Chad
> (*DS* 141)

These doctors run tests on the two brothers and put Gareth on drugs that are supposed to heal his eye sickness and fever. However, the doctors finally admit that there is no cure for this illness. The medication given to Gareth is in this sense related to the pollution of the region in "Grease," carried out by foreign ships that dump their waste in the Caribbean. In "Salvages," the pollution of the Caribbean is a pollution of human life through drug trafficking.

As a result of the ineffectiveness of the medication or drugs, Gareth decides to escape with his twin and a group of hostages, so that "he wd at least be controlling his own history & progression / as he had always wanted to do" (*DS* 151). In the cultural and political context of the Caribbean, Gareth's desire for independence mirrors that of the region's resistance movements such as *maronage* and Rastafarianism. In this sense, Gareth becomes a modern maroon figure. However, the sickness of his vision and the wish to escape into isolation also links Gareth to the scavenging individuals of *Trench Town Rock* and to the emotional desolation of "Pixie." The aspect of human scavenging reaches a drastic extreme in "Salvages" as Caliban turns cannibal.[17] In *ConVERSation*, Brathwaite explicitly refers to this reversal of Caliban back into cannibal in terms of a Sisyphean landslide:

> Yet by the last decade of this our first millennium – in the 500th year of Christophere Columbus' precipitation of us here – Caliban has become Cannibal if not 'again' then pretty close to it . so that our liberation & the sense of freedom in our hearts & homes
>
> earned by rebellions & maroons has been so gravely washed away to what some call 'our flawed but not yet failed society' –
> (*C* 276)

As a result of this cultural "amnesia," Gareth shows an acute lack of compassion and empathy for his fellow human beings. For him, people becomes soulless bodies (zombies) on which he feeds:

> & the guy was like shouting back at
>
> Gareth
>
> & his great clutching fingers that gripped. as we passed. into this poor man's loins. his sticky red fingers down into the nest of the man's heirs. whether thick or not didn't matter. & warp his hand round his wally as if it was a kind of towline or sail or rail rope & then curl his hand round it like tieing a
>
> **knot** - a bowline or granny or reef knot
>
> &
> . . . . . . . . . . . . . . . . . .

*DreamStories: The Far Side of the Mirror*

# pulled & the guy's cock was out from the roots

I watch the man who had been my twin & other
bring that cock to the gate of his mouth to his
thief & I watch him bite it like in half
like a small snake or shrimp or a fife of sound
& swallow the fat red bleeding part of it nearest
to him - **like the guy's protean shoots was
what he was after** - & toss-way the head...

(*DS* 157–58)

Continuing the thought on Caliban-turned-cannibal in *ConVERSations*, Brathwaite emphasizes the poet's responsibility to speak on behalf of those who have been mutilated in contemporary Caribbean Caliban-turned-cannibal society:

> But when that means my fragile only creativity –
> call god's gift what you will – rain-shadowed by hotels & supermarkets, bureaucracies
> & politicians, indifference & violence, persistent beggaring, the permanent structural
> dependence, it wd seem, on other people's aid – immune deficiency syndrome acquired
>
> thru the Middle Passage of rape & xploitation
> & choked now – overwhelmed – after some thirty years of Sisyphus – by my own brown
> bomber brothers' vvarts & bramble weeds into a ?nativised poetics of every little killing
> sound that startles in the night to this now hurt this Kurtz this common horror of the 90s
> w/its hope still clinging bitter aloes to these lips/ imploded faces that I have chronicle you
> this day upon these pages & stand up green & harrowed, let me tell you to be counted
>
> (*C* 276)

As in both versions of *X/Self*, in "Salvages," and in *DreamStories* in general, images are a site of struggle, open to often contradictory interpretations to reveal language as an instrument of power and to highlight the multi-accentuality of the image as sign. Thus the maroon is at once freedom fighter and cannibal, the serpent at once Damballah and Satan. Likewise, the "sea-doctors" on the coast guard ship change from corrupt scientists to the muses, who are in hot pursuit of Kamau the poet to rekindle the creative spark that vanished with Mexican's death. The muses catch up with the fugitives by a seawall, which in the dream functions as a boundary that separates the Caribbean from the world and can, at the same time, be read as the boundaries of the self. When the muses arrive, the Gareth persona becomes submerged in the sea:

> Garth slipped overboard & went down deep
> to the very roots of the sea-
> **Wall**
> as I knew he wd & that he must have been
> struggling to find down down down under
> there some insect or

> it that we knew wasn't there but still hoped
> there might be more & more desperately
> trying to find the breath to keep down...
> (*DS* 170)

His attempt to find a door in the wall is less an attempt to escape the muses than a search for a way to break out of the "crustacean boundaries" of isolation and to begin a new form of dialogue. Thus his submergence also links him with *nam* and the submerged history of the Caribbean:

> en-
> fetterments of clear air become water
> beyond this mutation. dissolving into this
> tinkle & oven & tide of the silence. dead
> arawaks drowned sailors drowned

> **steersmen my brothers drowned fishermen drowned Dahomean slaves w/ no glint or dream in their fishnets that cd not stop the time.**
> (*DS* 171)

The reference to the drowned sailor as well a the title of the story are, of course, echoes of T. S. Eliot. As Charles Pollard points out in his book *New World Modernisms*, Eliot is a major influence on Brathwaite's work as well as on that of other Caribbean poets of the same generation to the extent that he helped shape a Caribbean form of modernism. "Salvages" echoes "The Dry Salvages," the third part of *Four Quartets*. Eliot's preliminary note to the poem states that "The Dry Salvages," a group of rocks on the New England coast, is a corruption of *"les trois sauvages,"* which translates as "the three savages" (35). Brathwaite may have been thinking of the link between savage and Caliban, but I think the connection with Eliot has wider implications. Eliot is part of the imaginary dimension of *DreamStories*, sharing a "submarine unity" with Brathwaite's own work. As both writers come together they form a magical space or "creole cosmos." Both poets' voices merge into one in an instance of communion or possession (Brathwaite speaking with the voice of Eliot and vice versa). In this sense, Eliot emerges as part of Caribbean literary tradition, and this is how Brathwaite perceives him. *DreamStories* thus creates "forms of . . . inclusiveness" that bring together "the fragments of colonial legacy" in the form of magical or dream montage (Pollard 25).

The last three stories of *DreamStories* describe the journey back from the far side of the mirror. The act of writing, which follows the return, is literally an act of translating the experience of the imaginary into the language of the symbolic. In this sense, the page itself becomes the mirror surface, the magical space, where both realities converge.[18]

## Chapter 6
# "Oceans within": *Barabajan Poems, ConVERSations with Nathaniel Mackey* and the Utopian Space of the Text

◇◆◇

In *Barabajan Poems* (1994) and *ConVERSations with Nathaniel Mackey* (1999), Brathwaite looks back on his life and work, identifying influences and key experiences that shaped his poetry and thinking. *Barabajan Poems* centers mainly on the poet's life before the beginning of trauma in 1986, on his growing up in Barbados, his family homes, his life as a student in Cambridge as well as his years in Ghana and the revolution in his poetic vision which the confrontation with his African heritage entailed. Brathwaite employs his poetry up to and including *Sun Poem* (1982) to illustrate the interplay of autobiography and poetic vision. *ConVERSations* focuses on *X/Self* and his more recent works discussed in previous chapters as well as on the events in his life that accompany them. Both books together constitute a creative autobiography in which the author and his texts become one. In this sense, the text becomes open-ended and appears engaged in a dialogue with the poet's self, setting the tone for subsequent publications such as *Golokwati 2000* and the two volumes of *MR*. The open-ended text also functions as a possible bridge across the rift valley of trauma and shows the poet emerging from his dreams.

Significantly, both books begin as public events, *Barabajan Poems* as a speech, the "Twelfth Sir Winston Scott Memorial Lecture," delivered on 2 December 1987 at the Central Bank of Barbados, and *ConVERSa-*

*tions* as an interview conducted by poet and critic Nathaniel Mackey at Poets House in New York on 18 November 1993. Both books are in the first instance transcripts of voice recordings of these public events and have been subsequently extended by Brathwaite with comments, footnotes and appendices, which results in a gap of several years between the actual event and the final publication in print. Brathwaite regards these gaps in time not as gaps at all but as a continuing of the original conversation or event, an open-endedness of dialogue which becomes an open-endedness of the text and is mirrored in his use of the present continuous form or, as he calls it, the "present tense continuums" (*C* 15), the use of the word "continuum" instead of "continuous" illustrating the said open-endedness. Another clue to the importance of this sense of continuum or open-endedness appears right at the beginning of *ConVERSations*, where Brathwaite refers to an even earlier interview with Mackey, published in *Hambone* 9 (Winter 1991). In relation to this sequence of interviews, Brathwaite stresses that the conversation at Poets House "isn't a 'conversation' at all . . . / but really a continuation of Nate's own rap/port w/ me in / *Hambone* 9 (Winter 1991)" (*C* 14). Likewise, *Barabajan Poems* is an extension or continuation of the above lecture. The texts thus become palimpsests, and Brathwaite's meticulous listing of the several revisions of the texts illustrate their palimpsest-like nature, as here in *Barabajan Poems*:

```
                              Lecture Btown Dec 1987
             first (Eagle) draft IT Sept 1988-Jan 1989
                       first (Sycorax) Kng Ap-Nov 1989
                     second (Sycorax) version Kng Dec 1990
                                          third (Stark)
                      version NY feb 1993
 brand new Stark version, using NEW CENT SCHOOLBOOK as base,

 started 18 feb 93/'finished' Mon 15 March 93/ Fri 19 March 1993
           further rev & adjustments Kgn Tues 23 March 93

 txt has moved from orij ts of c15,000 through the 25,000 of Feb 93 to
 the present (Kingston Sunday 28 March 93 — New York Easter 93)
                                                      60,000words
                                                            400pp

                                    Rev again NY Ap 27-29 1993
                                                         399pp
                                                  60,000+ words

 and then thru Bajan, Ja & back to NY, my Birthday and the death of my last
     M&Q uncle (both 11 May) & on thru a 4th vision of the Index to Fri 21
```

"Oceans within"

May<br>
400+pp<br>
65+,000 words<br>
(*BP* 401)

That the word "finished" should appear in quotation marks again indicates that Brathwaite considers his work indeterminate, open-ended. Consequently, the text is not only looking backward in the sense of revising already existing material, but it also contains a space of anticipation intimated in "4th vision" rather than "4th revision." This space of anticipation has utopian connotations, as my reading of the books will hopefully reveal.

In the context of creating a sense of community, Brathwaite's notion of rapport and conversation is of crucial importance. In the opening paragraphs of *Barabajan Poems*, which retain the original speech form, Brathwaite rejects the term "lecture" in favor of "rapport," stressing the need to bypass what Wilson Harris calls "the tyranny of closure" (*The Mask of the Beggar* 53):

> ... There is no way that I could come stand here and 'deliver' something 'formal' when in fact what I was trying to say is so ?complex and so shifting elusive in meaning. So that I have to th ink this out with you, get your support – *your rapport, in fact* – and try my heart to make some charity out of the various strands of my 'title' *The Poet and his Place in Bajan Culture* (*BP* 21)[1]

Brathwaite also stresses here that the process of thinking, especially when it entails the nature of Caribbeanness, is not a solo act, but something reminiscent of the call-and-response nature of jazz. Brathwaite sees his own thinking in terms of this form of jazz structure, as a communication between individual and community, poet and audience. In his "Jazz and the West Indian Novel," he, in fact, presents jazz as a social metaphor:

> Jazz has been from the beginning a cry from the heart of the hurt man, the lonely one. We hear this in the saxophone and trumpet. But its significance comes not from this alone, but from its collective blare of protest and its affirmation of the life and rhythm of the group. We hear this in the bass and drums, piano comping, and in the full ensemble which hints some-

times at chaos, sometimes at anarchy. But the chaos is always resolved into order. The social sense retains its grip on anarchy. The individual, it says, still has his place within the whole, even, if, for now, it is a minor segment of that whole. (58)

In this sense, both *Barabajan Poems* and *ConVERSations* play on the antiphonic nature of jazz, and Brathwaite seems to have this social dimension of jazz in mind when he refers to his lecture as "a sharing" (*BP* 19). The act of thinking as an instance of sharing is a step towards not just communication and community but also towards communion and *Heimat*. In this sense, jazz itself can be read as an expression of *Heimat* in the sense of a longing for communion.

The concept of "conversation" fulfills a similar function in *ConVERSations*. Mackey elaborates on the use of the word, which corresponds to Brathwaite's above notion of "a continuation of Nate's own rap/ port w/ me":

Thinking about the series in which this evening is taking place, "Conversations", I thought about the fact that there's > been a conversation going on between me and Kamau Brathwaite'(s) work for quite some time now. In fact, that conversation began before I met Kamau, and in some ways it even began before I met his work. When I was a graduate student at Stanford, one of the people I took a course from was St Claire Drake, historian, anthropologist, sociologist. I took a course on the Caribbean from him. This was in the early seventies. One day I bumped into him and he said, "Where were you?" I said "What do you mean?" He said "Where were you the other day?" And I asked him again what he meant. He said "Brathwaite was here. Where were you?" I didn't know, first of all, who Brathwaite was, and I didn't know why I should have been there, but St Claire Drake, having a sense of some of my interests, felt like I should have been there. And he was right. I should have, but I wasn't. And certainly, in his mind, the conversation between some of my concerns and Brathwaite's work had already begun even though I didn't know that work. (*C* 18-19)

Brathwaite the poet becomes synonymous with his work, which is in conversation with the wider field of Caribbean literature. In this sense, the open-endedness of *Barabajan Poems* and *ConVERSations* echoes the interconnectedness of Brathwaite's poetry and cultural projects, such as the Irish Town maroon community and the "Bussa Centre" at CowPastor.

The idea of the open-endedness of the text is enforced by Brathwaite's liberal use of footnotes, which sometimes consist of independent essays and stories. These extensive commentaries add new facets, fragmenting the main body of the text and fracturing the linear reading process. The text functions, in fact, like Delany's jewel: in disturbing the linear reading process, the annotated texts of *Barabajan Poems* and *ConVERSations* "shatter unitary images" so that events and thoughts "become at once fragmented and multiple" (or prismatic in Brathwaite's magical realist sense), like the texts of a palimpsest.

In "Wordsongs & Wordwounds/Homecoming: Kamau Brathwaite's *Barabajan Poems*," Elaine Savory describes *Barabajan Poems* as "pangeneric," a term she derives from Édouard Glissant's concept of *métissage*: "*Barabajan Poems* is a compendium of writing styles and genres, a *métissage*, to use Edouard Glissant's term. It breaks down the artificial boundaries between academic and so-called creative writing.... I have used the term *pangeneric* ... to describe Brathwaite's more recent work" (751). *ConVERSations* can be included in this description. The "pangeneric" style of these works reflects the cross-cultural environment of the Caribbean, which enacts the "creole cosmos" on a regional scale as a "*métissage* of cultures" (Glissant, *Poetics* 163). In other word, in *Barabajan Poems* and *ConVERSations* the text is a utopian space that seeks to transcend the boundaries of its own textuality in order to become lived reality. In *Poetics of Relation*, Glissant states that "thought in reality spaces itself out into the world" (1). In other words, the text as an expression of thought needs to transcend its own boundaries, so that the journey to utopia can begin.

Apart from their function as examples of cross-culturality, both books represent a dialogue between orality and textuality. Set out as oral documents, they become, in the process of commentating the spoken with footnotes, documents that can only be fully conveyed to an

## A Creole Experiment

audience by fusing the act of hearing with the act of seeing, an "experience in terms of its impact as vision, as visual hearing" (*C* 176):

> I mean, is never only 'voice' or 'sound' or 'narrative' or 'rap' or what have you. I mean what's *song*, for goodness slake? or *ijala*? what goes on in Church or in the *oumfo* (r)/*oumfo* — Ogotemmêli. Homer. Kabuki. All of these aspects of Oral Tradition [OT] are total, are interdisciplinary, are transboundary . . . (*C* 211)

By using the terms "total" and "transboundary," Brathwaite suggests that the oral tradition encompasses all aspects of life and is, in fact, more a way of life than a form of literature. In view of the books as cultural documents expressing the diversity of Caribbean experience, the term "transboundary" can be extended to include the cross-cultural nature of the "pangeneric" text. In this sense, the term "pangeneric" implies a reaching out to other textual traditions. As his experimenting with fonts suggests, Brathwaite regards computer technology as engaging in dialogue with the oral tradition, bringing out the "*voice* of the fonts" (*C* 176) to "convert script into sound" (*C* 216). In this sense, the script becomes a "modern musical score" (*C* 215), which involves an act of precomposition, and Brathwaite himself states that "'oral poetry' . . . should not be confused with 'improvisation'" (*C* 227). Precomposition, then, moves the text away from an experience of immediacy. This fracturing of immediacy is also conveyed by the palimpsest character of the two texts, in their revisions, footnotes and appendices that interrupt the flow of the spoken word (the original voice recordings) in order to insert another, independent syntactical system. The textual components are opened up, thus making the text non-linear and labyrinthine.

Indeterminacy, non-linearity and precomposition are characteristic of hypertexts, as Jim Rosenberg, himself a hypertext poet, argues in his online essay "Poetics and Hypertext: Where are the Hypertext Poets?" *Barabajan Poems* and *ConVERSations* read like printed versions of electronic texts. In both books, footnotes function like hyperlinks, whether they are footnotes in conventional form, as highlighted numbers in the text with the additional information given in the "Notes" section at the end of the book, as in *Barabajan Poems*, or, as in *ConVERSation*, added directly into the sentence. Through these hyperlinks, an electronic text becomes indeterminate, since, as Rosenberg states, "the user is totally free to choose whether or not to follow a link, and the node sequence experience of each 'reader' . . . will be different." The use of hyperlinks, or in Brathwaite's case footnotes, "entails imposing a non-linear structure on a locally linear substrate" (Rosenberg). In other words, the text acquires a vertical axis in addition to its horizontal arrangement on the page usually associated with conventional reading. Rosenberg argues that precomposition entails "composing a work in layers, where work in one layer may affect the entirety of the succeeding layer." In Brathwaite's books under discussion, these layers correspond to the various stages of the document, from the original voice recordings to the fully annotated publication. Each successive layer of comments added by Brathwaite interprets the original text in a slightly different way. This is most obvious in the numerous rewritings of poems, which are reinterpretations of existing texts that predate the lecture and interview.

Rosenberg continues by claiming that "an important part of the hypertext act is the linking of pre-existing materials." In *Barabajan Poems* and *ConVERSations*, the rewriting of poems performs such an act of linking in that earlier publications are set into a new context and, therefore, into a new form of dialogue with each other, transforming Brathwaite's work into an organic whole. In becoming hypertextual constructions, *Barabajan Poems* and *ConVERSations* depart from the open field composition that characterizes *X/Self*. Rosenberg argues that open field composition expresses a "real-time poetics," i.e. the open field presents the poem as speech act, as transcript of an oral text form. The use of hypertext thus signifies the most significant break in Brathwaite's work, separating the "video-style" writing from his earlier poetry, which to a large extent sought to reproduce the act of speaking. However, the oral element is still present in the "underwaters" of *Barabajan Poems* and *ConVERSations*, in their original form which is the deepest layer of the palimpsest, creating a tension between the two textual forms, which expresses itself in the seemingly paradoxical notion of visual hearing mentioned above.

Thematically, both texts are attempts at remembering the self, and more specifically Brathwaite's written life obliterated in the destruction of the house and archive at Irish Town. The large number of primary texts that appear in both books are often revised versions of earlier poems and stories, which were not necessarily lost in the mudslide, but which represent the archive of his written life, obliterated metaphorically, as a death of creativity, in the period between 1986

## A Creole Experiment

and 1990. Brathwaite's reworking of "lost" poems creates a bridge across the mudslide, establishing conversations with aspects of his own writing and his personal history, which, as in all his other books, is intertwined with the history of the Caribbean as a whole. A large part of *Barabajan Poems* and *ConVERSations* is, therefore, devoted to a reinterpretation and re-evaluation of his written life and a contextualization of his work within the body of Caribbean writing at large.

The act of remembering and reinterpreting self and history involves, yet again, a journey to the "most ancient place" of memory. In terms of his creative life, this is also a journey to the heartland of inspiration, which in *Barabajan Poems* has an actual geographical location in Ghana and in the interior of Barbados. In *ConVERSations*, this heartland becomes the "most ancient place" of written language, where Brathwaite compares the visual quality of his "video style" to hieroglyphic writing and the Amerindian rock art of the *timehri* (C 201). This chapter will focus on these sources of inspiration and how they serve to create a utopian space of the text.

### 6.1. Barabajan Poems

*Barabajan Poems* consists of seventeen chapters. Thirteen of these chapters describe various kinds of journeys into the heartland of inspiration, whereas the rest comprises appendices, notes and references, an index, and what Brathwaite entitles "A brief vertical interview" (Chapter XVI). In this interview, Brathwaite describes his work on *Barabajan Poems* as a journey of discovery not only into the hinterland of inspiration but also into previously unknown regions of the imagination:

> The first significance, I think, is TIME the second LABOUR and the two are combined, as I worked, into the image of Balboa of all people hacking his way through the Isthmus of Panama towards – towars, really – that peak in Darien where he wd beheld the Pacific. In this enterprise – I can say this now since on this video version alone (not to mention the lecture itself and the more monolithic firstdrafts) I worked almost 3 months nonstop – similar to Balboa's time/ space – in such a way that that thick forested tropical Isthmus became what it must always have been from the beginning of geological time, since it is this unique corridor & neck-

> lace between oceans – there is none such other on this earth – this Isthmus becomes a Muse – allowing me to discover oceans within myself, if I can put it this way, that I did not know before were there (*BP* 378–79)

The Spanish conquistador Vasco Núñez de Balboa was the first European explorer to set eyes on and stand in the waters of what came to be known as the Pacific Ocean in 1513, although it was Magellan who actually named the ocean "pacifica" (peaceful) ("Vasco Núñez de Balboa"). Brathwaite's "oceans within" represent new worlds within his mind, the discovery of which he regards as paralleling the European discovery of the far side of the Americas. Brathwaite's "oceans within" are utopian spaces, infinite and open-ended, a stage for a future creative output that has not yet become conscious and still lies beyond the horizon of his creative vision, beyond the "horizon of utopia" (*PH* 1: 202). Moreover, beyond this horizon is the location of Eldorado. Balboa's Amerindian guides described to him a land of infinite riches to the south, which echoes the myth of Eldorado.

Intimately linked to the reality of conquest and colonization, the story of Eldorado also resonates with the idea of utopia, which echoes Bloch's own sense of the myth "as the spatial possibility of a new heaven and a new earth. The intention towards the earthly paradise thus focused on a golden space which could still be expected in the outflowing world, at the delta of the world" (*PH* 2: 794). Here Eldorado becomes the space of tomorrow, latently present in the space of today, where alienation ends and *Heimat* begins. Eldorado as utopian space is implied in Brathwaite's "oceans within." Moreover, since *Barabajan Poems* and *ConVERSations* embrace all of Brathwaite's previous work, including the utopian aspects within them, the books themselves become oceans, or golden spaces, fed by the rivers of his life's work.

Brathwaite's choice of identifying with Balboa harks back to the vision of the first *X/Self*, and the poem "Titan" in particular, where he superimposes the messianic figure of Quetzalcoatl with the conquistador Cortez. In this way, Brathwaite established a dialogue between the two opposing forces, creating an image of creolization that recognizes "the other in the self and ... the self in the other" (Greenblatt 135). Balboa is of the same destructive nature as Cortez (in "Titan" both conquistadors are even briefly identified with each other) as he cuts his way through the forest towards the unknown southern ocean. Brathwaite's play on "towards" and "to*wars*" intimates the destruction Balboa causes to the indigenous population he encounters, and indeed to the land itself, as Brathwaite suggests in the idea of "hacking" a path through the forest. In repeating Balboa's journey through the forest or palimpsest of the text, Brathwaite recognizes the other in himself. Balboa's journey of destruction is redeemed in Brathwaite's journey of inspiration. Consequently, the raped forest is healed and becomes again the muse of inspiration.

In "Caliban's Guarden," Brathwaite describes the journey to the sources of inspiration in terms of a venturing out into a geographical, historical, and psychological hinterland:

> The garden, that community, that hinterland, not only hinterland in the Guyanese sense of a place where you have resources, but the resource place from which one receives hints and guesses as Eliot would say. Hints of a world which we have almost forgotten. Hints of a submergence which is at the basis of one's metaphor and therefore of one's poetry and consciousness, because you see the whole history of the Caribbean is based upon submergence. The islands, cordillera submerged, the Amerindian presence submerged. The Europeans coming into the Caribbean altered the garden and therefore much of their achievement submerged. Africans brought dumb into the Caribbean and therefore their drum Sycorax submerged. The whole process it seems is to sink below the waters and discover submergence. And this is what we began to do when we began to get to know the garden better. (6)[2]

Brathwaite's journey to the hinterland of his imagination parallels his journey into the interior of the island of Barbados, to the village of Mile&Quarter, the home of Brathwaite's aunts and uncles to whom *Barabajan Poems* is dedicated. This journey mirrors the movement into the "underwaters" of the unconscious around which *DreamStories* centered. The village of Mile&Quarter can thus be read as the location of the island's dreaming psyche. As in *DreamStories*, the space of dreaming is an ancestral as well as a utopian place. Moreover, the village and the carpenter shop of Brathwaite's great-uncle Bob'ob become the "wall-less structure" and communal space that for Brathwaite is the unique quality of the Caribbean house. Thematically, therefore, *Barabajan Poems* is linked to *Shar* and *DreamStories*.[3]

## "Oceans within"

The title of Brathwaite's lecture, "Caliban's Guarden," suggests that Caliban "guards" the Caribbean "garden," the interior of the islands with their submerged histories of slavery and maroon resistance. This garden or sanctuary (a space that "guards" something sacred or valuable) has the potential to become a utopian space, as Caliban is the beginning of an "alter/native" Caribbean self, one that has transcended the binary opposition of master and slave:

> Those children of Caliban who begin to conceive of something other than simple rebellion. Who seek beyond the physicality or the naturalness of Caliban for a cosmos or for the restoration of a cosmos which includes their mother Sycorax. Because Sycorax is that one submerged feature of Shakespeare's play that we are very much involved with in the Caribbean. (4)

The "alter/native" Caribbean self is thus one that moves "tidalectically" backwards into the past towards its *nam* and its guardian Sycorax in order to move forward into Caliban's future. In "Caliban's Guarden," Brathwaite illustrates this opening of the past into the future by describing the canefields of Barbados as an ocean: "The whisper of the sugar cane itself is an ocean much larger than Barbados. An ocean which stretches back in the north to Europe, along the west, Amerindia; to the east, to Africa, and in the south, into my own imagination" (6).[4]

Despite the violent history of slavery, which connects Africa, Europe, and the Americas, Brathwaite argues that history is a narrative and can, therefore, be opened up to revisions and new visions in the "south," in the space of the poet's imagination, which parallels Balboa's unseen land of infinite riches. In other words, the imagination is an Eldorado, a magical space. Moreover, it has the potential to transform the legacy of slavery into a vision of cultural coexistence. The link that Brathwaite establishes in his narrative between the Caribbean, himself, and the world also implies that he regards the Caribbean islands not as isolated but as related to other islands and continents, to other human communities on the globe, thus creating a web of communication. In this sense, Brathwaite returns to the concerns of the first edition of *X/Self*, the web of Ananse or the coconut's traveling root. In *Barabajan Poems* and *ConVERSations*, the horizontal connection of cultures through oceans (of the world and the imagination) creates a totality that is communion or *Heimat*.

## A Creole Experiment

Brathwaite's own journey backwards into the canefields of history and forward towards the ocean of his imagination involves a process of what he terms "de/education" (*BP* 68), i.e. an unlearning of colonial education, which includes the rediscovery of mother Sycorax. In Chapter III of *Barabajan Poems*, Brathwaite describes the effects of the colonial education he received as a boy in Barbados and as a student of history at Cambridge on his understanding of history and his notion of selfhood. The first part of Chapter III can be regarded as Brathwaite's reading of his own book *Masks*, in which he records his confrontation with African culture in Ghana, where he worked for the Ministry of Education between 1955 and 1962. *Masks* imagines Brathwaite's Caribbean self returning to the mother continent three hundred years after his ancestors' deportation as slaves to the New World. In joining in the daily life of Africa, the *omowale*, "the stranger returned after three centuries of disaster," learns about an ancestral heritage that was eclipsed by his colonial upbringing in Barbados and England (Rohlehr, *Pathfinder* 138). In the following passage from *Barabajan Poems*, Brathwaite illustrates this by pointing out the differences in everyday habits and customs between Africa and the Caribbean:

**the morning I lost the imperial ass/umption that Goldie Flake co rnflakes makes the Best Breakfast**

**when I was told by my Takoradi friends that out here in our country is yam & okro make the meal**

**like**
**what you grow in yr own backyard**

> like
>
> when I first saw through the eye
> of the navel/ heard the drum sp-
> eak God & cd talk of drum belly
> drum centred earth sounding cult
> ure . . . (*BP* 68–69)

Here Brathwaite illustrates Glissant's notion of "consumer colony," which characterizes the neocolonial dependence of the Caribbean on western culture and economy, undermining the islands' formal status of political independence (*Caribbean Discourse* 43). "Goldie Flake cornflakes" represents consumer capitalism, which floods the local market with foreign produce, disabling the local economy and potential self-sufficiency. The above passage from *Barabajan Poems* is thus a reflection on societal models and echoes the concerns of Rastafarian culture outlined in chapter four, which sought to achieve independence from the west by cultivating local produce. In this sense, Brathwaite's "de/education" in Ghana involves a profound rejection of capitalism as a modern form of imperialism, of "biospheric" exploitation, to use Gary Snyder's term again. As a result of this awareness, a network of "ecosystems" becomes Brathwaite's utopian vision not only for the Caribbean but also for a global "creole cosmos." The idea of interrelated communities or "ecosystems" in *Barabajan Poems* creates a space, where the text enters into conversation with lived reality.

Despite this new vision, Brathwaite is far from idealizing Africa. One concern of *Masks* is the *omowale*'s coming to terms with Africa's involvement in the slave trade. The *omowale* feels betrayed by his own people, in particular the *Asantehene*, the Ashanti king, who conducted the trade in slaves with Europe. Brathwaite describes the city of Kumasi in the heartland of Ghana, the seat of the *Asantehene*, as the "city of gold" (*Arrivants* 138), as the "golden space" of the Ashanti nation. The king is regarded not only as wealthy but also as a utopian Eldorado figure in the spiritual sense of a perfect human being, having responsibility for the well-being of his people. In the poem "Tutu" of *Masks*, King Osei Tutu is described as clothed in "gold, that the sun may continue to shine / bringing wealth and warmth to the nation" (*Arriv-*

*ants* 141). As "city of gold," Kumasi becomes the African equivalent of the South American Eldorado. In the end, however, Kumasi turns into a dystopian place, its golden space belonging to the "Africa of dreams" (*BP* 76) as Brathwaite writes in Chapter III of *Barabajan Poems*, where he describes how he and a friend traveled into the heartland of Ghana to ask for an audience with the *Asantehene*. Their request is refused and regarded as "a ceremonial insult" (*BP* 76–77):

> ... since we – Citizens of the World and now would-be Africans and Diasporans – did not know that it was the West India Regiment, hurriedly summoned from its Caribbean stations in 1895 or thereabouts [this info was supplied, after imprecations as to why we could not meet w/
>
> Nana, by his okyeame] that had brought about the defeat of the nation & th(e) banishmant of Prempeh to the Seychelles in 1896 at what the history books claim to be 'the hands of the British'. But the Ashanti knew better . and here were their brothers & cousins back again in a re/warped nightmare of history; and as he was being ferried over the River Pra into captivity, the Asantehene swore a solemn oath never again to
>
> look upon the faces of *cane-suckers* . (*BP* 77)

The golden space of Kumasi becomes a space of betrayal, "paved with silver" (*Arrivants* 138) (silver being the metal of betrayal), in a double sense. On the one hand, the *omowale*'s ancestors have been betrayed by the *Asantehene* as he sold them into slavery. On the other hand, the descendants of slaves, out of a lack of historical understanding, betray their motherland Africa by becoming instruments of empire. Through a growing awareness of these historical circumstances, Brathwaite begins to regard the trip to Kumasi as an "*interior journey* into the history & cul ture of our *selves*" (*BP* 77). As has been pointed out before, selfhood for Brathwaite is a result of historical awareness brought about by a questioning of received notions of history. Unwillingness to question, therefore, perpetuates dependence and creates the conditions under which "human scavenging" can happen:

> For without the river of an answer here, the drought and desert of our past continues – Independent Africa crippled by a new slave trade, more guns, more greed, more coups, more murders & abductions in the night, more starving

millions...
... more finding of my friends' part-body in the gully – his arm, his thighs, his head – his **skull**, that is, in a crocus bag full up of maggots maggots maggots – the maggots that we ate as slaves – salt fish saltfish salt flesh of maggots – slave trade the new slave trade Passage Mid-

dle Passage the new Middle Passage Passages flowing out across Atlantic now not the factories of cotton sugar flash but to new industries of

fa$x$ – computer processes – flowing out from/ flowing in towards a new

world New World that was always here although we couldn't see it . though we sell it (*BP* 80)

This passage, in its depiction of human life debased into waste, echoes the anguish of *Trench Town Rock*. Again, the old empire, the plantation, has given way to a new form of global imperialism, which perpetuates violence and creates new economic dependencies. Therefore, the possibility of a new world order remains invisible and is even betrayed ("we sell it") in the "darkness of the lived moment," which is the dread and despair of the present.

The image of the river in the above passage bears the connotations of the Akan concept of *sunsum*, the bloodline that connects the generations of a family. Brathwaite uses the idea of *sunsum* in *Sun Poem*, and again here in *Barabajan Poems*, in an attempt to restore the broken connection between Africa and the Caribbean and between the Caribbean's plantation past and the present. In *Masks*, the *sunsum* is seen as broken due to the *Asantehene*'s participation in the slave trade:

> Why did our gold, the sun's
> *sunsum*, safe against termites, crack
>
> under the white gun
> of plunder, bright bridge-
> head of money, quick bullet's bribe? (*Arrivants* 149)

*Barabajan Poems* restores the *sunsum*, the bloodline between Africa and the Caribbean, in a fever vision that overlaps the landscapes of Ghana and Barbados:

> ... I wi
> sh you to vision me five thousand miles away on the other end of the
> Middle Passage/ but about to turn the corner back to Brown's Beach

and Mile&Quarter. For is here, high up in the forests of the Volta, with my first real attack of malaria & dreaming, within the miasma, of water&river&coastline&blue/green&whitewaterbreaker&ocean, that I saw, in the dream, as it were, not Elmina, not Accra, not Keta, not Lomé, not Lagos, but the sea & not just the sea but *my* sea Brown'(s) Beach & the morning & meaning of *home* with which I began, I begin and that now – I knew – I could sing – (*BP* 82–83)

The fever vision moves beyond a mere recollection of the past. It becomes an instant of creative daydreaming that gives new meaning to Brathwaite's poem "South" (*Rights of Passage*). In *Rights*, the poem has no specific location but merely describes a river flowing from a forest through a plain into the sea. The poet follows the journey of the river in his mind, describing his passage from exile, "where the shadows oppress me / and the only water is rain and the tepid taste of the river" (*Arrivants* 57), to the seashore, his home. In *Barabajan Poems*, the poem follows the above passage of the vision, giving the river and the shore a geographical location. The place of oppressing shadows becomes the forests of the Volta, the seashore Brown's Beach on the west coast of Barbados, where Brathwaite grew up. In this sense, the African river, the river of *sunsum*, of African heritage and history, flows into the Caribbean Sea, thus reflecting not only the poet's restored connection with the heartland of the past but also the connection of the past with the oceans of the poet's imagination. The African river and the concept of *sunsum* thus take up the image of Damballah as *Grand Chemin*, the road that connects the past with the future, the dead and the *loa* with the living and the unborn.

Chapter III of *Barabajan Poems* concludes with Brathwaite's reflections on a Barbadian literary tradition, which can be read as another manifestation of the river, originating in another ancestral bloodline, that of Europe. Brathwaite investigates the work of a white Barbadian, M. J. Chapman, who in 1833 published a poem entitled "Barbadoes," which for Brathwaite reflects Chapman's sense of belonging to the island.[5] Brathwaite's concern, as he stresses in his opening remarks to *Barabajan Poems*, is to express "how I walk talk & *think* Barabaja (n)" (*BP* 23). At the same time, he laments "the (dis/graceful really) absence of *Bajan* critical discussion the absence of a *Bajan* critical *dimension*" (*BP* 23) with regard to his own work as well as that of other Barbadian authors. His discussion of Chapman's poem "Barbadoes" alongside his own poem "The Dust" (*Rights of Passage*) attempts to show the existence of a "Bajan culture," which he defines as "this shared collective xperience on a rock of limestone, half-way from Europe, half-way (?back) to Africa" (*BP* 21).

"The Dust" is a poem of intermingling voices. It records a conversation of women gathering in a local shop to socialize, to discuss herbal remedies and, above all, to reminisce about "May Dust," a cloud of ash from a volcanic eruption that drifted to Barbados from a neighboring island. Chapman's poem, too, records this experience of "May Dust." In a footnote to this section of Chapter III, Brathwaite provides historical detail concerning the eruption, recording the evolution of volcanic eruptions in the region into a "shared collective xperience":

> . . . Chapman's poem would have referred to the 90-mile-away eruption of Souffrière in St Vincent, which started on 27 April 1812 My 'Dust' Dust' would (or might) have been this + the one of 1902 (assuming that our people kept the memory – and the vials of dust – of both of them. We also know from Chapman that dust from the May 1812 xplosion reached Barbados (hence 'May Dust') What I don't yet know is whether the 1902 Souffrière gave off the same effect. That same year (1902), in also nearby Martinique, there was the apocalyptic xplosion of Mt Pelée, that completely destroyed the town of St Pierre and killed 40,000 people. This I am sure also became part of the Bajan legacy. The St Vincent Souffrière erupted again in 1979 and gave us Shake Keane's **Volcano** poems (1979), but there was no repercussion of dust in Barbados . . . (*BP* 305 n27)[6]

Brathwaite emphasizes that the environment and not an established canon inspires the poetry of the Caribbean region. Consequently, he states that he wrote his poem "The Dust" "without then even *knowing* of Chapman" (*BP* 86) at the time. Brathwaite's argument is that a response to the landscape and cultural environment indigenizes, culture and "tradition . . . being what filters & fuses in/to you from yr landscape people happenings mysteries fossils histories time" (*BP* 86). Barbadian identity is no longer merely defined by a harking back to the rivers of ancestral tradition, but also by looking out into the space of the ocean. Unlike the steady progressive flow of continental cultures, symbolized by the river, the Caribbean rhythm of life is measured by the sea and the dialogue of sea and land on the shores of the imagination.

Brathwaite's engagement with the work of Chapman can be regarded as a desire to bridge the divide between black and white that he perceived in Barbados when writing *Contradictory Omens* (1974). He considers Chapman not as a member of the colonial ruling class but as native to Barbados precisely because he identified with the island. The landscape had filtered into his consciousness and metaphor.

Chapman had become calibanized, and like Caliban, both Brathwaite and Chapman are "alter/natives," new identities, indebted to, but not imprisoned by, the ancestral cultures of Europe and Africa. As a contemporary cousin to Chapman, Brathwaite mentions Julian Hunte, a white Barbadian, who between late 1992 and early 1993 swam around the island. Brathwaite relates his story, mostly in Hunte's own words, in a footnote. He refers to Hunte as "a white ITAL Baje for those who glad to note that some at least white Bajans continue — increasingly so, I think, since the 80s — to contrib to Bajan life & letters" (*BP* 289 n14). Brathwaite thus revises his claim made in *Contradictory Omens*, which refers to the political realities of the 1970s, that "white creoles in the English and French West Indies have separated themselves by too wide a gulf . . . to give credence to the notion that they can . . . meaningfully identify . . . with the spiritual world on this side of the Sargasso Sea" (38). Within the space of his creative imagination, therefore, Brathwaite succeeds in breaking down the barriers between the races, which is his vision in the first cosmology. Thus he also counters critics such as Peter Hulme, who accuses him of racial bias on the grounds of his arguments in *Contradictory Omens*, disregarding all of Brathwaite's subsequent works.[7] Hunte becomes a "native" or "alter/native" of Barbados because of "the truly nativist knowledge he reveals of tides, beaches & landfall" (*BP* 289 n14). In this, he is twinned with Mexican, who at the end of *The Zea Mexican Diary* is celebrated for precisely this "nativist knowledge" and who consequently becomes the spirit of the land. Being thus in communion with the environment, Brathwaite's "alter/natives" become the inhabitants of an "ecosystem." In this sense, he has achieved a utopian vision for the island of Barbados. However, as he states in his opening remarks to *Barabajan Poems*, his overall vision is of a web of islands (which echoes his desire for cultural wholeness voiced in *Caribbean Man in Space and Time*), a vision of "culture as web . . . [w]hich means that we'll have to widen our definition to include generosity and an awareness not only of i/sola i/land/ hole, but of **Caribbean** as a **whole**" (*BP* 23). On a textual level, Brathwaite opens the closed form of the poem, creating a wider web of meaning in juxtaposing his poems with those of other authors and his own reflections. Thus he goes beyond merely retrieving the lost archives of his written life. His "pangeneric" approach fragments and reconnects works in new ways, creating new archives.

    Chapters VI and VII take up the image complex of river and sea. In Chapter VI, Brathwaite focuses on his childhood memories of his great-uncle Bob'ob, a carpenter, who appears in *Islands* as the artisan

"Oceans within"

Ogoun in the poem of the same title. Bob'ob is both a carpenter and an artist:

And this Bob'ob, my Ogoun, this carpenter – and it is significant also

...that he was a carpenter –

the word has such deep religious & mythological significance – I mea(n), a carpenter does not only mean a man who does *that* you know [acting it out] shubbin the plane, hearing the sissle of shavings; a carpenter is a parson in touch, through his wood, with Nature, with Super Nature. Christ was a carpenter, for instance. And in Hebrew that means he was a powerfully spiritual person, one who dealt, as the Vikings said of their woodgod Wodin or Oudin, in magic or wode; the tree or cross or crossroads connecting the cosmos: sky through air + electricity + thunder + wind into water + earth + metal + mineral + vegetable word –

So that Bob'ob not only taught us, subliminally as it were, about other wheres, other wares, other cultures – something of Egypt & Ethiopia & modern Babylon, for instance; **but he himself, I discovered, in addition to his 'plantation' carpentry...**

...**was quietly & seecreetly – carving something out of wodin...**

...a **local carving of an African image & a nommo/ name (*mkissi*)** (*BP* 155)

The *mkissi*, the remembered African mask, is thus connected to the unconscious, the "underwaters" of *nam*, where, as has been shown in *DreamStories*, the *loa* or gods of the Middle Passage reside. The river of divine inspiration originating in Africa deltas into the consciousness of the rural carpenter Bob'ob in a form of spirit possession. Bob'ob becomes Ogoun, the warrior and artisan, a deity originating in West African Yoruba culture and surviving in Haitian voodoo and Cuban santería.[8] In this sense, the *mkissi* itself can be regarded as a sea, one that, paradoxically, opens in the heartland of Barbados.

Moreover, since in *Barabajan Poems* the sea represents the confluence of cultures in the Caribbean basin, Bob'ob is not just Ogoun, but also Christ and the Germanic deity Wodin or Odin, who embody similar aspects of other ancestral cultures of the region. Within this counterpoint of personalities, Bob'ob becomes a redeeming figure, transcending the "hubris of totality," which is Wilson Harris's expression for the hegemony of one culture over another (*The Womb of Space* 51). In addition to this, Bob'ob/Ogoun is also the keeper of an archive. He owns a collection of newspaper cut-outs, photos of Marcus Garvey, Haile Selassie and other figures of resistance against European imperialism.[9] These slips of ancestral memory disappear after his death. The loss of Bob'ob's archive is thus an echo of Brathwaite's own loss recorded in *Shar*, but the *mkissi*, like the forms of incantation in *Shar*, survives and functions as an alternative, oral, avenue of memory that proves to be more durable than the written archive.

In Chapter VII, Bob'ob's carpenter shop has become a meeting place for the Barbadian Zion Baptist Church:

When I return to Barbados in 1972 . . . the beautiful large woden upstairs Ogoun house . . . was . . . in ruin

But the place where Bob'ob's workplace had been, the large square concrete floor area, had been converted into a Zion meeting place – a Wednesday Night Prayer Meeting place – and remember that wood or wode = Wodin or Wednesday = a polytone-&-polyrhythmic-handclap tie-head tambour / ine-& sing / ing place . . . (*BP* 166)

Brathwaite witnesses how the Christian Zion meeting place becomes a voodoo *houmfort*:

it had started in fact before I entered the shop:/ before i entered the hounfort – increased nasalization, deeper & deeper vertiginous fallings & flattings of octaves as if they were singing not even in the Parish of St Peter anymore with fruit trees canefields Brevitor hills gullies the sea at Six Mens Bay . so that, as I say (and I can only say, I say) it takes me back & drags me tidalectic into this ta

ngled urgent meaning to & fro . like foam . saltless as from the bottom of the sea . dragging our meaning our moaning/ song from Calabar along the sea-floor sea-floor with pebble sound & conch & wound & sea-sound moon

It could have been Yemanjaa . That night it was Damballa . dancing with that whisper of a sound inside a simple unsuspecting shop in Mile&Q, Barbados (*BP* 182 )

In one sense, the *houmfort* with its center-pole or *poteau mitan* representing the world axis or *Grand Chemin* can be read as the delta where the ancestral rivers of Christian and African beliefs meet to create a cross-cultural religious expression. Therefore, Damballah, like Bob'ob's *mkissi*, has a composite, hybrid, identity. The Caribbean identities of the woman possessed by Damballah and of Bob'ob carving the *mkissi* subconsciously fluctuate between their different origins, thus creating the "tidalectic" movement Brathwaite indicates in his observation, which echoes the refractive quality of Delany's jewel. Above all, the reference to the seafloor as the location of residual ancestral memory echoes not only Brathwaite's own poetry of *Islands* and *Sun Poem* but also the work of other Caribbean writers, who describe the Atlantic Ocean as an archive of the Middle Passage.[10]

Through the refractive quality of the jewel of *nam*, Bob'ob's shop becomes related to the "Palace of the Peacock" in Wilson Harris's novel of the same title. *Palace of the Peacock* describes the journey upriver into the heartland of Guyana of a racially mixed crew representing the racially mixed society of Guyana. They are in pursuit of a group of escaped Amerindian farm workers. During the course of the journey, the manhunt is transformed into the desire for union with the spirit of the land, here represented by the Amerindians, a desire, in other words, to perceive the land as *Heimat*. The crew's journey comes to an end as they encounter a waterfall. The "Palace of the Peacock" is situated above the waterfall, in, as Benítez-Rojo describes in *The Repeating Island*, "the rainbow's spectrum, a place where the colors' identities are generated as the light's rays decompose" (188). Like Delany's jewel, the water of the falls fractures the light, transcending the binary opposition of light and darkness, and in racial terms of black and white. The rainbow can, therefore, be read as symbolic of racial coexistence, and thus of the "creole cosmos."

As rainbow, Damballah becomes the utopian space of Bob'ob's shop/*houmfort*. In his collection of interrelated stories, *Damballah* (1981), the African-American writer John Edgar Wideman describes the transformation of the *loa* into space. The story from which the passage below is taken centers on Orion, an African-born slave refusing to adapt to plantation life, and a boy, drawn to Orion's African spirituality as a source of resistance and liberation. In the following passage, the intersection of divinity and humanity becomes the *houmfort*:

> Orion drew a cross in the dust. Damballah. When Orion passed his hands over the cross the air seemed

to shimmer like it does above a flame or like it does when the sun so hot you can see waves of heat rising off the fields. Orion talked to the emptiness he shaped with his long black fingers. His eyes were closed. Orion wasn't speaking but sounds came from inside him the boy had never heard before, strange words, clicks, whistles and grunts. A singsong moan that rose and fell and floated like the old man's busy hands above the cross. Damballah like a drum beat in the chant. Damballah a place the boy could enter, a familiar sound he began to anticipate, a sound outside of him which slowly forced its way inside, a sound measuring his heartbeat then one with the pumping surge of his blood. (21)

In *Barabajan Poems*, not only Bob'ob's shop but also each individual within it is a crossroads or rainbow space. As the Zion congregation is drawn into the center of the shop, from outside to inside, from Christian worshipper to possessed servitor, so the *loa* moves from outside the individual to the inside in the instance of possession. In this context, Bob'ob's shop is linked in another way to the archive/*houmfort* of *Shar* in that the carpenter shop is transformed into the "wall-less structure" of the Caribbean house that allows for communion between individual and community, between the human and the divine. The instance of possession is thus a Blochian moment of "arrived-at Being," of *Heimat*. This instance of arrival is emphasized by the association of Bob'ob not only with Ogoun but also with Legba:

... Bob by O'Neale, known to our world as Bob'ob – not only as a 'diminutive' for Bobby (?Robert but because one of his feet was slightly shorter or smaller than the other ... and (so) in my life he became (I know this now) the Legba or Toussaint Louverture/ crippled god & alter/native of the doorway (and he was always standing there/at the door of his shop & greeted me like that when I first went to the Mile&Quarter that I can remember) the entrance (the entrance into his 'shop' was like going into a cave into an underworld into another world) the crossroads ...
... of my imagination my possibilities my passibilities into the world of poetry and in my poetry he has become the avatar of iron & carpenters & creativity, Wole Soyinka's favourite poet, the African (Yoruba) god, Ogoun
(*BP* 152)

"Oceans within"

Bob'ob/Legba opens the door to the rainbow space of *Heimat*, which is illustrated in the subsequent chapters entitled "Barabajan Landscapes" (VIII–XI), where Brathwaite cites those of his poems that express a sense of *Heimat* and "passion for the land" as Glissant puts it (*Poetics* 151). *Barabajan Poems* describes how in the "geography of Brathwaite's soul" the ancestral rivers have arrived in the delta of the Caribbean.[11] "Barabajan Landscapes" is thus a celebration of this arrival. However, Legba also opens the door to the future, a new departure, which is indicated in the title of the last chapter of *Barabajan Poems*, "Beginning" (Chapter XIII). Chapter XIII ends with a series of Barbadian proverbs, expressions of an indigenous identity, the last of which reads:

And then there is the great small-ilann

saying

sea

doan have no

BACKDOOR

(*BP* 282)

Brathwaite contradicts this generalizing statement with personal memories:

X -

cept that our house on Brown's Beach was just

that - the sea's

BACKDOOR

(BP 283)

In Brathwaite's font, the letters of "backdoor" appear as wooden planks to create the impression of the backyard fence of Brathwaite's house, from which the door opens out to the beach and the sea. The back door to Brathwaite's childhood home at Brown's Beach can be read as opening towards the "oceans within."[12]

The image of the open backyard door echoes with Brathwaite's idea of "transboundary" art. This quality of the "transboundary" is mirrored in the book's form in that *Barabajan Poems* transcends its own margins. The text does not finish on the last page but continues across the inside and outside back cover. *Barabajan Poems* thus "begins new meanings of the / MARGIN(S)" (*BP* outside back cover). On the inside back cover of *Barabajan Poems* Brathwaite writes of the Caribbean as being "the very redge of space," which also bears the connotations of utopian space in that the word "redge" implies both "edge" and "ridge." Ridge suggests the edge of a high place, a mountain like the one in Darien perhaps, from where Balboa could see far into the distance. On the other hand, Brathwaite emphasizes that "edge" of space is not synonymous with the "margin of Western culture / . . .

since it contains significant fections of / ANCESTOR / — Amerindian, African, Oriental, Pacific, Australasian" (*BP* inside back cover). In this sense, Caribbean space is open-ended, "transboundary," and so is the space of Brathwaite's Barabajan or Caribbean book.

## 6.2. ConVERSations with Nathaniel Mackey

*ConVERSations* repeats the poet's questing journey to the heartland of the imagination, but at the same time it goes beyond the concerns of *Barabajan Poems*. *Barabajan Poems* investigates "how metaphors come from 'raw material'" (*BP* outside back cover) and traces the poet's journey to the places that inspired his poetic language. In *ConVERSations*, language itself becomes the landscape through which the poet travels to the "most ancient places" of the written text, investigating the influence of Egyptian hieroglyphics and Amerindian petroglyphs (*timehri* or stele) on contemporary Caribbean writing. The computer is a vital element in this investigation in that it functions as a means to re-access and reactivate these early forms of expression:

```
            . . . from the fist of my broeken hand
and begin what I call my 'video-style', in which I tr
(y) make the words themselves live off - away from - the 'pa-
ge', so you can see . . .
                . . .like see their sound - techno
logy taking us 'back', I suppose', to the Urals - which is why
I continue to think of the MiddleAges  -  what was happening'
in Europe, the Mediterranean, the Middle East, the Islamic wo
rld of the ILLUMINATED MANUSCRIPTS when the written word
could still hear itself speak, as it were And beyond that, ev
en to the possibility of
```

# HIEROGLYPHICS

> – Egypt, Maya, Aztec – and 'beyond' that even unto *timehri* before fire. (*C* 166-67)

Brathwaite describes *ConVERSations* as a "return, for the first time ... to the Other" (*C* 196-97). The other here is no longer the ancestor as person but the poetic language of ancestral cultures, the "unexplored, ignored, unknown, INCOGNITA areas of Caribbean/American experience" (*C* 197). The return to the other is also a return to the Caribbean imaginary and this in turn is accompanied by a longing for communion, a longing to break out of the boundaries of the self. In *Barabajan Poems*, this breaking out is achieved in the form of the "transboundary" book and in the image of the sea into which the ancestral rivers of the Caribbean flow. In *ConVERSations*, water again appears as a connecting element, but less obviously so, encrypted in the *timehri*. Two references are crucial in creating this new web of cultural interaction. Brathwaite presents a list of authors and artists that have investigated the region's Amerindian heritage in their works. Of particular interest to him are the Guyanese artist Aubrey Williams and the writer Ivan Van Sertima, author of *They Came before Columbus* (1976). In this book, Van Sertima investigates "West and East African explorations of/contact with the Americas — and Pacific Asia and Australasia" (*C* 198) in pre-Columbian times. In other words, the web of connections between the Caribbean and other parts of the world exists independently of European imperialism.[13]

In "Timehri," Brathwaite discusses Aubrey Williams's artistic engagement with Amerindian petroglyphs when he lived among the Warraou Indians of Guyana:

> ... high up on the rocks at Tumatumari, at Imbaimadai, people who were perhaps of Maya origin — the ancestors of the Warraou and others in the area — had made marks, or *timehri*: rock signs, paintings, petroglyphs; glimpses of a language, glitters of a vision of a world, scattered utterals of a remote *Gestalt*; but still there, near, potentially communicative. Sometimes there were sleek brown bodies that could have been antelope or ocelot; there were horns and claws of crabs. There were triangular forms that might have been the mouths of cenotes. But hints only; gateways to intuitions; abstract signals of hieroglyphic art. To confirm that these marks were made by man, imprints

of the etcher's palm were left beside the work; anonymous brands in living stone, imperishable witnesses from past to conscious present. (40)

The underground reservoirs of the *cenotes* encoded into the *timehri* can be read as openings onto the ocean, connecting the Americas with other parts of the globe, linking Amerindian *timehri* to Egyptian hieroglyphs. In this sense, *cenotes* are also "oceans within" the land and are thus in dialogue with Bob'ob's *mkissi*. For Brathwaite, the art of the *timehri* is related "to what we find also preserved in the caves and high ground of other parts of the dry world" (*C* 201), such as the cave paintings of Europe, Africa, and Australia. These art forms express, as Brathwaite suggests, "a way of 'history' before books" (*C* 201). They record an alternative history to colonial history, a web of global connections before colonialism. Brathwaite thus deconstructs the notion of the "prehistoric" as suggestive of the idea that the non-European world was without history until the arrival of the Europeans.

In *ConVERSations*, he relates the art of *timehri* to contemporary creative expression:

```
So I begin to conceive of poetry itself as a kind of timehri:
a human imprint with all that's recorded in and by that impr-
int, into a kind of enduring enigmatic silence - the poem si-
nging back to life when you see it, say it; but that 'silenc
(e)' encoded with that ancient memory - the sound of the fir-
st (forest) trees and rivers, slant of sunlight on the slopes
of mountains, anima of dream and nightmare, the voices of all
those voiceless generations. . . (C 201)
```

The poem as *timehri* becomes a record of the silenced, subjugated and dispossessed people of the world. *Barabajan Poems* and *ConVERSations* can, therefore, be regarded as Caliban's books. In her reading of *Barabajan Poems*, Elaine Savory suggests that "to enter fully into *Barabajan Poems 1492–1992*, it is necessary to understand it as a magic book, in a real sense an answer to the old colonial landlord (Columbus)Prospero's book of spells from *The Tempest*" ("Wordsongs & Wordwounds" 750). Brathwaite's aim is to create an alternative to Prospero's book in his use

## A Creole Experiment

of alternative forms of writing. The *timehri* are "buried far within" the monolithic narrative of colonial history. They are "patches and traces, palimpsests, of cultures some of whose visible signs lead to riches" (Reiss, "Realisms of the Fictive Imagination" 258). In a sense, *timehri* are fragments of Eldorado or "oceans within" Prospero's book, and it is the task of Caliban to create "new events from those breakages ... so that even Eldorado's violence ... can be transformed" (Reiss, "Realisms of the Fictive Imagination" 260).

The *timehri* are thus rivers of ancestral heritage. They extend into the past but also flow into the future. Brathwaite presents an evolution of the concept of *timehri* that mirrors the movement of creative expression through history. From stone-age rock art to poem it proceeds to "prosepoem" (*C* 204) and from there to "video." For the tradition of the poem, Brathwaite cites the poetry of W. B. Yeats and Derek Walcott as representative and Wilson Harris's novels and poems for that of the "prosepoem." Yeats and Walcott work in conventional verse forms, whereas the forms used by Harris move beyond a mere description to an enactment of the movement of consciousness, rendering into visual form "aspect(s) of time/space" (*C* 205). Brathwaite thus distinguishes poem from "prosepoem" in that for him the latter is an open, "pangeneric" form:

I mean one can still write poetry (often a form now *calculated* in ?tranquillity) but there's so much more now to be said, and so many ways of saying it, that, even *within* a poem. . . some. . . . many of us now introduce other forms. Some people introduce clippings, quotations, contextual information, footnotes, video! – all of this so-call 'prose' – so that it's difficult sometimes/often now to know what you're dealing with – except of course the *metaphorical life*, which is where the poem truly resides, within its name, and, without any further excuses or delays, within its **nam** (*C* 231)

In this sense, the "prosepoem" ventures beyond the rigid categories of poetry and prose towards a dynamic, "transboundary" art form, which is a way of decolonizing both genres. That Brathwaite's understanding of "prosepoem" is, to a large extent, informed by an enactment of movement becomes clear in his remark on Harris: ". . . Harris . . . moves us from the vivid but static 'grecian urn' tendency of the antillean 'timehr i,' into closer what I have in mind — carrying the memory of this primeval, translating it into the 'present' . . . " (*C* 203). What Brathwaite has in mind is the idea of "video," which represents "even further movement — like *quetzalcoatl* flying" (*C* 205). In other words, the computer, like "the video of television" (*C* 208), has the potential to transform the written word, so that it can again "*hear itself speak*" (*C* 167).

Brathwaite intends his "video-style" documents to function in the same way as the ancient *timehri*, as public art, as "large-scale statements sh ared at important visible levels by all (many? most?)" (*C* 207). The computer, especially in the form of the world wide web, the hypertextual structure of which Brathwaite imitates, is a more public space than the conventional, printed book, allowing for immediate interaction and dialogue. Brathwaite's "video-style" texts open a new space of poetic expression that can be immediately responded to or shared in by an audience (which is something that the *Save CowPastor* blog makes very poignant). In this sense, the "video style" voices the need to transcend "the present concept of the **4 ½" x 7 ½"** margin **book** with a certain uniform **face**," which, however, "won't interest and therefore can't/won't/won't entertain — hence my struggle with publishers and printers over the presentation . . . of all my new 'Sycorax video-style' stuff" (*C* 167–68). This difficulty in finding publishers ultimately prevents a wide audience from sharing in Brathwaite's creative thinking and also makes a critical engagement with his work very difficult. However, the "video-style" writing is *intended* to be shared as a communal document and thus represents the utopian space of an "ocean within" into which the tradition of the *timehri* and its related art forms flow. The analogy of virtual reality with Quetzalcoatl, the winged serpent of Aztec mythology, exceeds even the utopian image of Damballah, in that Quetzalcoatl lifts off into new dimensions of time and space, "live[s] off — away from — the 'page'" (*C* 166), towards something very different from the conventional book. In his dual nature (snake and bird), Quetzalcoatl bridges the divide between the elements and echoes the connecting ocean of *Barabajan Poems*. Cyberspace is thus another "ocean within," another space of creative or fictive imagination.

## A Creole Experiment

In pointing at the open-ended space of virtual reality in *Barabajan Poems* and *ConVERSations*, Brathwaite succeeds in breaking down the barrier between book and world, writing and the writing life, and thus continues, albeit on a very different level, the Irish Town maroon project. Moreover, he re-establishes communion with the muse, Sycorax, the spirit in the machine. In *ConVERSations*, Sycorax remains submerged in the "underwaters" of the unconscious, in the sea of the computer's virtual space. However, "[t]he invisible mother is one who can inform from afar and through silence" (*C* 191). In this, she becomes one with Mexican, who still functions as muse but is separated from Brathwaite through death.

Finally, the computer becomes the stage for the performance of a jazz suite, which returns us to reflections on sharing and rapport, on the interaction between poet and audience discussed at the beginning of this chapter. Brathwaite illustrates the jazz structure of his poetic language in the poem "Bird: ascending," published in *ConVERSations* and later republished in both versions of *Words Need Love Too*:

> Now the first hills at the darker mountains of english . the sea below
> all shard & silver like our shadow . the
> beacon topaz eyes unblinking even through all the shudder
> the wings now stretched across all space openly & awesomely . so that we are
> not beating any. more but ahh sailing something like singing . because at last
> I have been able
>
> to use all the wounds in the language . as long as I lay them out softly &
> carefully
> like these unfluttering feathers of song . like the sea below turning into a
> grey ball of wine
> without fishes or sperm . like the darkness no longer lingering above us
>
> but we moving towards it as part of its fuse & its future . the àxé & ayisha of
> sails one last time in our ears ... (*C* 206)

The passage echoes one of Brathwaite's jazz poems, "Miles" from the collection *Jah Music* (1986), reprinted in Chapter I of *Barabajan Poems* to illustrate Brathwaite's fascination with the music of Miles Davis:

> *He grows dizzy*
> *with altitude*

> "Oceans within"
>
> *the sun blares*
>
> *he hears*
> *only the brass*
> *of his own mood*
>
> *if he could fly*
> *he would be*
> *an eagle*
> *............*
> *he would see*
> *how the land lies*
> *softly in contours*
>
> *how the fields*
> *lie striped*
>
> *how the houses fit into the valleys*
>
> *he would see cloud lying*
> *on water, moving*
>
> *like the hulls of great ships over the land*
> (*BP* 38)

In his article "Too good for this world?" Jonathan Jones compares jazz, and especially Miles Davis's album *Kind of Blue*, recorded in 1959, to "the flowing lines and improvisational brilliance of Jackson Pollock, who in the late 1940s started to place his canvas on the floor and loosely, rhythmically move around it, flicking, throwing, pouring paint" (5). Jones concludes that "like the great jazz musicians, he was able to loop, stretch and twine his thread of improvisation so that it was both free and somehow structured" (5). The structure of *Barabajan Poems* and *ConVERSations* can be described in the same way, as free and at the same time structured, which echoes the tension between the original oral nature of the texts and their subsequent transformation into hypertext.

Moreover, the idea of sharing that Brathwaite associates with jazz can be read as an expression of the longing for communion and thus for "arrived-at Being" or *Heimat*. In this context, "Miles" merely describes the soaring of the solo act, implying that the soloist has to descend to earth to resume the dialogue with the ensemble. "Bird: ascending," on the other hand, sweeps soloist and ensemble towards the space of *àxé*, towards a new heaven and a new earth, beyond the "darkness of the lived moment." Music, in a sense, becomes *àxé*, the life-force of the universe: ". . . ase is 'the light that crosses through the tray of the earth, the firmament from one side to the other, forward and backward'" (Dos Santos 2 qtd. in Gates 8). Through *àxé* or *ase* the Yoruba creator god Olodumare formed the universe. *Àxé* is also the creative force that works through the "golden space" of the poet's outflowing imagination. Penetrating the horizontal as well as the vertical plane of the universe, *àxé* retraces the two directions in which Ananse spins his web, uniting the ocean and the world tree, thus bringing together all aspects of Brathwaite's vision of utopian space into a single totality.

## Chapter 7
# "The spirits of GOLOKWATI... have led me to this place": *Words Need Love Too* and *Born to Slow Horses*

◇◆◇

### 7.1. "Write it upon my oumfô body": *Words Need Love Too* and the Spirit of Namsetoura

If Brathwaite's work culminating in the publication of *X/Self* (1987) represents a "first cosmology" and his subsequent works record its destruction as well as intimations of a new vision, then this new vision comes into its own in his writings beginning with the first version of *Words Need Love Too*, published in 2000 (*Words* [2000]). This second cosmology is less pristine and optimistic but closer to the notion of "concrete utopia" and closer, too, to what Stewart Brown in his introduction to the second edition of *Words Need Love Too* (*Words* [2004]) calls the "dread and carnage and despair" (xix) that characterizes the reality of life in the Caribbean. In this new vision of the "creole cosmos," place, especially the place where writing happens, becomes central. Moreover, the events and repercussions of 9/11 impact significantly on this second cosmology and on the way the local is perceived in relation to the global.

Brathwaite's recent work is as open-ended and "transboundary" as *Barabajan Poems* and *ConVERSations* and continues to revisit and recontextualize existing poems as well as adding new ones. What is new to these works is that they all contain a reference to Namsetoura, the spirit of CowPastor. Many of the poems also address a community of poets, either regional or global, and thus also echo *Golokwati 2000*.

In *Golokwati 2000*, Brathwaite looks back on his life and work on the occasion of his seventieth birthday. The text assembles an archive of his poems while setting these poems into the context of memories and revelations of how they came to be. Golokwati is a village in Ghana that acquired special meaning for Brathwaite during his Ghana years. Golokwati means "a resting place on a journey" in the Akan Twi language. Much in the same way as *Barabajan Poems*, *Golokwati 2000* is a powerful insight into the development of the poet's imagination and spirituality. Like *Barabajan Poems* and *ConVERSations*, *Golokwati 2000* is a reflection on a public gathering of artists, writers, performers and politicians. The book is also a meditation on the realized space of writing.

Significantly, the acknowledgements page of both versions of *Words Need Love Too* states that *Words* was inspired by the spirit(s) of CowPastor, i.e. its people, its spiritual presences as well as its flora and fauna. *Ancestors*, which reimagines the Barbados of the first cosmology, is likewise dedicated to this place. Although place has always been an important factor in Brathwaite's life and work, dating back to very early pieces such the unpublished "Boy and the Sea," a memoir of the author's growing up in Barbados, place becomes a prominent theme in works written since the author's move to CowPastor. From the very beginning, CowPastor has been a contested place, the poet's right of residence there challenged by the government's decision to build a road through his property, an old plantation ground, allegedly for easier access to the nearby airport. Like Irish Town, CowPastor is more than just a place of writing for the poet as individual. On the website *Save CowPastor*, set up by the Cambridge poet Tom Raworth in support of Brathwaite's battle with the government of Barbados, Brathwaite writes of his dream of establishing a "Bussa Centre":

> The dream the vision was to in-gather the scatta archives (Ja & NYC) here, try heal them and from this wound of miracle, set up a BUSSA CENTRE for us all — enough peace & space & beauty surpassing any other in the world — in a small sacred bless — to build a place to live to love, a place for the LIBRARY OF ALEXANDRIA, a conference room, performance outdoor places, chalets for writers, artists — that kind of possible dream — because we had the dream

"The spirits of GOLOKWATI . . . have led me to this place"

> we had the space we had the means — destroyed by my own Govt - w/out DISCUSSION — and digging us down and STRANGLING the holy past & constellation flute & future of this place.... ("Kamau Brathwaite and CowPastor")

In this sense, CowPastor, "my nation here — my maroon town, resistance palenque" ("Kamau Brathwaite and CowPastor"), continues the maroon project of Irish Town and is another vision of community through writing.[1]

*Words Need Love Too* imagines and celebrates a community of Caribbean artists in the style of the "Bussa Centre." Not only do the poems themselves speak of this community, but the design of the book, too, demonstrates a communal effort. In the first edition of the collection, the poems are interspersed with digital illustrations by various Caribbean artists. The book is an exchange of words and other creative gestures, which in essence is still there in the second edition but less obviously so as it does not feature the art work. However, throughout both versions dedications to loved ones, fellow poets and critics create a sense of dialogue and community. There is more than one voice speaking and there are other listeners and witnesses apart from the reader. The book is full of "presences" in both a physical and spiritual sense. Moreover, some pieces are inspired by music and painting and create a dialogue across creative disciplines. Both editions of *Words Need Love Too* are divided into four parts, the first and the fourth comprising a single poem each. Apart from the digital illustrations, which are absent in the second edition, the two versions differ from each other in that the sequence of poems in Part 3 has been changed in the 2004 version, the "video style" is exploited more fully in this second version, and individual poems have been revised.

Both versions of the collection begin with the record of a telephone conversation between Brathwaite and Jerry Ward in the poem titled "JerryWard & the fragmented spaceship dreamstorie." Jerry Ward had heard a lecture given by Brathwaite at the "Southern Black Cultural Alliance meeting" in Mississippi and subsequently telephoned the poet with comments. Brathwaite himself states that he had forgotten about the incident. The poem thus celebrates the power of words, which lies in their capacity to create their own cosmos:

> ... what i had said thought & felt
> that evening & had allowed it to be cost

*A Creole Experiment*

> by the wayside/ someone unknown & unexpected
> had picked one of the green shoots of metal or mental
> fragment up & planted
> it & it had grown & spread & **flourish**
> perhaps in his own work & person/ality...
> (*Words* [2000] 4)

The words of the poet are not owned exclusively by the poet. They become, in fact, independent entities once they have been uttered by the speaker/writer.

The poem indicates that Brathwaite's lecture revolved around his image of the missile, his metaphor for colonization and conquest. In the course of the poem, the poet's words, too, become missiles sent out into the space between speaker and listener. Brathwaite thus proposes an alternative reading of his own metaphor. Touching down in another person's mind, the image has the power to alter that mind and change that person's world just as the colonial missile did when it touched down in the New World at the end of the fifteenth century (the poem makes a reference to 1492). However, whereas the colonial missile silenced and extinguished the desire for (cross-cultural) exchange, the missile of the poet's word encourages the other to talk back. In *Fantastic Metamorphoses, Other Worlds* (2002), Marina Warner argues that the encounter with the New World profoundly influenced European perceptions of self by "produc[ing] ... rich new materials to think with" (21). "JerryWard" rethinks Brathwaite's metaphor of cultural encounter on a personal level, pointing towards the utopian, mind-changing quality of art, the potential of words to create a world. What we are given here are again the two possibilities of the "creole cosmos," the reality of domination and dependence versus the utopian possibility of a new world order of freedom and a communion of cultures, here condensed into the space of writing, reading and listening.

The theme of love to which the title of the collection refers is most clearly expressed in the last two poems of Part 2, "Défilée" and "Words Need Love Too." "Défilée" is set in Haiti in 1806, two years after the island's independence from France, and is told in the voice of Jean-Jacques Dessalines's lover Défilée. Défilée scours the countryside in search of Dessalines's dismembered body. As a monologue of a lover whom grief and violence have driven to the brink of madness, the poem encompasses the very "dread and carnage and despair" Stewart Brown observes. Défilée's words appear as a dialogue but do not achieve any form of communication with the addressed beloved, who is dead. In this sense, the poem represents the antithesis of "JerryWard." On another level, however, Défilée's words communicate with the reader in the same way as Brathwaite's lecture communicates with Jerry Ward. Moreover, by assuming the voice of Défilée Brathwaite reveals aspects of Haitian (and by extension Caribbean) history that would not find their way easily into the official versions of events, both colonial and anti-colonial. He creates a woman's version of events, a "herstory," a word he later uses in relation to Namsetoura. By focusing on the intimate and private, he reveals just how devastating the impact of violence that followed the Haitian struggle for liberation was. He also concedes that there are aspects to the Haitian slave rebellion that are less than glorious and which are often forgotten or evaded in more celebratory accounts.

Part 2 concludes with the title poem. It is, in the first instance, a poem that celebrates Brathwaite's marriage to his second wife Beverly. But it also, once again, returns to the concerns of "JerryWard." "Words Need Love Too" is an invocation of the power of words to transcend suffering and is thus a direct response to "Défilée." Significantly, the poem begins on a rather violent note:

> you crush my skull
> you force o open cry
> my mouth. red teeth. the deep thought of the gullet
> (*Words* [2000] 22)

In his introduction to the second edition, Stewart Brown reads these lines as "an horrific image of the slave forced to speak even the words of love in that broken *other* tongue of the plantation" (*Words* [2004] xix), an apt association, given that the preceding poem speaks from the context of emancipation. The rest of "Words Need Love Too" becomes a "quest for recovery" (*Words* [2004] xix) of Caliban's own tongue (an echo of "Nametracks"). The poem is a way of making sense of the violence and carnage that pervades life in the Caribbean but also goes beyond that. "Words Need Love Too" is a quest for a new world created through the medium of language.

If the poem opens with Caliban again setting out in search of his tongue as he does in "Nametracks," the remainder of the poem departs from that earlier work, although we find some echoes in the way Brathwaite uses images of water:

> green lakes
> bright flasking rivers. curled quiet rivulet
>
> & glaciers. chipped scented ice in cones. caves
> deep within the limestone soil of sea anemone
> (*Words* [2000] 24)

Brown states that the poem tries to recover the "language that knows the lime-stone caves of Barbados" (*Words* [2004] xx). From *Mother Poem* we know that these caves take on a similar function as the *cenotes* of Mesoamerica. As pointed out in the discussion of "Carab," without the *cenotes* the development of Mayan civilization in Yucatan would have been impossible. By equating words with water, the poet implies that language shapes civilizations, which relates to the image of mud in "Nametracks." In *Mother Poem*, water is an image of the mother, the feminine, Sycorax, and the word "mud," earth mixed with water, itself a play on "mother" ("mudda"). From this fertile ground Caliban grows his own sense of self and his language. This is the soil that nurtures his roots.

"Words Need Love Too" departs from "Nametracks" in that the language sought and found is not so much a form of creole or nation, as it was in "Nametracks," but a language that transcends and at the same time unites all speech communities. In one section of the poem, Brathwaite draws together a list of poets and thinkers who all partake in the struggle to heal the "rotting city" (*Words* [2000] 25), reminiscent of the dystopian cityscapes of *Trench Town Rock* and "Pixie," with words of love.[2] What unites the poets listed by Brathwaite is their love for the language of poetry and their concern for their people. In *Coming to Writing*, Hélène Cixous, herself from a multiracial and multilingual background, speaks of this language as "at once unique and universal":

> There is a language that I speak or that speaks (to) me in all languages. A language at once unique and universal that resounds in each national tongue when a poet speaks it. In each tongue, there flows milk and honey. And this language I know, I don't need to enter it, it surges from me, it flows, it is the milk of love, the honey of my unconscious. (21)

By focusing on the power of poetic language to shape the world, the absence of love and responsibility for that language implies a threat to human civilization, to a people's inspiration, here represented by the

"The spirits of GOLOKWATI . . . have led me to this place"

image of the "rotting city" with its "*monstrous messengers the raped the dead the leprou (s) scavengers*" (*Words* [2004] 32). However, at the end of the poem the poet reaffirms the transformative power of words, speaking on behalf of the community of all poets:

> bringing our lips at last out
>
> not to resist not to resist but kiss
> kiss shapes back into their proper pout
> & speech into their proper sounds
>
> & even beyond these proper sounds
> soft song soft songs
> (*Words* [2000] 28)

This passage also echoes *Shar* in a manner that will frequently recur in the remaining parts of *Words Need Love Too* and in *Born to Slow Horses*: the emphasis on the song that rises out of the "darkness of the lived moment" and transcends the labor of Sisyphus.

In Part 3 of *Words Need Love Too*, Brathwaite revisits a concern that goes back to his early work, such as "Boy and the Sea" and *Islands*, and increasingly engages with, or rather revisits, ecological issues affecting Barbados and the Caribbean at large. Tourism again emerges as a major representative of the region's neocolonial dependence on the affluent west, destroying local "ecosystems," both environmental and cultural. Brathwaite claims that the pasture surrounding his house is the site of an old slave burial ground. He substantiates his claim by pointing out a grove of trees, which would have been held sacred in Africa at the time of slavery. In this grove, the poet encounters the spirit of Namsetoura as he inadvertently stumbles upon her grave.

"Namsetoura" brings together two issues, the already mentioned concern with ecology and independence and the "tidalectic" connection between past and present. "Namsetoura" is the poem that has been most significantly altered in its transition from the first to the second edition of *Words Need Love Too*. One reason may be that Brathwaite simply had more time to make sense of this extraordinary encounter and appropriate the poem's form accordingly. Whereas in the first edition the poem appears as one among many, it becomes the focus of the second edition in such a way that the other poems seem to gravitate around this central event. It is the one poem that makes the most extensive and drastic use of the "video-style" range. Large fonts and extensive "prose" passages set it off from the other poems and mirror the impact this event had on Brathwaite's life.

The circumstances leading up to the poet's encounter with the spirit remain sketchy even in the 2004 edition of *Words*. *Words* leaves out why he felt compelled to take her picture in the first place, but another document, *The Namsetoura Papers* (*NP*), first published in *Hambone* 17 (2004) and also available on the *Save CowPastor* website, gives a detailed account of the event.[3] In *The Namsetoura Papers,* Brathwaite chronicles the acquisition of CowPastor as well as the threat of its loss. The document begins with a detailed atmospheric description of the flora and fauna surrounding the place, almost mirroring the act of photographic record keeping that becomes the subsequent focus. When Brathwaite first hears of the government's plans to build a road through his land, he and Beverly/Dream Chad resign themselves to the fact that they may have to leave CowPastor. In McSweeney's *Raintaxi* interview, Brathwaite states that what he felt for the place was nostalgia and that, as a result of this, he decided to create a photographic record of every detail of the house and surrounding pasture, which was to serve as a memorial to the pasture and the inspiration Brathwaite received from its spiritual presences. This record keeping harks back to the beginning of Brathwaite's work as he himself states. He sees it connected to the writing of *Barabajan Poems* and the first editions of *Mother Poem, Sun Poem* and *X/Self*:

> we be- gin making an inventory of everything in our hearts as I had don those 100 years before when i know i would be leaving this same said eyeland for the first time & not knowing then that it wd be my last
>
> then I walk all the roads & beaches. thirsting up all our images in- to flute into metaphorical harp into what wd become the last will & testament. My hinterland. MotherPoem. SunPoem. BarabajanPoems. X/Self (*NP* 43)

Brathwaite's early memoir, "Boy and the Sea," performed a similar kind of record keeping, as did his walk around the island with a group of friends, which Brathwaite alludes to in the above passage. "Boy and the Sea," which provided material for many of his subsequent texts, comes to stand for a sense of *Heimat* as well as loss and exile — or more precisely, a sense of *Heimat* because of the imminence of loss and exile, a feeling that repeats itself at CowPastor.

"The spirits of GOLOKWATI . . . have led me to this place"

In *The Namsetoura Papers*, CowPastor emerges as a spiritual place, and the everyday flora and fauna, so lovingly detailed, hide its numinous energy. This other reality is revealed when Brathwaite attempts to take a picture of a spider in its web that happens to be in the same spot as Namsetoura's alleged grave. As a manifestation of Ananse, the spider itself holds numinous significance for Brathwaite. But as he looks through the camera lens, the spider is nowhere to be seen. Two cameras mysteriously break before he can take the picture and then he captures not the spider, but the face of Namsetoura herself, whose name is a combination of *nam* and Ananse: "we get this pic. ture. not of spiders spiderwebs. but this. the one shot out of a whole wide roll of blacks & blanks of flim. this **Nam- / setoura**" (*NP* 45). The photo of the spirit appears in *The Namsetoura Papers* and on the dust jacket of *Born to Slow Horses*. The camera seems to open a window onto another, a spirit reality, "its sun's eye illuminating my own eye into the at last spirits & magicals I've nvr known before tho they are here" (*NP* 43). Namsetoura's grave itself, which she claims is in this spot, is a portal to a magical reality and in many ways reminiscent of a *houmfort*. As such it becomes a portal through which the Caribbean imaginary can be accessed. Brathwaite himself describes the "Bussa Centre" as an "oumfô" (*NP* 40), using an alternative, more recognizably creole spelling of *houmfort*. This idea of the place of writing as sacred space links CowPastor to Irish Town.

Interestingly, Namsetoura plays on the two related meanings of possession and thus creates a link to concerns that run through all of Brathwaite's work. The word she uses when addressing the poet is *gyaNyamebiriw*, which has its origins in the Akan Twi language. In the second edition of *Words Need Love Too* Brathwaite states that *gyaNyame* means "only God," Nyame being the Akan supreme deity. The second half of the word, *biriw*, implies possession "in both its senses" (*Words* [2004] 78), i.e. spirit possession and possession in terms of ownership. Both types of possession acquire a sacred quality due to the presence of Nyame in the same word. Brathwaite traces both meanings back to related words in the Twi language: *abíribiriw*, "epilepsy. sacred insanity. possession" (*Words* [2004] 78), and *biribíwa*, "the little property which is (still) left to me" (*Words* [2004] 78). The poet himself reads this last meaning "like a ref to CowPastor" (*Words* [2004] 78) where her grave is situated. Echoing many other instances in his work, Namsetoura is an African spirit who has taken possession of the Caribbean soil, reminding the poet of his duty to defend his and her plot of land:

## A Creole Experiment

> *yu tink dey*
> *dispossessin u? Yu tink u tall? you tink u*
> *rastamouttamassacouraman?*
>
> . . . . . . . . . . . . .
> *Write dis in flash*
> *befo de nex red season come*
>
> *Doan write it down in coral . dat is water .*
> *dat will spill*
>
> *Write it upon my oumfô body*
> *berry berry burnin coal*
>
> (*Words* [2004] 83-84)

Namsetoura's injunction compels Brathwaite to fight for his right to remain resident at CowPastor and to prevent the destruction of the pasture, including the grove of sacred trees that allegedly harbors her grave. Interestingly, in Namsetoura's command, writing becomes synonymous with political action; the word is believed to have the power to shape reality. As her body is inscribed, her grave is marked; it becomes real. Writing will give Namsetoura a reality and visibility she would otherwise lack. Her inscribed body becomes witness to what has been written out of official colonial records. As discussed in chapter three, Brathwaite argues that the body of the slave was an archive that preserved the memory of his/her ancestral heritage: "The knowledge is withim. . . . There could be no 'forget' since there was 'nothing' to forget and <u>nam</u> is immemorial. The gods, therefore, do not 'survive', they wait they listen they remain as ancient and as modern as the morning star" (*Gods of the Middle Passage* 7).

Despite her centrality to his project, there seems to be no archaeological evidence that a grave actually exists in the spot where Brathwaite encounters Namsetoura, although for him a grove of what he calls sacred trees is suggestive of African burial customs:

and right on the ridge. behind the old ruin of the slave attendant cabin a calabash a clammacherry an old cordial. nunu. nuni. and a dark obscure i don't even kno.

> some croton and a small army of the smallest cactus you have ever seen.
>
> and all these in a space & time *relation* to each other and now to somehow *me*. these xtrasensory & semination < *signs* that usually mark the graveyards of the Africas (*NP* 5)

However, an excavation site exists not far from CowPastor at Newton, which contains the oldest and largest slave graveyard in the Caribbean, often compared in its importance to the one that was found in Manhattan. In *The Namsetoura Papers*, Brathwaite creates a connection between CowPastor and Newton. Both are old plantation grounds with still existing slave outhouses. Newton also contains the only "prone burial" in the area, which is referred to as "Burial 9," "unique not only to Newton but also to early African cemetery sites in the Americas" (Handler). The grave contains "a young adult female, around 20 years of age ... probably interred during the late 1600s and early 1700s" (Handler).

Publications on West African burial practices reveal that prone burials were only performed under exceptional circumstances, usually when "the person was considered to have socially negative traits or had been convicted of witchcraft, a criminal offence in all West African societies" (Handler). The archaeologists, therefore, conclude that Burial 9 contains a "witch or sorceress — in any case, someone who, following African custom, was feared or socially ostracized because she was a vehicle of supernatural contagion" (Handler). These passages from the *African-American Archaeology Newsletter* discussing the Newton graveyard are cited verbatim in *The Namsetoura Papers* and are followed by a description of Brathwaite's encounter with Namsetoura. The poet superimposes both sites, and the woman of Burial 9 becomes a twin to Namsetoura, if not Namsetoura herself.

If we accept this identification, then Namsetoura is a witch and sorceress and thus closely related to Sycorax, chiding Brathwaite/Caliban for "eatin de backra culcha" (*Words* [2004] 83), i.e. giving in to the government's demands to surrender his, and most of all her, land. Hand in hand with this act of "eatin de backra culcha" goes Brathwaite's use of the standard language, which Namsetoura viciously attacks. She is, therefore, a much angrier version of the Sycorax of "Nametracks." What is most striking about Namsetoura's language is its explicit sexual nature, which she combines with a deeply sacred meaning. When she alerts the poet to his duty to save her "little property," she does so by reminding him that she is his (fore)mother and, pointing to her sexual organs, that he was born from her "sacred pussy" (*Words* [2004] 79). She puns on "Bosomtwi," the name of a sacred lake in Africa (in many ways similar to Brathwaite's image of Lake Chad), saying "bosomtwa" instead, which Brathwaite translates as "the sacred lake of pussy" (*Words* [2004] 79). What is implied here is the nurturing and life-generating quality of Namsetoura's female body. She is, like Brathwaite's other mother figures, associated with water and the physical as well as spiritual sustenance this association implies. Brathwaite frequently refers to a "wet-season pond," which is of crucial importance to the ecosystem of the pasture and was essential in sustaining the lives of the slaves in previous centuries ("from Kamau: TWO SMALL VICTORIES"). This well is close to the sacred grove of trees, the place of Namsetoura's grave. Construction work for the aforementioned airport expansion had filled it with rubble when Brathwaite was writing about these events in 2005/6. Echoing the empty *cenotes* of "Carab," the filled-in well becomes an epitome of the threat to Caribbean culture and human civilization for which the struggle over CowPastor comes to stand.[4] In a sense, the pond is an echo of Namsetoura's "sacred pussy," and this she asks the poet to protect.

Although Namsetoura is a manifestation of Sycorax, Brathwaite also aligns her with Oya, santería goddess of the storm, and Erzulie Dantor, the Petro aspect of the Haitian *loa* of love, because of her independent, outspoken nature. We first encountered Erzulie as goddess of love and consort of Xango at the end of *X/Self*. In her Petro aspect she is often depicted as a black Madonna with a child in her arms. According to voodoo tradition, Dantor fought in the Haitian slave rebellion, and some writers perceive a distinct link between the rebellion and the rites of the Petro cult. Maya Deren writes:

> It was the Petro cult ... which gave both the moral force and the actual organization to the escaped slaves who ... swooped down upon the plantations and led the rest of the slaves in the revolt that, by 1804, had made of Haiti the second free colony in the western hemisphere, following the Unites States. Even today the songs of revolt, of "Vive la liberté", occur in Petro ritual as a dominant theme. (62)

"The spirits of GOLOKWATI . . . have led me to this place"

Dantor embodies the spirit of rebellion, the desire to throw off the yoke of enslavement. Despite being an inspiration to the slaves of Haiti, she had her tongue cut out by her own people, who feared she would betray their secrets if she were captured by the French (Brown, *Mama Lola* 229). Therefore, when she appears among worshippers, Dantor does not speak but communicates through guttural sounds and body language alone, forced into silence by those closest to her.

The ostracized individual of Burial 9 echoes Dantor's mutilation. Namsetoura, too, is mutilated. Her photo shows her with only one human eye, the other is a bright disk. In the poem, Brathwaite refers to her as "brutalize":

> yr sweet mouth bash
>
> & brutalize
> my sister mother o my aunt my ancestor
> the one eye sink away from her(s)
> -tory
> (*Words* [2004] 81–82)

Namsetoura's unconventional, rebel sexuality brings her closest to Dantor. Dantor refuses marriage with any of the *loa* who are regarded as her sexual partners and raises her daughter on her own. However, she frequently participates in ritual marriages with the living, and some of these marriages are with women.[5] Thus she emerges as an independent childbearing woman, who defies conventional sexuality and the authority of the patriarchal family (Brown, *Mama Lola* 228–29). Instead she offers the possibility of having a child without a man. In doing so she also offers an alternative family structure — one which reflects the all-female households characteristic of many Caribbean societies, where urban unemployment forces women to rely on their own resources and husbands and fathers are often absent.[6] Hand in hand with the economic situation of the Caribbean goes the fact that many traditions and customs are handed down through the female line, from mother to daughter. Brathwaite alludes to this tradition by frequently stressing the role of women as guardians of *nam*. In this context, Namsetoura's refererence to her childbearing capacity but not to a husband or lover is interesting to note. Equally significant is Brathwaite's explicit mentioning of the term "herstory." Although a dated concept, Brathwaite's use of "herstory" shows his concern with silenced individuals and eclipsed histories as well as an awareness of how the mechanisms of silencing have historically affected women to a greater extent than men.

Another Erzulie figure, who, as mentioned earlier, also tells "herstory," is Défilée. "Défilée" and "Namsetoura" overlap in a variety of ways. The context of the Haitian slave rebellion is very prominent in both poems as Haiti and Barbados are superimposed upon each other. The rebellious character of Barbadian Namsetoura echoes the slave rebels of Haiti, and Brathwaite's struggle against the Barbadian government is set in the same context. He refers to the time when he takes her picture as "March 1804 — under threat of xpropriation from the Govt of France" (*Words* [2004] 78). The Haiti of "Défilée," on the other hand, acquires characteristics of the Barbados pastures: "Cows on this dry pasture all my strife provide me meat goats. / **blackbelly** sheep are here" (*Words* [2000] 19). (Blackbelly sheep are a type of goat native to the pastures of Barbados.) Moreover, Dessalines is wearing a "ruby ring," a sign that he has undergone ritual marriage with Erzulie. As a warrior he is also reminiscent of the *loa* Ogoun, one of Dantor's lovers. Thus Défilée emerges as a very strong manifestation of Erzulie.

As sorceresses and madwomen, Namsetoura, Défilée, and Dantor are women on the margins of their communities. In this sense, they would usually remain invisible, like Sycorax, who in *The Tempest* is present only as an absence. By making them visible and heard, Brathwaite creates what can be called a feminist counter-image to Caliban. Dantor/Namsetoura is in my opinion a stronger image than his invention of Caliban's Sister Stark. Stark remains a somewhat flat and underdeveloped character in Brathwaite's gallery of plantation types (see *Barabajan Poems*), whereas Erzulie is actually claimed by many feminist Caribbean writers as an embodiment of their very own experience of history. Joan Dayan, for example, argues that "Erzulie ... tells the history of women's lives that has not been told" ("Erzulie" 43). Dayan criticizes the prominence of Caliban as an image of Caribbean identity because it eschews the female perspective (Torres-Saillant, *Caribbean Poetics* 71 ff). Therefore, she proposes Erzulie as a female counterpart. In this context, the fact that "Défilée" is partly dedicated to Joan Dayan seems to be no coincidence.

By describing Namsetoura in terms of the rebel spirit Dantor (and also Nanny, whose name Namsetoura herself mentions), Brathwaite sets Barbados in the context of other Caribbean histories. Whereas Jamaica, where he built his first creole maroon home, actually has a tradition of maroon resistance, Barbados, Brathwaite argues, has always been a "total plantation" ("Xtendting the CP Dicscourse" 13). The slaves and their descendants never owned the pastures on which they lived, unlike the maroons in other parts of the Americas: "... historically the black people of this island, descendants of slavery, were not allowed to own land — were not even permitted to build unless the houses were of a certain dimension, made of a certain material and shd have no foundational connection w/the earth — a terrible metonym in itself" ("Xtendting the CP Dicscourse" 6). These chattel houses are a unique phenomenon of Barbados, and together with the pasture they are, at least for Brathwaite, the island's only "spiritual alternative" (13) to the modern plantation of tourism and foreign capitalism. What is significant in this context is that Brathwaite's project of the "Bussa Centre" envisages a set of chattel houses that could be used by writers and artists.

Another feature unique to Barbados and significant in Brathwaite's struggle to preserve the pastures and their history is Thyme Bottom, "what in Ja we wd call a Free Village," the closest thing Barbados has to maroon heritage: "... the slaves of this plantation lived along this ridge and what we had here until a few weeks agao was their descendants — who turned to independent cattling (hence CowPasture) and blackbelly sheep herding, gardening, welding, seamstresses etc and a foreday morning horizon of cocks..." ("Letter... to... Mervyn Morris"). Brathwaite's struggle to preserve this heritage through the "Bussa Centre" becomes a form psychological *maronage* in opposition to capitalist interests in the island, and Namsetoura's grave emerges as the spiritual hub — the *houmfort* — of this project.

The pasture is also the only arable area on the island and its eradication through the creation of new roads and golf courses is of considerable political significance. As Brathwaite and many other writers from the Caribbean and Latin America have argued, sugar introduced a monoculture economy, "consuming the alluvial pockets & terraces for centuries," making sustainable farming and local self-sufficiency virtually impossible (Brathwaite, "Letter... to... Mervyn Morris").[7] However, Brathwaite's idea of self-sufficiency, which has its roots in the history of the maroon communities and their descendants, the Rastafarians, goes beyond the purely economic. First and foremost he is concerned with cultural and spiritual independence, and for this reason the preservation of Namsetoura's "little plot of land" is so vital to his project.

"Namsetoura" brings together the feeling of dread and despair that pervades some of the other poems, but the perception of her grave site as magical space also points to the utopian potential within this "darkness of the lived moment." Brathwaite even goes as far as to say that catastrophe often leads to magical realism or a magical reality.[8] This comes very close to Bloch's idea of "concrete utopia" which begins in darkness, the "dread and carnage and despair" of the here and now, and moves towards the light of a new dawn. In this context, the position of "Namsetoura" in the collection is significant. As mentioned before, in the second edition of *Words Need Love Too* the sequence of poems in Part 3 has been altered. In both versions "Namsetoura" is followed by "Xango at the Summer Solstice" but preceded by different poems: in the first edition by "Bamako Poem," an impression of the city of Bamako in Africa, and in the second edition by "Praise Poem," which in the first edition preceded "Bamako Poem." This shift of "Praise Poem" alters the tone of the entire collection.

Dedicated to Brathwaite's sister Mary Morgan, the poem gives a sense of closure to the poet's "time of salt." In one respect, the writing of "Praise Poem" is another instance of "walking back across this broken ground" that was taking place between himself and his sister after Mexican's death. Although the poem evokes these past sorrows, the reader has a sense that the "time of salt" is over once and for all when the poet says:

> Give thanks & praises for the scars. for those
> recovering us our names. nourbese & richard allsopp
> all bruce st john's insistant bajan studyation of our pebble
>
> tongues.... (*Words* [2004] 76)

The poem is a form of stocktaking and also an appraisal of the community of Caribbean artists. In many ways, "Praise Poem" echoes the Golokwati gathering and is thus also connected to "Mountain," which appears towards the end of *Born to Slow Horses* and makes direct reference to the meeting in Jamaica. At the same time, "Praise Poem" reflects Brathwaite's sense of defeat in the face of the government's plans to destroy CowPastor and the surrounding pasture land and is thus connected to the nostalgic record keeping at the beginning of *The Namsetoura Papers*. The poem is an elegy to times gone by, to a Barbados of the past, and marks that point of deep despair that is challenged when he encounters the anger and rebellious energy of Namsetoura. The poem also represents a point of closure. In a final backward glance it evokes the Barbados of the first *Mother Poem*, the first cosmology and the "time of salt" that followed.

"The spirits of GOLOKWATI . . . have led me to this place"

The last poem of the collection, "Agoue," is in many ways also a praise poem, celebrating the *loa* of the sea. The poem harks back to the first vision of the "creole cosmos," not least in its celebratory tone, but it also creates a bridge to the vision of *Born to Slow Horses*. Also published in *Jah Music* (1986), "Agoue" sums up the endeavor of the whole collection, combining "the music [of] im brooks. the vision [of] temne callender. the painting gérard valsin" (*Words* [2004] 91) with the words and vision of Brathwaite himself. In this sense, the poem becomes a communal arts project, bringing together works from different artists and disciplines and thus summarizing the endeavor of the collection as a whole.

The beginning of "Agoue" echoes the creation story in Genesis. The biblical tone is sustained throughout the poem but its meaning is frequently undermined by references to voodoo. Agoue himself is introduced as "king of kings" (*Words* [2004] 94), "offering to us the leaves & fishes / of his peace" (*Words* [2004] 95), which associates him with Christ. In this respect, the arrival of Agoue echoes the arrival of Xango at the end of *X/Self* (1987). Both are imagined as creole messiahs. Agoue is also described as the center of "the world's kingdooms" (95), which links him to the messiah of "Kingston in the Kingdom of this World" (*Trench Town Rock*), imprisoned in his suburban home. Agoue, however, has left the "rotting city" behind. In his divine authority with which he oversees creation he is closer to the Xango of the "first cosmology." However, as a creation of Brathwaite's "post-salt" period, Agoue himself carries the experience of the poet's "time of salt," which makes the celebratory tone at once mellower and more intense.

The arrival of Agoue among the worshippers marks the beginning of a voodoo ceremony. In this sense, too, it is closely related to "Xango," which begins with creation through sex and ends with an instance of possession, but whereas "Xango" ends with X/Self's homecoming to himself through possession, "Agoue" ends with the poet departing to "the distance ilannn of sounn" (*Words* [2004] 103). Here possession is explicitly linked to the act of writing and the search for dreams and inspiration. The island from which the *loa* arrives and to which the poet departs as he is writing the poem is at once the Guinée of the ancestral spirits and the poet's own personal space of writing — a space that has not yet been reached, of writing that is yet to be done. This dream island is the magical location, where the imaginary and the symbolic, spirit possession and writing come together. It is the "Bussa Centre" realized on the page and in the mind of the poet. His departure for that place also adds a new dimension to the idea of homecoming and "arrived-at

Being": *Heimat* contains within itself the possibility of new destinations, of other utopian spaces, which is the focus of *Born to Slow Horses*.

## 7.2. "Approaching the new life of Eleuthera": *Born to Slow Horses*

*Born to Slow Horses* (*BTSH*), published in 2005 and winner of the Griffin Poetry Prize in 2006, begins with three seascape poems, thus thematically relating to the end of *Words Need Love Too*. Yet *Born to Slow Horses* is more ambitious in scope and scale than *Words*. Structured in seven parts, the book is described by Joyelle McSweeney as "a composite text, including prophecy and anecdote, drum song and jazz riffs, unconventional forms working personal, national, and international events into the mother matter of history and memory." Although the dust jacket of *Born to Slow Horses* shows the picture of Namsetoura, the poem of the same title is not the main focus of the collection. Instead the events of 9/11, dealt with in the longest poem of the sequence, "Hawk," take precedence. Therefore, whereas *Words Need Love Too* emphasizes the local, Barbadian context, *Born to Slow Horses* concentrates on how the local relates to the global.

The events of 9/11 add a new dimension to the "creole cosmos." In this sense, *Born to Slow Horses* harks back to the political concerns rather than the mythical themes of *X/Self*. Like *X/Self*, which read creolization as a global phenomenon, *Born to Slow Horses* views world politics through a particularly Caribbean lens. We see events unfolding in the same "labyrinth of past/present/future" applied in that earlier book, but the "post-salt" "magical montage" adds elements that are not yet fully developed in the first edition of *X/Self*. *Born to Slow Horses* not only fuses different voices but also different styles, genres, and art forms, such as "audioglyphs" (of which later). Thus we are confronted with a more developed "video style," an element already there in *Words Need Love Too*, a form that has managed to fulfill Brathwaite's vision of simultaneous perception.

An example of the simultaneous perception of past, present and future is the last poem of the first section, "Guanahani." It pictures the poet in an airplane "flying over the Bahamas 12 Oct 1492" (*BTSH* 7). This, together with its title, places the poem firmly within the context of the Columbian colonization of the region. "Guanahani" describes the poet surveying the geography of the post-9/11 world. The plane leaves from the east coast of North America, Brathwaite's second home, heading for "the Bahamas where it will be light" (*BTSH* 8) via central

"The spirits of GOLOKWATI . . . have led me to this place"

Asia, the new "enemy" of the west. The subheading of the poem states that "the cold front from the North we are leaving is following us South bringing this kind of history" (*BTSH* 7), implying that the history of imperialism moved (and still moves) from north to south and west to east. The weather, the "cold front," becomes a carrier of culture, which is reminiscent of Brathwaite's observations about the *harmattan* discussed in chapter one. Here as there nature mirrors culture, and geography and meteorology are metaphors of historical processes. In *X/Self* the *harmattan* is a metaphor of the Caribbean's ancestral connection with Africa, posing an alternative frame of reference to the "christian ocean," the colonial connection between the Caribbean and Europe. In *Born to Slow Horses*, the "christian ocean" has become the "cold front" that envelops the globe, thus linking the imperialism of earlier centuries with contemporary forms of globalization and neocolonialism. The post-9/11 freedom fighters/terrorists of central Asia mirror the Vietcong and maroons of *X/Self*. Mt Blanc, too, has acquired a more contemporary twin, Guantanamo Bay. Even more so than in *X/Self*, the United States emerges as a major, if not *the* major, global imperial force, the global "cold front" moving south. Guantanamo itself is described as a place exposed to the vagaries of the weather and the seemingly random legislation of the United States government:

unplacated in cages
their heads & faces. their full souls & bodies. xpose to the weather. not

even like horses or cattle w/out rights against torture
& the soft hiss of injustice & patience & poultice

(*BTSH* 11)

Guantanamo echoes Toussaint's cold prison and eventual grave in the Jura Mountains. Therefore, the fact that Mt Blanc is mentioned only two lines above the passage just cited is no coincidence. Brathwaite seeks to create an obvious parallel between the two imperial forces and the two cultural metaphors of imprisonment.

The poet's flight in the airplane is not just a survey of the map of world politics unfolding below him but rather a meditation on the history of the Americas to which central Asia has been tied ever since 9/11. Moreover, the phrase "flying over the Bahamas 12 Oct 1492" suggests that Brathwaite sees himself in the position of Columbus just before landfall or "touchdown," watching the Caribbean from the cockpit of the colonial missile, glimpsing the "sweet sweep of the land to the sea before the building of houses. no / tourisses yet surfing" (*BTSH* 10). Yet this supposedly pre-Columbian landscape already encodes post-Amerindian history, "how it is formed from unknown but not forgotten African fingers" (*BTSH* 10). In fact, the landscape reveals past, present and future simultaneously. Time is a spatial arrangement rather than a line of successive events. The landscape also keeps a record of Brathwaite's own writing life, particularly his writing of *Mother Poem*. Landscape and book become one and the same. Guanahani is thus also Barbados, with the island selling its beaches to tourists in many ways an echo of that first island claimed by Columbus for the monarchs of Spain.

The idea of landscape as text is a theme that harks back to the notion of *timehri* in *ConVERSations* and the landscape as repository of creative inspiration that was the focus of *Barabajan Poems*. In "Guanahani," the poet sees the "landscape unfolding like scroll like metaphor" (*BTSH* 12). This is reminiscent of Wilson Harris's notion of "living landscapes," an idea he first conceived when he was a land surveyor in the interior of Guyana: "The landscape possessed a life, because, the landscape, for me, is like an open book, and the alphabet with which one worked was all around me" ("The Music of Living Landscapes" 3).[9] The landscape of "Guanahani" exists in a space-time continuum of past, present and future. The latter enters the poem as Brathwaite travels from central Asia back into the Caribbean, where he discovers "causeways into another continuum" (*BTSH* 12). As he finds himself "approaching the new life of Eleuthera" (*BTSH* 12), the future acquires a utopian dimension and the landscape becomes a place where the texts of the past and present are reimagined and rewritten.

Like Guanahani, Eleuthera is an island that belongs to the Bahamas. Its name, derived from the Greek, means "freedom." It becomes the utopian space of the whole collection. Mentioned in a number of poems, Eleuthera is closely related to Guanahani but also goes beyond it, releasing the utopian potential of the historical moment the latter island stands for. As Brathwaite rewrites his own image of the missile in "JerryWard," he now rewrites Columbus's first landfall in the Americas, imagining it as a utopian moment as well as an act of (literary) creation. Brathwaite states that "the first ever light ... will be Guanahani" (*BTSH* 12), echoing again the biblical creation story. Columbus's first landfall in the Americas on 12 October 1492 was the moment when the Caribbean as it now exists was first created. However, since here landscape and history are also text, the text can be opened to new readings. Creation can begin all over again, and this is what happens in the last two sections of "Guanahani," where Brathwaite begins to write "the first poem," which is filled with "so much hope" and appears "like schools / of fish migrating towards homeland. into the bright / light of xpectation" (*BTSH* 13), evoking the connotations of *Heimat* and "arrived-at Being."

By pointing to the utopian potential of the Columbian "discovery," Brathwaite's work echoes that of Wilson Harris, who focuses on the utopian dimension of the Eldorado legend. It marks not only a new vision of Caribbean history — a way of thinking differently about that history — but also ushers in the new, "post-salt" phase of Brathwaite's own work, of which "Guanahani" is, figuratively speaking, the "first poem." Thus Eleuthera itself is less important as an actual geographical location than as a space of writing, where freedom from colonial bondage can be imagined and created. Therefore, Brathwaite's listing of names such as Bogle, Michael Manley and Bob Marley towards the end of the poem, people who have fought for the region's freedom and independence, is no coincidence. Eleuthera is also a space where the poet is allowed to dream of these new possibilities. However, for a dream to be more than an individual endeavor it needs a space where it can be shared and converted into collective vision. CowPastor and the "Bussa Centre" are envisioned as such a place.

The theme of landscape as text and source of metaphor is taken up again in "MMassaccourraamann," a piece in which Brathwaite responds to three collections of poetry by the Guyanese-Canadian poet Cyril Dabydeen. Focusing in particular on Dabydeen's *Stoning the Wind* (1994), the form of "MMassaccourraamann" is a mixture of personal observation, academic essay and letter. Leading on from the "missile" theme, Brathwaite's reading of Dabydeen centers on "cultural icons" and the way their perception is influenced by the poet's changing environment. He also reflects on two different generations of Caribbean writers, represented by Sam Selvon, of whom Dabydeen creates an intimate portrait, and Dabydeen himself. Both writers moved away from the Caribbean, Selvon first to Britain, then to Canada, but whereas Selvon felt in exile in both places, Dabydeen begins to undergo a change of consciousness induced by the landscape of Canada, "the tropical colonial adjusting to the new << landscape of colder alien metaphor" (*BTSH* 51).[10]

Significantly, Dabydeen's and Selvon's interaction takes place in a hotel room, a place symbolizing transit if not exile and thus for Brathwaite related to the Middle Passage. In this hotel room, both poets relive the Middle Passage together on a number of different levels:

"MiddlePassage of history . African/East Indian . Middle Passages into the Atlantic of the prairies . into the prayers & xpensinve xpanses of xile . MiddlePassages of career & tired hopeful talent . MiddlePassages of middlelife . two ships crossing each other's meridiam in a living hotel of sleep" (*BTSH* 50). Moreover, both poets are "shipmates," recognizing kinship through the ancestral experience of the transatlantic crossing. Brathwaite uses a Caribbean paradigm to read human experience, but he also implies that these regional paradigms are fluid and that their meanings evolve as the poet enters a different environment. Dabydeen's own metaphors are beginning to change, although Brathwaite finds him "still clinging to the old colonial ikons. glim(p)sing the northernAmerindian alliance. but not yet ready for it. not yet ceritain how to handle it and if handling it makes sense in im own personal/cultural situation" (*BTSH* 51). To highlight the connection between the poet and the Amerindian presence, the poem's title refers to an Amerindian spirit, the same spirit Brathwaite sees embodied in Carl Abrahams's Columbus, depicted on the dust jacket of the 1987 edition of *X/Self*.

In section iii of *Born to Slow Horses*, where "MMassaccourraamann" appears, Brathwaite introduces the dark side of the utopian prophecy represented by Eleuthera. This dystopian aspect and by now well-known, even essential element of his "video-style" work dominates the middle parts of the collection with foreshadowings "of the Middle-Passage-conseQuences in what is now call <9/11>" (*BTSH* 53). He perceives echoes of these events in the title poem of Dabydeen's collection, where we see Dabydeen's father

> a Muslim . . . /
> Non-believer –
> . . . who stood aloof,
> . . . . . . . . . . . .
>     tearing at the silhouette
>     of the wind –

and his "mother / collapsing / on ruinous ground" (Dabydeen 30–31 qtd. in *BTSH* 53–54). The twin towers themselves, of course, are cultural icons, the destruction of which dramatically rearranges the "cosmological equilibrium" (*BTSH* 53 n17) not only of New York and the United States but of the whole world. The destruction of the towers also radically changes the constellations of power within Brathwaite's "creole cosmos."

"The spirits of GOLOKWATI . . . have led me to this place"

The central poem of the collection that deals with the 9/11 attacks is "Hawk," which is closely related to "MMassaccourraamann" not only thematically but also through the "simultaneous multiple representation" (*BTSH* 50) of time and space. This space-time continuum creates the "magical realism" that resonates with Brathwaite and which he believes to be "[t]he very heart of jazz & metaphor" (*BTSH* 50 n12). Jazz also provides the underlying theme and structure of "Hawk." Brathwaite conceives the poem as an "audioglyph" (*BTSH* 115), a piece that combines the visual and the audible. Like the pieces of *Words Need Love Too*, "Hawk" is the product of many artists, especially musicians, such as the jazz saxophonist Hawk (Coleman Hawkins) himself, as well as Bob Marley, John Coltrane and Nina Simone — to name only a few. Here we really hear the "*voice* of the fonts" (*C* 176) if we imagine the music of these artists as we read the poem. Here Brathwaite succeeds in "convert[ing] script into sound" (*C* 216). More so than any other poem in this or others of his collections, "Hawk" is a work imagined as performance. Brathwaite states in his conversation with Joyelle McSweeney: "It was performed here in Barbados to a soundtrack of Coleman Hawkins' 'Body and Soul', and I used some video from the 9-11 disaster, and I had children's voices, and the collapsing of the towers, things like that" (McSweeney).

In his note at the end of the poem, Brathwaite writes that "in the performance or audioglyph version of this poem. there shd be two murals corresponding in spirit to the *MARASSA* (Twins) of the twin towers" (*BTSH* 115). One of these murals is meant to consist "of sound. grounded on Hawk's Body & Soul . . . falling shimmering & rising continuously behind the poem" (*BTSH* 115), the other of "the names of the beloved dead . . . spoken in all the various accents tongues of speech of the bereave" (*BTSH* 115). *Body & Soul* is regarded as Coleman Hawkins's master piece, recorded in 1939, and its solo consists of two perfectly balanced improvisations, "these future towers of his solo master piece" (*BTSH* 97), as Brathwaite calls them, thus mirroring the structure of the rising and falling twin towers. This idea of doubling or twinning is carried over into the time structure of the poem. "Hawk" begins on 11 September 1967 with Brathwaite attending a concert given by Hawkins in London. The concert features *Body & Soul*. In a similar way to "Stoning the Wind," Brathwaite perceives foreshadowings in *Body & Soul* that hint at the events of 9/11 in its rising and falling double structure. In 1967, the poet finds himself not only reading but also listening to the future. Both past and future happen simultaneously, running next to each other in parallel (twin) columns.

## A Creole Experiment

Brathwaite's reference to the twin towers as Marassa, the twins of voodoo culture who are believed to be the parents of the race, adds a curious twist to the collection as a whole. The World Trade Center is the icon of a culture that Brathwaite has thus far labeled as imperial and hegemonic. However, describing the towers as Marassa dismantles the all too easy binarism of oppressor and oppressed. The Marassa themselves represent a concept that undermines or transcends duality, an idea discussed in relation to "Dream Crabs": "In Voudoun one *and* one make three . . . ; for the *and* of the equation is the third . . . part . . . , the relationship which makes all the parts meaningful" (Deren 41). In this sense, they represent a different way of thinking to the "us" versus "them" ideology that pervades the post-9/11 world in various guises.

In this context, also significant to note is that Brathwaite lived only a few blocks away from the twin towers when the attack happened. Therefore, his comparing the catastrophe around him to the destruction of his Jamaican home by Hurricane Gilbert, "the debris falling from the air of shar" (*BTSH* 98), comes as no surprise. He subsequently aligns the attack on the World Trade Center with a number of world catastrophes, both natural and man-made. In the process, the New Yorkers running from the falling debris become witnesses to all those other catastrophes gone before: "our souls sometimes far out ahead already of our surfaces / and our life looking back / salt. as in Bhuj. in Grenada. Guernica. Amritsar. Tajikistan" (*BTSH* 101). Brathwaite's use of the pronoun "our" in this context is of interest. In a similar movement to "Dream Haiti," the poet has joined the people around him in their suffering, suggesting that the citizens of New York are part of *"the poor & the helpless the cold the hungry / les damnés de la terre"* (*BTSH* 107).

Asking "what is the word for this high rafter of suicide," the poet admits that there is no word for it; what he is experiencing is "the tsunami loss of my Mother the Noun" (*BTSH* 101). In the face of this human catastrophe, language fails the poet and the society in which he lives. This repeats the notion of the intimate connection between language and civilization that was the major theme in *Words Need Love Too*. That language should fail that part of the world that is the heir of centuries of European colonialism, which was experienced in the Caribbean as linguistic oppression as much as anything else, is of immense significance. 9/11 has been perceived as an attack on a whole civilization, hitting its most prominent icon, its "crystal crash cenote" (*BTSH* 97). Although echoing the water resources that made possible the Mayan civilization on the Yucatan peninsula, the shimmering crystal

"The spirits of GOLOKWATI . . . have led me to this place"

towers are only an illusion of water. The association of the towers with a *cenote* encodes Brathwaite's metaphors of missile and circle. As tall structures the towers are missiles, indicative of the imperial power of the United States. Certain of its superiority, the missile stands out and becomes a target easy to destroy. Water, on the other hand, is pliable and thus a prime image of survival. The pliability of water is echoed in the music of Coleman Hawkins. Jazz, an expression of another circle culture, is able to rise, fall and rise again, to build anew from the ashes of devastation (echoing the idea of singing in *Shar*), whereas the towers of the missile culture can only rise and fall once.

"Hawk" is at once personal commemoration and public memorial. As a personal statement it encodes Brathwaite's time in London at the beginning and the loss of Mexican at the end of the poem:

> my beloved
>
> aXe
>
> aXe
>
> àXé
>
> before these worlds falling clawes
> i lose
>
> u
>
> (*BTSH* 113)

At the same time, the loss of Mexican becomes the loss of all loved ones in the attack. "Hawk" is a public statement of great compassion, and the mixing and intertwining of metaphors that in other works by Brathwaite represent distinct cultures shows how his vision of the "creole cosmos" is changing into something altogether new. "[T]his poem's world" is one in which "New York Rwanda Kingston Iraq Afghanistan" (*BTSH* 105) are joined in the same calamity of loss, and the distinction between oppressor and oppressed ceases to exist.

In this context, Brathwaite's foregrounding of women's suffering is interesting. The widows of the New York firemen stand side by side with the women of the third world who see themselves forced to abandon their babies on hospital steps. Brathwaite seems to imply that the present state of the world plunged into chaos and destruction is a result of a neglect of the "mother," who appears under a variety of names (Sycorax, Namsetoura, Barbados, or simply "my mother") but is essentially the same source of spiritual sustenance and survival. The metaphorical return to the mother in such poems as "Namsetoura" and "Kumina" forms a counter-narrative to the dominant narrative of dispossession and despair that pervades most of *Born to Slow Horses*. The return to the mother is an appeal for a return to the healing powers of spirituality, the seat of which, in Brathwaite's cosmos, is Kilimanjaro or Africa in its widest sense, acting as a counter-force to Prospero's materialism in both this new world order and the original "creole cosmos."

"Kumina" in particular shows how a personal crisis — the death of Dream Chad's son in a road accident — can be overcome when one has recourse to a spiritual framework, in this case the Afro-Jamaican *kumina* cult. Moreover, showing female suffering and survival as global erases the cultural boundaries between the Caribbean and western imaginary. The imaginary becomes exclusively the realm of the mothers. In this sense, the imaginary is also reaffirmed as the source of magical transformation and utopian possibility. Here the new "creole cosmos" of global suffering can be healed and reimagined.[11]

For Brathwaite, the destruction of the World Trade Center echoes in the destruction of CowPastor. Part iiii of *Born to Slow Horses* deals with local issues that are reminiscent of the CowPastor events. "Dear PM," for example, opens with a record of environmental devastation with the poet as witness "on this promontory where we keep looking out" (*BTSH* 63), the location being suggestive of CowPastor. With obvious allusions to Eliot's *The Waste Land* ("but there are no pearls / of eyes in prospero plantation..." (*BTSH* 63)), Barbados is depicted as an ecological, spiritual and human wasteland, not only in this poem but in all of section iiii, again echoing the "dread and carnage and despair" of *Trench Town Rock* and "Pixie." In this context, it is significant that Brathwaite claims that "this new sudden wanton destruction of the pasture" exhibits a "falluja mentality" and he asks for this and his other statements, made in an email, to be copied "verbatim... to the PM" of Barbados ("from Kamau; reply to email").

The reference to the Iraqi city of Fallujah sets Barbados and CowPastor into the context of the post-9/11 so-called "war on terror," with the exception that Brathwaite calls this "falluja mentality" itself an "act of terrorism" ("from Kamau; reply to email"). The parallels

"The spirits of GOLOKWATI . . . have led me to this place"

between CowPastor and Fallujah are obvious. In 2004, allied troops destroyed much of the Iraqi city, the seat of a major group of Sunni "insurgents." The legality of the weapons used in the assaults has since been questioned (Reyhani). Brathwaite implies that the means and motives behind the destruction of CowPastor are equally questionable. (Interestingly, Brathwaite chooses not to mention the burnt and dismembered bodies of the American contractors who were hung from the city's main bridge, an equally atrocious act and the reason for the assaults on the city in the first place.)

Another parallel between Fallujah and CowPastor is the spiritual significance of both places. Fallujah is known as the "city of mosques," many of which were destroyed. The allied attack is thus, implicitly, also an attack on the cultural and spiritual values of the Muslim world. Again, the analogy to CowPastor is obvious: for Sunni insurgents read CowPastor "squatters" — according to Brathwaite a term applied to the residents of the pasture by the government of Barbados ("Letter . . . to . . . Mervyn Morris"). The alleged grave of Namsetoura and its surrounding plantation ground have an equally important significance not only for Brathwaite himself but for the island as a whole, and the destruction of the site shows a sense of "cultural DISRESPECT" ("from Janice Whittle"). In this sense, Brathwaite implies that the local and the global are controlled by the same forces. Unlike *X/Self*, which has a similarly global scope but still with many references to the empires of the past, *Born to Slow Horses* is firmly situated in the post-9/11 world.

In one of his contributions to *Save CowPastor,* Brathwaite states that "i know now that the spirits of GOLOKWATI to who(m) i was introduced in Ghana and again at Limuru in Kenya by Ngũgĩ wa Thiong'o grandmother, have led me to this place and to the vision of Namsetoura" ("April 29th"). In "Mountain," the penultimate poem of *Born to Slow Horses*, Brathwaite returns to the original event of the Golokwati gathering. In this context, "Mountain" becomes not only a poem about the act of writing but also about the kind of environment that makes writing possible. As a celebration, "Mountain" is the antithesis of "Hawk" but related to the latter in its evocation of an "imagined community." "Mountain" is the utopian possibility of the global community united by loss that we encounter in "Hawk." Marking the end of "these salt years of the fast" (*BTSH* 131), the experience of the Golokwati gathering reopens the door to the muse that Brathwaite saw closing on him in *The Zea Mexican Diary*. Significantly, the last section of "Mountain" reiterates the last section of the *Diary* with its vision of the afterworld on the other side of the valley from which Brathwaite felt cut off at the time.

The middle parts of "Mountain" represent the poet's resumed conversation with the muse or his re-established contact with the "presences" — as he calls them — of the spirit world. Golokwati itself comes to stand for this new beginning in both his experience of community and in terms of his writing projects. It becomes a generic term, indicating more a togetherness in spirit than an actual gathering: "even tho we long-distance ourselves from the hills / creating these ghosts. these ghosts of beginnings" (*BTSH* 129).[12] "Ghosts" is not only suggestive of tentative beginnings but also of ancestral connections, and the connection to literary forebears in particular: "no / golokwati in sight till we reach Claude McKay's sad fiery apples of song" (*BTSH* 128). Above all, "ghosts" echoes "the spirits of golokwati" who connect the different communities of writers, past and present. Golokwati, in other words, becomes a *houmfort* of the mind, and since Golokwati or "golokwati" happens within the space of the poem, the text itself, once again, becomes that sacred or magical space of communion and transformation.

In this context, the poem as a record of the poet's "confession to the muse" (*BTSH* 132) echoes his encounter with Namsetoura and the new direction it gives to his writing and life. As in "Namsetoura," writing and life become one, and Brathwaite realizes, through the guidance of the muse, that "the poem 'finish' but not yet complete" (*BTSH* 132). In other words, his writing remains open-ended. Human life, too, is experienced as open-ended, especially with regard to the spirit realm and the afterlife. At the end of "Mountain," the poet finds himself in the same place as he did at the end of *The Zea Mexican Diary*, experiencing the same sense of uncertainty: "i do not know / that i will reach the mountains of tomorrow / tho i can see them" (*BTSH* 134). At the same time, he is now able to bridge the divide between here and there that seemed final at the end of the *Diary*, for the last section of "Mountain" is not an exact restating of the "Anyaneanyane" chapter of the *Diary*. Whereas the *Diary* emphasizes loss and a coming to terms with that loss, "Mountain" celebrates communion and "arrived-at Being": "you here we here" (*BTSH* 135). To underline the aspect of communion, the whole section is written in the present tense (whereas the past tense is used in the *Diary*), and the poem ends on a note of celebration and an affirmation of peace.

The last poem, "Robin," brings the collection back from a vision of the spirit world into everyday life. Lost love (in the form of the

"The spirits of GOLOKWATI . . . have led me to this place"

dead female robin) is buried; the vision of "Mountain" has become grounded. For a moment, we as readers feel that "here both flight and message end" (*PH* 3: 1311) in a moment of "arrived-at Being." This is compounded by the postscript that takes us through the various stages of Brathwaite's life and work, ending with the mentioning of *Born to Slow Horses* and *Words Need Love Too* as examples of his new, "postSalt" (*BTSH* 143), creative phase. "Robin" thus sums up the poet's work discussed in this study. Closure, however, is only temporarily achieved. The postscript again hints at open-endedness, the poet giving us an indication of future projects, "continuing from *Words need love too*, perhaps another tripartite exploration" (*BTSH* 143).

# Notes

## INTRODUCTION: Kamau Brathwaite's Creole Experiment

1. Brathwaite has published under the names Lawson Edward Brathwaite, Edward Brathwaite, Edward Kamau Brathwaite and Kamau Brathwaite. All of his work after *X/Self* (1987) has been published under Kamau Brathwaite.

2. As Brathwaite's "video" work relies on a strong visual impact, I have attempted to reproduce the original typescript in longer quotations in order to convey this visual effect. However, since a lot of his work has been composed on an Apple computer, the reproduction can, in some cases, only be approximate, since Apple uses fonts that are incompatible with Windows. Shorter quotations, of four lines or less, have been blended into Times New Roman font.

3. In "An Alternative View of Caribbean History," Brathwaite is explicit about the consumption of God implied in *nam*:

   > Onyami, meaning the supreme God of the Africans, is there embedded in the concept of Nam; which is also a very personal concept, meaning to eat.... "Nyam" is an African word meaning "to eat," and to eat is connected with the concept of God, so that in most cultures at the very most sacred moment of the culture you tend to eat your God in order to identify with him or her. (56)

4. I agree with Nana Wilson-Tagoe, who argues that in Brathwaite's *Mother Poem*, for example, "woman is not always a character in her own indi-

vidual right but a representative figure": "... in *Mother Poem* a waterless rock seed, the porous limestone of the land whose rootedness shows up the outward pulls and wanderings of the male figures" (250). However, in the case of "Nametracks," the black man shows passivity while the black woman exhibits agency in the form of casting magic spells. In this sense, slave women are cells of resistance, though often unacknowledged, an argument put forward by Édouard Glissant. Glissant suggests that among Caribbean slaves "collective dependence reinforced the 'reproductive' machismo of male slaves but did not authorize the appearance of femininity as a spiritual counterforce, even if women were frequently centers of resistance" (Glissant, *Poetics* 60).

5. Brathwaite acknowledges that Édouard Glissant was the first who wrote about nation language in his "Free and Forced Poetics" (*Caribbean Discourse*). Even though Glissant does not use the word "nation language," he distinguishes between the creole spoken by white settlers and that used by the slaves and their descendants. The crucial difference is that the latter draw on a folk/oral culture that has its roots in Africa whereas white creole speakers do not.

6. This pre-occupation with language confirms Silvio Torres-Saillant's observation that the region's "quest for decolonization" takes place first and foremost in the "battle for language" (*Caribbean Poetics* 7). For this reason, Caribbean poetics, unlike its western counterpart, celebrates "the virtues of logocentrism," and language itself forms the basis for all other forms of cultural expression (124).

7. In his introduction to the 2005 edition of *The Development of the Creole Society in Jamaica*, B. W. Higman points out that the notion of creolization has been considered as a global model within "the broader fields of anthropology and globalization studies" (xix). Brathwaite's idea of a "creole cosmos" moves in a similar direction. However, he would insist that cultures actually do retain a distinctiveness, as he exemplifies in his analysis of the folk culture of the slaves, a chapter in *The Development of the Creole Society*.

8. In *The Development of the Creole Society*, Brathwaite argues that the maroon societies during his period of investigation were formed mainly by African-born runaway slaves. Cutting themselves off from the plantation and retaining a strong affiliation to all things African, their "development ... did not involve them significantly, during this period, in social interaction with others outside their group; did not involve them ... in the process of creolization" (Higman xxxi). However, as a genuine New World phenomenon, the maroon community is creole in the sense that

it is "Caribbean-born" and as such "an African-influenced creole form (Afro-creole)" (Brathwaite, *The Development of the Creole Society* 231).

9. Originally published in German in 1959 under the title *Das Prinzip Hoffnung*.

10. In chapter two of the first volume, significantly entitled "Coming to the Americas," Alma Norman writes: "We who live in the Caribbean might be called 'people on the move.' Our people have always migrated from the Caribbean to other regions. In the past, people also migrated in great numbers *to* the Caribbean. They came from Africa, from Asia, and from Europe" (6).

11. Recent book-length responses to Brathwaite's writing include Emily Allen Williams's *The Critical Response to Kamau Brathwaite* (2004) and Annie Paul's collection of essays *Caribbean Culture: Soundings on Kamau Brathwaite* (2007). The former gives an overview of the critical reception of Brathwaite's work, the latter is a selection of the papers presented at the second Conference on Caribbean Culture in honour of Kamau Brathwaite.

# CHAPTER ONE: *X/Self* and the (Re)invention of the "Creole Cosmos"

1. The main modernist influence on Brathwaite's work is T. S. Eliot. Throughout *X/Self* we find numerous echoes of passages from Eliot's major poems and essays. The very fact that Brathwaite decided to provide "Notes" to *X/Self* (and to *Mother Poem* and *Sun Poem* for that matter) in the style of Eliot's notes to *The Waste Land* shows the strong influence of Eliot on Brathwaite's imagination and style. Much of Brathwaite's work can, in fact, be classed as modernist in its desire to achieve a sense of cultural as well as personal wholeness, and in this it is related to the work of other major Caribbean writers, most notably that of Derek Walcott. The appropriation of Eliot has been instrumental in the creation of a particularly Caribbean form of modernism. Brathwaite's use of magical montage echoes most clearly Eliot's ideas of tradition and time. In *New World Modernisms*, Charles W. Pollard argues that "Eliot conceives of tradition, not as a struggle between the past and the present, between the community and the individual, between continuity and originality, but as a collocation of the past and present, of the community and the individual, and of continuity and originality in a new contingent whole" (26). This, in many ways, intersects with Brathwaite's notion of "tidalectics" as well as his

understanding of magical realism, which "involves the immanence of the PAST ... as part of the present-future (present/future) & (therefore) the immanence of SPIRITS" ("MR" 25).

2. My reading of the poem is in part derived from Mark McMorris's article "Provincial Subjects in the Classical Labyrinth: the Challenge to Tradition in Brathwaite's *X/Self*":

> "Alphs" — i.e., alpha, the first letter of the Greek alphabet – is put for the unexpressed "Alps." ... this substitution allows Brathwaite to unite the African invasion of Europe with the origins of the Greek and therefore of the Latin alphabet, the technology that launches the "mental canoe" of literacy and literature. The logic of the series "alps alphs" inserts the Carthaginian Hannibal into a narrative of the development of the western mind at its beginnings. But the series mis-maps historical territory: Hannibal reached Italy in 218 BC, and by then the alphabet with its Phoenician base had been in use in Greece for at least 500 years. Furthermore, the general is implicitly aligned with black Caribbean possibility (indicated in the word "vodoun"). Could the region, given its brutal history and its current poverty, produce a dream such as Hannibal dreamt? (119)

McMorris also argues that the characters that appear in *X/Self* are "creolized by Caribbean capacity" (115), which echoes my own reading of the creole personae of, for example, Vercingetorix and Hannibal himself. Imperial language, too, is thus creolized, although McMorris does not explicitly say so.

3. In his article "The Role of Africa in the Construction of Identity in the Caribbean," Mervyn C. Alleyne points out that in Aimé Césaire's rendition of Shakespeare's *The Tempest*, *Une Tempête* (1969), Hannibal is a name given to Caliban by Prospero as an approximation of cannibal, Prospero's initial name for Caliban. In Césaire's play, Caliban rejects both cannibal and Hannibal and names himself X (186). Brathwaite seems to play on this succession of names, although for him Hannibal is the more assertive persona, whereas the X in X/Self's name represents, initially, a sense of dislocation, a loss or lack of selfhood, which is indicated by the slash that ruptures the name.

4. Other calendar gods that Brathwaite may have had in mind are the *bolón-ti-ku*, the "nine lords of the night," who rule over a certain period of the solar year (Cordan 186). The *Popol Vuh* includes an episode similar to that in "Titan," a challenge of the underworld Xibalbá by the Mayan hero twins.

# Notes

5. That the Aztecs mistook Cortez for Quetzalcoatl seems almost common knowledge. All the major books on the conquest of Mexico mention the fact, for example, the sources cited in this chapter: Tzvetan Todorov in *The Conquest of America*, and Hugh Thomas in *The Conquest of Mexico*.

6. In Mayan mythology, there is also a period in which titans ruled the earth. They are likewise associated with chaos and the state of the world before human civilization. In the calendar, they correspond to the five days without names, the *xma-kaba-kin*, which reappear every fifty-two years. The Maya dreaded these days and spent them in fear of a possible return of the primordial world chaos (Cordan 181).

7. See in particular the chapter "The Battle for Tenochtitlan" in Hugh Thomas's *The Conquest of Mexico*.

8. Open field composition is a concept of writing poetry first conceived by Black Mountain School poet Robert Creeley and later developed by Charles Olson, also of the Black Mountain School, in his essay "Projective Verse" (1950). In open field composition, structure or form is not imposed on the content but emerges from the content.

9. In this way, the poem's content extends into its form. Olson writes:

    ... the *principle*, the law which presides conspicuously over such composition, and, when obeyed, is the reason why a projective poem can come into being. It is this: FORM IS NEVER MORE THAN AN EXTENSION OF CONTENT. (Or so it got phrased by one, R. Creeley, and it makes absolute sense to me, with this possible corollary, that right form, in any given poem, is the only and exclusively possible extension of content under hand.) (240)

10. C.L.R. James gives an account of the Haitian revolution in *The Black Jacobins: Toussaint L'Ouverture and the San Domingo Revolution* (1938). James reads the Haitian revolution from a Marxist perspective, viewing colonial oppression not in terms of racial oppression but as an expression of class struggle or class antagonism. Paul Gilroy, for example, criticizes such a reading, arguing that colonial oppression was and is fundamentally a racial issue (46–49). Brathwaite himself reads the Haitian revolution in terms of racial and cultural liberation, arguing that Toussaint's power derived from his role as spiritual leader:

    *l'ouverture*: Toussant L'Ouverture, slave rebel leader who liberated St Domingue/Haiti from France and the French plantoc-

> racy (1791–1804). He was given the sobriquet 'L'Ouverture' in acknowledgement of this; he created an opening for his people. Or, in terms of *vodoun*, the Dahomean culture of the St Domingue slaves, he was *legba* . . . , *loa* of thresholds and beginnings. Some portraits of Toussaint picture him, in fact, dwarfed, apparently deformed and unprepossessing, like Legba. (*X/S* 114)

In his connection with voodoo, Brathwaite's Toussaint expresses a genuine New World identity, an aspect that is lacking in James's Toussaint.

11. Césaire is, of course, one of the major exponents of the Négritude movement rejected by the more fashionable theorists of creolization for its apparently easy binarisms and exclusivist aesthetics. Much of Brathwaite's work, with its focus on the African presence in the Caribbean, is deeply indebted to Négritude. Very much in line with Négritude tenets, Africa in the form of Sycorax appears as the salvation of Caribbean man, the only power that can free him from Prospero's prison. For this reason, Brathwaite's work cannot be classed as magic realist in the same way as that of the writers of the "Latin American boom," although Brathwaite tries to make a case for a form of magical realism inherent in Négritude, wondering whether one could indeed speak of such a thing as "**Black** MR" ("MR" 12). As he himself observes, critics see his work as "trapped in the SIS" ("MR" 24), i. e. the Sisyphus tradition, because of its many instances of social realism — or rather social and cultural pessimism. However, for Brathwaite it is precisely the entanglement of the social with the magical reality that lends magical realism its power and concrete utopian, i.e. transformative, potential.

12. Brathwaite writes in a note to "The African Presence in Caribbean Literature": "*Vodun* is the largest and most public African-derived (Dahomey: *vodu*) religious form in the Caribbean, centered in Haiti. See also *shango* (in Trinidad), *poco* (in Jamaica), *santeria* (in Cuba) and the *candomble or macumba* (in Brazil). Often, in this text, the term *vodun* is used to apply to Afro-New World religions generally" (216 n60). All forms of religious expression listed by Brathwaite have in common the element of spirit possession. As there is no set spelling of voodoo / vodu / vodun, I have decided to use the most commonly known, voodoo.

13. Rohlehr suggests that "'huh,' 'hah,' 'hah' are explosions of breath connected . . . with the primal sounds of the loa's lovemaking" ("The Rehumanization of History" 283).

14. ". . . our Lady of the Sorrows has come to represent Ezili-Freda-Dahomey because the jewellery with which she is decked and the sword transpierc-

ing her heart evoke the riches and love which are the attributes of the Voodoo goddess" (Métraux 325).

15. Métraux gives a detailed description of the instance of possession (*Voodoo in Haiti* 120), as does the last chapter of Maya Deren's *Divine Horsemen*.

16. The association of X with coming to selfhood is, of course, reminiscent of Malcom X, who, when he joined the Black Muslims changed his name from Malcolm Little to Malcolm X: "The Muslim's 'X' symbolized the true African family name that he never could know. For me, my 'X' replaced the white slavemaster name 'Little' which some blue-eyed devil named Little had imposed upon my parental forebears" (229). The idea of liberation from domination through an assertive act of renaming the self is a connotation that Brathwaite certainly intended in *X/Self* and which is already there in "Nametracks." However, X/Self also moves beyond himself to become Xango, just as Malcolm X himself moved beyond Malcolm X to become El Hajj Malik El Shabbaz. (Interestingly, "Xango" is a revised version of "Shango," a poem that appears in *Black + Blues* (1977), one of the volumes of Brathwaite's "Kingston poetry" of the 1970s. The *Black + Blues* version of the poem is, in keeping with the general tone of the collection, much more subdued in comparison to the celebratory *X/Self* version.)

17. The mother-daughter issue, in terms of cultural as well as familial belonging, is also a major theme in the work of many female Caribbean writers, the most prominent being Jamaica Kincaid, especially in her novels *Annie John* (1985), *Lucy* (1990), *The Autobiography of My Mother* (1996) and also in the story "My Mother" from the collection *At the Bottom of the River* (1984).

18. "Crab" is the penultimate poem of *Black + Blues* (1977), followed by "Koker," and the last of *Third World Poems* (1983). As "Carab" differs from "Crab" in only a few words and phrases, the reading of "Crab" that Gordon Rohlehr has given in "Songs Of The Skeleton" can be drawn on to a considerable extent in a reading of "Carab." *Black + Blues* was reissued in 1995 by New Directions in New York.

19. Gordon Rohlehr perceives this dimming of creative vision already in his reading of *Black + Blues*, which suggests that a dystopian undercurrent exists side by side with utopian vision in Brathwaite's work. Rohlehr argues that the crab is a shadow or double of the poet's writing hand and thus of his inspiration: "'Candlelight' suggests that the poet sees his vision as uncertain; the light of the candle isn't particularly strong. The candle casts a shadow of the poet's hand on the page. It is this shadow, its

fingers legs, that scuttles across the page and becomes the crab. So literally the crab issues from the poet's hand and from his vision's uncertain light" ("Songs of the Skeleton" 315).

20. Rohlehr points out this change of image from bird to crab with reference to Brathwaite's poem "Dawn" (*Islands*), suggesting that "the unconscious is thought of as ground, so the crab or the snail is a more appropriate guide than the hummingbird" ("Songs of the Skeleton" 314). Rohlehr seems to refer to the following passage from "Dawn," the snail and the hedgehog echoing the crab of "Carab"/"Crab":

> the mouth-organ drool of the snails'
> slow passage, discretion, through zones
> that the hummingbird's swiftness
>
> that is stillness, knows not, knows not;
> and the lourd
> hedgehog, following the mongoose and the mangrove trail, reaches
>       the green
> pool (*Arrivants* 238)

21. Brathwaite's cultural paradigms often tend to simplify or idealize African and Amerindian societies in order to set them off from European expansionism as alternative ways of living and thinking. The Aztec empire, for example, never appears as a form of imperialism but always as a victim of European conquest. Africa is portrayed in a more complex light, acknowledging African complicity in the slave trade (see *Masks* and *Barabajan Poems*). However, here, too, Brathwaite tends to emphasize the aspect that shows Africa as victim of Europe and African traditional societies as alternatives to European political structures.

22. Snyder thinks along similar lines as Brathwaite in his perception of America as *Heimat*. In *Turtle Island* (1974), which won the Pulitzer Prize in 1975, Snyder draws on Native American mythology. For him, Turtle Island is a place where immigrants may be transformed into "native" Americans. In this sense, America becomes not a place of migration, a "biosphere culture," but an instance of Blochian "arrived-at Being," an "ecosystem." In *Poetics of Relation*, Glissant employs a similar distinction between biosphere and ecosystem, missile and circle. He calls it "arrow-like" and "circular" nomadism (12).

23. In *Folk Culture of the Slaves in Jamaica*, Brathwaite points out that in some cases this did actually happen: "Interment took place in Negro burial grounds, if these were provided by the authorities, or 'promiscuously in the fields, and [near] their near and dear relations at the back of their huts, and sometimes under their beds'" (Moreton 162 qtd. in *Folk Culture* 9).

24. Inga Clendinnen remarks that one should not conflate the Aztec notion of pollution and cleansing with that of Christianity. Whereas in Christian belief, the act of ritual cleansing creates a link between humanity and God, in Aztec culture it is pollution that functions as a gateway for divinity. Drunkenness and excessive sexuality, for example, made an individual a danger for society because society was threatened by an eruption of the sacred into the mundane world through the individual who had momentarily lost control over his or her self and could thus be seized as a vehicle by the gods (52). For an understanding of "Carab," this difference between Aztec and Christian notions of pollution and cleanliness is not essential, although worth pointing out is that Brathwaite emphasizes the mundane, i.e. the social and cultural, dimension of the "creole cosmos" and not the communion of the human with the divine as in "Xango." Brathwaite most likely was aware of the difference mentioned by Clendinnen, considering his knowledge of Mesoamerican cultures he demonstrates in many of his texts. Therefore, "Carab" makes a deliberate cultural statement by giving preference to a non-European perspective rather than to Christian symbolism.

## CHAPTER TWO: Death, Marriage, and Maroons: *The Zea Mexican Diary*

1. Brathwaite taught in the History Department of the University of the West Indies at Mona, Jamaica, from 1963 to 1991.

2. Zea Mexican may well be derived from "zea mays," the most important seed crop among the early pre-Columbian Americans. From this type of corn sweet corn was later developed (Norman 7). Brathwaite's choice of an Amerindian name for his first wife is significant. Mexican was of part Amerindian descent and embodied, for him, the Americas as *Heimat*. With similar intent, his second wife Beverly, who is of African descent, is renamed Dream Chad in honor of the sacred lake in Africa.

3. In his preface to the 1996 edition of *Maroon Societies*, Richard Price traces the origin of the word "maroon" beyond its traditional association

with the *cimarrones*, the wild cattle that roamed the island of Hispaniola during the emergence of the first rebel slave communities:

> Since the original publication of *Maroon Societies*, the Cuban philologist José Juan Arrom has pushed back the origin of the word maroon beyond the Spanish *cimarrón* that was first used in Hispaniola to refer to the Spaniards' feral cattle, then to enslaved Amerindians who escaped to the hills and, by the early 1530s, mainly to the many Africans who were escaping from slavery on the island. That New World Spanish word — which spawned English *maroon*, as well as French and Dutch *marron* (and English *Seminole*) — actually derives, he now argues, from an Amerindian (Arawakan/Taíno) root, making it one of the earliest linguistic coinages in the postcolumbian Americas (Arrom 1986). (xi–xii)

4. Some of the original maroon communities still exist and still form independent enclaves within contemporary societies of the Americas, such as the Saramaka "Bush Negroes" of Suriname. After independence from Europe, there has been a "trend toward gradual assimilation into national populations," which "has been successfully countered by sporadic expressions of Maroon identity and specificity in diverse places such as Colombia and Jamaica" (Price xiii).

5. Benítez-Rojo refers to two kinds of repression:

> . . . Caribbean societies are among the most repressive in the world. I'm not referring necessarily to political repression, although we'd have to agree that the Caribbean's history, colonial and contemporary, exhibits a gallery of governors, captains-general, dictators, and fathers of the fatherland of hardly surpassable ironhandedness. In reality . . . the Caribbean's economic and social structures favor this type of political option. But I'm referring here to another kind of repression, and this is the one that every Caribbean person experiences within himself and which impels him to flee from himself and, paradoxically, which leads him finally back to himself. (249)

Whereas for Benítez-Rojo, this latter, psychological repression is more illuminating in his reading of the maroon experience in Caribbean literature, my reading of Brathwaite focuses on the political definition of repression.

## Notes

6. In associating Mexican with Legba, Brathwaite moves beyond the European conception of the muse as an aspect of the divine feminine. In her juxtaposition with Legba, Mexican's gender becomes secondary and her power to connect to the spiritual comes to the foreground.

7. See, for example, Ismith Khan's novel *The Jumbie Bird* (1961), which opens with the cry of the owl that announces the general sense of foreboding that pervades the novel as well as the death of one of its main protagonists and with him the end of an historical period. In Ian McDonald's *The Humming-Bird Tree* (1969), the jumbie bird is heard at the end of the novel and accompanies the end of childhood innocence and also the end of childhood's possibility of transcending race and class boundaries.

8. Mexican's death would thus be a form of the "loss of Eldorado," a phrase V. S. Naipaul employs in *The Loss of Eldorado* (1969) to characterize the impact of European colonization on the Caribbean.

9. The repetition of "yes" and the lack of punctuation in the cited passage from the *Diary* echoes Molly Bloom's monologue at the end of James Joyce's *Ulysses* (1922), where it signifies an acceptance of life. In a similar way, Brathwaite's sequence of "yes yes yes" is also a sign of beginning acceptance, which later in the *Diary* emerges as a concrete acceptance of Mexican's death. In his identification with the affirmative female character of Molly Bloom, Brathwaite becomes a mirror image to Mexican/Legba, the female/male muse.

10. Of particular interest in this context is the first chapter of *Myth, Literature and the African World*, "Morality and aesthetics in the ritual archetype", and the appendix, "The Fourth Stage."

11. Gabriel Okara's novel *The Voice* (1964) echoes a similar isolation of the poet. The Nigerian poet and novelist describes how Okolo, which, as it reads on the back cover, translates as "voice," is in search of *it* (the novel is not explicit about the meaning of *it*) and is subsequently ostracized by his society that has abandoned traditional African values as well as the possibility of a cross-cultural existence for the western promise of social prestige. Okara presents a protagonist in search of new meaning for a culture that has become hybrid and multi-accentuated in the process of colonization. Okolo's quest for *it* is thus a quest for a new space of rootedness. In this sense, Okolo is very similar to Brathwaite and his quest for a cross-cultural identity.

12. George Lamming portrays such an instant of denial in his novel *In the Castle of my Skin*: "He told the teacher what the old woman had said. She was a slave. And the teacher said she was getting dotish. It was a long, long, long time ago. People talked of slaves a long time ago. . . . It had nothing to do with people in Barbados. No one there was ever a slave, the teacher said. It was in another part of the world that those things happened" (49).

13. The full title of Chapter VII of the *Diary* is "The working muses nourish Hector/Hero of Time," which is a line taken from the poem "Troy" by Wilson Harris (*Eternity to Season* 11–12). In his review of the book, Brathwaite writes about the classical hero figures that abound in these poems: "In Harris' genesis, we find no people we can recognize. There is Hector, but he is hero not of Troy but of *time*. . . . The concern is with Symbol: with the Hero: figures which, like Henry Moore's stand or sit in great landscapes, partaking of and lending beauty to the grandeur of the elements, but powerless, passive and pre-determined from the start" ("The Controversial Tree of Time" 111). During the course of the *Diary*, Brathwaite emerges as a similarly isolated figure, severed from the nourishing muse.

14. In *African Art & Literature*, Duerden writes: ". . . a man who has had the special qualities which enabled him to regulate his social group's behaviour in their environment may be induced to come back in a new incarnation, and his qualities may be remembered for a few generations" (58). In Haitian voodoo, the dead are reincorporated into the human community through a rite that Maya Deren in *Divine Horsemen* calls "retrirer d'en bas de l'eau," the extraction of the soul from the abysmal waters (46). Haitian folk culture reworks many aspects of traditional African religious thinking, including ancestor worship, into a New World religion. In this context, Brathwaite's use of "dream" is interesting. According to Frank Collymore, the verb "to dream" is a Barbadian idiom: ". . . someone who has dreamt of a dead relative or friend will say, for example, *My old grandmother dream me last night and tell me wasn't to have nothing to do with the business*. It will be seen that the narrator speaks of himself as having been dreamt by the deceased person who is the active agent in the matter. Is this a relic of African tribal lore?" (34).

15. In "Nanny, Palmares & the Caribbean Maroon Connexion," Brathwaite argues that historians have tried to deny Nanny's historical existence "because she was a visible woman living at the end of the 17th century — a period when 'visible' women — apart from a few White Queens — were almost impossible to conceive of & therefore to perceive in PUBLIC FUNCTION AND PERSONA" (122). Brathwaite also argues that, contrary

to the popular myth, she could not catch bullets with her buttocks, but that she was

> *buttockicized* (& that the word is awkWEIRD & ungainly is no accident) because she was black & therefore a slave no matter what & therefore how could she possibly be a leader, far less a *black* leader — far less a black *woman* leader — & physically & metaphysically so successful that by 1720 the Br (certainly some key planters in the Port Antonio area — on the GrandeeNanny firing line, as it were) were contemplating abandoning their Plantation Xperiment in Jamaica ... (122)

Despite this, Brathwaite acknowledges that she has become a national hero, although he laments that no statue of her has been erected and that she does not even figure on a postage stamp (123). However, Price confirms that her image appears on the Jamaican five-hundred-dollar bill (xiii).

16. In the same source Brathwaite states that Roderick Ebanks, "The Maroons of Jamaica," is an unpublished manuscript.

17. However, this characterization of women is not homogenous. Men in Brathwaite's work also have Sycoraxian qualities, like Brathwaite's great-uncle Bob'bob, who appears in *Barabajan Poems*.

18. In his notes to *Barabajan Poems*, Brathwaite provides a list of what he calls "PLANTATION PERSONALITY TYPES" (*BP* 315), of which Sister Stark is one:

> **Stark** / Sister Stark, Caliban's sister, is my own imagination's invention and although I have been thinking of her for some time now ...
> ... she did not walk clearly away from me until the October evening 1991 at NYU when I spoke of Paule Marshall's then new book, **Daughters** and recognized Stark in what Marshall was doing – the first time that the Plantation has a black woman w/ firm feet, sensitive / aggressive breasts and a space & plan if not always a room of her own She begins in James Carnegie's Mary **(Wages Paid)** and now makes her way in & through the wonderful efflorescence of STARK WRITING since Mary Prince since Mary Seacole since Walker since Morrison since Brodber since Kincaid since Condé since Warner since Carolivia Heron since Cynthia James/ to name only a few
> (*BP* 316)

As opposed to other plantation personality types, which comprise more than just the characters from *The Tempest* (he adds, for example, Antoinette of Jean Rhys's *Wide Sargasso Sea* (1966) and Fola of George

*A Creole Experiment*

Lamming's *Season of Adventure* (1960)), Sister Stark is the only character entirely Brathwaite's own.

## CHAPTER THREE: The Poet's Archive as Houmfort: *Shar*/Hurricane Poem

1. *Shar* has no page numbers. I have added the page numbers myself for easier reference, page 1 starting with "Saving the Word."

2. In Jamaica, "John Crow" is a name for "the turkey buzzard, *Cathartes aura*." As "John Crow's nose," the name refers to a parasitic plant, "*Scybalium jamaicense*" ("John Crow," *The New Shorter Oxford English Dictionary* 1: 1452).

3. Another rendition of Herron's speech, complete with Brathwaite's comments and interjections, appears in Appendix V of *Barabajan Poems*.

4. In this context, Brathwaite cites Ian McDonald's *The Humming-Bird Tree* (1969), John Hearne's *Stranger at the Gate* (1956), and V. S. Naipaul's *A House for Mr Biswas* (1961).

5. Brathwaite uses *houmfort* and *tonnelle* interchangeably to designate "vodoun space/time place/continuum and by extension the area set aside and used for ?formal Afro-Caribbean religious expression" ("Caribbean Culture — Two Paradigms" 52).

6. This reflection on the nature of the *houmfort* appears as part of an account in which Brathwaite describes how he witnessed a Revival Zion night prayer meeting in his great-uncle Bob'ob's former carpenter shop. Brathwaite describes how a woman is successively possessed by the voodoo/santería spirits of Yemanjá, Erzulie, Damballah and Shango (see *Barabajan Poems*, Chapter VII). The woman's possession by the spirits is Brathwaite's own cross-cultural reading of the event and may not strictly correspond to the celebrants' understanding of the ceremony. Voodoo originates in Catholic Haiti, and the *loa* are identified with the images of Catholic saints. Revival Zion churches, on the other hand, occur in Protestant areas of the Caribbean but nonetheless involve possession by the spirit, in their case the Holy Spirit (see, for example, Earl Lovelace's *The Wine of Astonishment* (1982), a novel about a Trinidadian Spiritual Baptist community, who encourage possession by the spirit and were therefore outlawed). Revival Zion churches, to which the Spiritual Baptists belong, form part of an African-Caribbean expression of spirituality.

Brathwaite draws the parallel to voodoo because these Protestant-based religions are less well — or not at all — known outside the Caribbean. He thus attempts to demonstrate that "even" Protestant Barbados "**had recognized its other heart** — in Africa" (*BP* 169). The spirit as descending dove, which Brathwaite refers to in *Barabajan Poems*, echoes a line from "Little Gidding" in T.S. Eliot's *Four Quartets*:

> The dove descending breaks the air
> With flame of incandescent terror
> Of which the tongues declare
> The one discharge from sin and error. (57)

The dove represents the Holy Spirit descending as fire on the day of Pentecost when the disciples speak in tongues. Possessed voodoo devotees are said to speak *langage*, a "sacred language, probably African words" (Deren 331), which is another form of speaking in tongues. In this context of remembering the language of the ancestors, Brathwaite's own research on Jamaican *kumina*, *Kumina: The Spirit of African Survival in Jamaica* (1982), reveals that for Miss Queenie, the *kumina* initiate Brathwaite interviews, only the African language (Kikongo in her case), allows her to commune with the ancestors and spirits.

7. In their studies of Haitian voodoo, both Maya Deren and Alfred Métraux stress that the appearance of a *houmfort* can vary greatly depending on the financial resources of a *houngan* (priest) or *mambo* (priestess), on whether the *houmfort* is situated in the country or the city, and also on whether voodoo is tolerated in a particular region or not. Deren's description of a *houmfort* corresponds to Brathwaite's idea of a "wall-less" structure. Deren's *houmfort* also conveys a sense of living architecture, of humanity in communion with nature, which the ordinary house, built of dead material, lacks (181). Métraux's description of a *houmfort* reveals its communal nature and a sense of community that includes the divine (77). Due to the oral nature of voodoo culture, the spelling of voodoo terms varies greatly. I have chosen the spelling *houmfort* as its sound echoes "home" and implies *Heimat* ("the *hoom* of psyche" (*C* 154)). Brathwaite uses both spellings, *hounfort* and *houmfort*, and most recently *oumfô*.

8. The reference to Golokwati takes on a particular resonance as it echoes or foreshadows the Golokwati theme of the recent book of the same title as well as in *Born To Slow Horses*. In this sense, the African journey continues into the present.

9. In *The Repeating Island*, Antonio Benítez-Rojo argues that "the cultural discourse of the Peoples of the Sea attempts . . . to neutralize violence" (17) via the interaction of individual and society, which he refers to as "performance" and which corresponds to Brathwaite's description of the *houmfort* as a space for ritual dance: "In any event we can say that the Caribbean performance, including the ordinary act of walking, does not reflect back on the performer alone but rather it also directs itself toward a public in search of a carnivalesque catharsis that proposes to divert excesses of violence . . ." (22). The interaction between individual and society in performance can thus be read as a definition of Brathwaite's "wall-less" alternative to the enclosed space of the house, where everything a person does reflects back only on him- or herself.

10. At the end of the novel the prostitute Dinah, one of the main protagonists of *The Children of Sisyphus*, fails to escape the ghetto, illustrating Patterson's notion of the futility of the Sisyphian struggle. She is described as scrambling up a mound of rubbish, where she dies, which echoes the notion of "human garbage" that is particularly graphic in *Trench Town Rock*.

11. Pauline Melville's novel, *The Ventriloquist's Tale* (1997), relates a similar tale, establishing a link between the food-bearing tree and Mount Roraima, a table mountain located at the border of Guyana with Brazil and Venezuela.

12. In a voodoo ceremony the initial incantation and drumming are called *prière Guninée* and *battérie maconnique* respectively (Deren 208–9).

13. In *ConVERSations with Nathaniel Mackey*, too, Brathwaite links "drum" and "computer" and argues that oral tradition ("drum") and written tradition ("computer") can no longer be clearly separated in the world of electronic media.

14. John H. Taylor states:

> In the Old and Middle Kingdoms the coffin was normally positioned in the burial chamber with the head pointing northwards and the long left side towards the east, so that the mummy, placed on its left side within the coffin, faced towards the part of the tomb where the funerary offerings were made and towards the land of the living. As a magical aid for the deceased, a pair of eyes was painted or carved on the exterior head end of the coffin's eastern side. It was believed that the dead man could

look out through these eyes into the tomb, thus maintaining a link with the world of the living.... (15–16)

15. In this passage, Dayan refers to pages 33, 34, and 36 of *Shar*.

# CHAPTER FOUR: Zombies and Messiahs in the Kingdom of this World: *Trench Town Rock*

1. "Trenchtown was a housing scheme, built after the 1951 hurricane had destroyed the area's squatter camps. These camps, which had gradually grown up around west Kingston, had been built around the former Kingston refuse dump, where the country folk and displaced city dwellers would scavenge for whatever they could find." ("Trenchtown," *Bob Marley*)

2. In the late 1950s there was a growing undercurrent of opportunism in Jamaica: people were redefining themselves, working out who they were with a new confidence. The guilty, repressive hold of the British colonialists was becoming increasingly uncertain; already there were whispers of independence being granted to the island. A new era was beginning. The cauldron of Trenchtown epitomised one of the great cultural truths about Jamaica — and other impoverished Third World countries: how those who have nothing, and therefore nothing to lose, are not afraid to express their talents. These people seem to have a pride and confidence in their talents — a pride and confidence that western educational and employment systems seem to conspire against. ("Trenchtown," The Life of Bob Marley)

    The *Bob Marley Sound Archives*, from which this quotation was originally taken, no longer exists. For a similar website see *Bob Marley: Home: The Official Website*. 2008. <http://web.bobmarley.com/index.jsp>.

3. Brathwaite highlights the absurd presence of American consumer goods in the face of the extreme poverty of downtown Kingston in his poem "Starvation" (*Black + Blues*):

    de eart' cole, you see me hyah
    de goodyear tyre dem tek flight
    a dust, a nasty water
    fram de pat 'ole, from de hasphalt,

> an' lan' pan tap de sufferer dem,
> standin' by pan de sidewalk,
> inside de wayside cabin dem a-kall
> a bus stap, hadvertisin,
> SHERATON HOTEL (23–24)

4. Campbell refers to Nkrumah's book *Neo-colonialism, The Last Stage of Imperialism* (1965).

5. This scene is similar to that of the violently awakened sleeper of the tribe in the poem "The visibility trigger" (*X/Self*), whose disrupted sleep is reflected in the disharmony of the world he awakens to:

   > and i was dreaming near morning
   >
   > i offered you a kola nut
   > your fingers huge and smooth and red
   > and you took it your dress makola blue
   >
   > and broke it into gunfire
   >
   > the metal was hot and jagged
   > it was as if the master of bronze
   >
   > had poured anger into his cauldron (*X/S* 48)

6. Marcus Garvey as well as the Rastafarians after him perceived Haile Selassie as a messiah figure because he was among the first rulers of an independent African nation. As such, he posed an alternative to the white English king and thus colonial subjugation. When Italy invaded Abyssinia in 1935, identification with the African ruler unified a large part of the African diaspora in their opposition to European colonial rule. Campbell writes in *Rasta and Resistance* that "as far as the mass of black people in the world were concerned, the defence of Ethiopia was the defence of black dignity" (73). He also states that "at their Sunday night meetings the brethren waved the black, red and green flag of Garvey, beat their drums and sang with fervour that the Lion of Judah shall break every chain and bring us the victory again and again'" (77). Thus after the defeat of Italy, Haile Selassie had indeed become the "*Conquering Lion of Judah*" (78) for the Rastafarians. Independent of this, Rastafarians identified with the lion as a symbol of black pride, confidence and strength, and as a reaction against the apparently docile Quashie or Anancy (Ananse) personality of

the slave, which was characterized, especially in the case of Anancy, by cunning (99). The Rasta dread locks are also compared to a lion's mane (99) as well as to the hairstyle of the Kenyan Mau Mau warriors with whose struggle for independence the Rastafarians identified (95).

7. Wheeler cites Brathwaite's poem "Starvation" to illustrate her argument.

8. In *Divine Horsemen*, Deren emphasizes the notion of alienation:

> The popular notion — outside Haiti — pictures the zombie as an enormously powerful giant who, being soulless and incapable of moral judgement, is inaccessible to reason, entreaty or any other dissuasion if he is directed to a malevolent purpose by his controlling force. This notion reflects a confusion as to the function of a zombie. Actually, the very essence of magic is *psychic* rather than physical force, and it is by such relatively subtle means that a magician would attain his malevolent ends. The choice of physically powerful individuals for zombies is precisely because their major function is not as instruments of malevolence, but as a kind of uncomplaining slave-labor to be used in the fields, the construction of houses, etc. While the Haitian does not welcome any encounter with a zombie, his real dread is that of being made into one himself. This is not because he fears hard work.... The terror is of a moral nature, related to the deep-rooted value which the Haitian attaches to powers of consciousness and the attendant capacity for moral judgement, deliberation and self-control. (42–43n)

9. The Jamaica Labour Party (JLP) represents the conservative opposition to the People's National Party (PNP) in power in the early 1990s.

10. Brathwaite has encoded two references into this passage, which provide a backdrop to *Trench Town Rock* and his work in general. The first reference is to the Jamaican film *The Harder They Come* (1973), the second to the Bandung Conference (1955). *The Harder They Come*, starring reggae artist Jimmy Cliff, is set in Kingston and tells the story of a young man, who comes to the city, hoping to become a reggae star. After being exploited by a record company, he turns to crime, while his music, released without his knowledge, achieves fame. *The Harder They Come* was the first successful film to come out of Jamaica and has been praised for its realistic depiction of Kingston ghetto life. In his attempt to transcend ghetto life through music, the young reggae artist can be seen as one of the children of Sisyphus.

## A Creole Experiment

The Bandung Conference was the first meeting of the leaders of newly independent African and Asian countries in order to establish economic and cultural links among the so-called third world nations, ways of maintaining their independence from neocolonial powers, which is a central issue in *Trench Town Rock*, and neutrality between east and west. The successor of the Bandung Conference was the Non-Aligned Movement, founded in 1961.

11. Another version of the poem also appears in Kamau Brathwaite, *Third World Poems*. In 1949, the Cuban novelist Alejo Carpentier published a novel entitled *El Reino de Este Mundo* (*The Kingdom of this World*) about the Haitian revolution. Brathwaite's adoption of this title for his poem suggests its revolutionary concern.

12. In *Divine Horsemen*, Deren describes the origin of the Petro cult as follows:

    > Petro ... is the rage against the evil fate which the African suffered, the brutality of his displacement and his enslavement. It is the violence that rose out of that rage, to protest against it. It is the crack of the slave-whip sounding constantly, a never-to-be-forgotten ghost, in the Petro rites. It is the raging revolt of the slaves against the Napoleonic forces. And it is the delirium of their triumph. For it was the Petro cult, born in the hills, nurtured in secret, which gave both the moral force and the actual organization to the escaped slaves who plotted and trained, swooped down upon the plantations and led the rest of the slaves in the revolt that, by 1804, had made of Haiti the second free colony in the western hemisphere, following the Unites States. Even today the songs of revolt, of "Vive la liberté," occur in Petro ritual as a dominant theme. (62)

    Deren supports her argument by citing Maximilien (134) on the role of the whip in Petro rites and Rigaud and Denis (no pag.) on the songs of revolt employed by the cult.

13. Campbell argues that the term "sufferer" was adopted by the Jamaican poor during the capitalist depression that hit the island in the 1930s and finally led to a general strike in 1938. He states that working conditions were comparable to the times of slavery: "The planter monopoly over most of the arable land and over the reward for work meant that the working people of Jamaica, like the majority of colonised workers, suffered from a special kind of super exploitation" (78). Workers had no right to vote and no right to strike for better wages as this was consid-

*Notes*

ered a crime by law. Consequently, the poor called themselves "sufferers" as an "attempt to define their location in the international system" (79).

14. "Dis" is the name of the fictional city in Dante's lower hell. It is also an alternative name for Pluto, Roman god of the underworld.

15. Again, this passage is reminiscent of Dinah, who herself becomes garbage, climbing up the mound of rubbish in the Dungle of Patterson's *The Children of Sisyphus*. Brathwaite is also alluding to the title of a collection of poems by LeRoi Jones (Amiri Baraka), *The Dead Lecturer* (1964), no doubt picturing himself as the dead lecturer on the garbage heap, thus referring to his own near-death in Chapter 4 of *Trench Town Rock*. In the book, as opposed to my reading of it, the burglary of Brathwaite's apartment precedes this quotation of Kingston as rubbish dump. In relation to the Dantean theme that pervades *Trench Town Rock*, he may also have had in mind LeRoi Jones's *The System of Dante's Hell* (1966), Jones's own interpretation of the canonical European text. As Amiri Baraka, LeRoi Jones became involved with black nationalism, which in the form of Garveyism and Rastafarianism also informs Brathwaite's *Trench Town Rock*.

16. This is a reference to *The Zea Mexican Diary*. Brathwaite and his sister seem to mean the souls of the dead or messengers from beyond the grave. Originally, as Adrian F. Chatfield points out, it is a reference to Hebrews 12.1, where the Christian community is seen as a "cloud of witnesses" (221).

17. The spelling of Ananse varies and can also be found as Anansi, as in this story, or as Anancy. I have decided to use Ananse, as it corresponds to Brathwaite's own spelling.

18. According to Gates, the tradition of Signifyin(g) is related to Esu's interpretation of the Ifa oracle, the sacred texts of the Yoruba. Interpretation, Gates argues, is by nature open-ended. Esu, as Legba's Yoruba twin, is thus also related to Ananse.

19. In this sense, Brathwaite adopts Walter Rodney's critique of the Rastafari movement, which he saw lacking in knowledge ("grounding") of everyday African life, identifying too much with an idealized Haile Selassie and the imagined splendor of ancient African kingdoms: "Even within those Kingdoms the historical accounts often concentrate narrowly on the behaviour of elite groups and dynasties; we need to portray the elements of African everyday life and to comprehend the culture of Africans irrespective of whether they were resident in the empire of Mali or an

Ibo village" (Rodney 53 qtd. in Campbell 129). Campbell also points out the Rastafarians' ignorance of the political realities of Africa when referring to their incentive to learn Amharic, which for them was synonymous with Ethiopian culture as a whole. Campbell maintains that "Rastafari in Jamaica ... were not to know that the linguistic and cultural diversity of Ethiopia was much richer than Amharic, and that the promotion of Amharic as opposed to other Ethiopian languages was part of the cultural chauvinism of the Ethiopian ruling class" (77).

# CHAPTER FIVE: *DreamStories*: The Far Side of the Mirror

1. "Eastern Africa," *Encyclopaedia Britannica*:

   Too rigid for folding to take place, the platform on which eastern Africa rests has been buckled by subterranean forces into broad basin-and-swell structures hundreds of miles across. Associated with these tensional forces, extensive faulting has raised and lowered vast blocks of land, leaving prominent escarpments between them, and extruded lavas have formed elevated plateaus and have spread across the plains as well as forming numerous volcanoes. The most striking of these features is the East African Rift System, of which the main branch, known as the Eastern Rift Valley or Great Rift Valley, extends from the junction of the Red Sea and the Gulf of Aden, crosses the summit of two centres of uplift in Ethiopia and Kenya, and enters northern Tanzania, where it largely disappears only to reappear in the south of that country in the Lake Nyasa trough (Lake Nyasa is also known as Lake Malawi).

2. Higgins draws particular attention to the 1974 find of the skeletal remains of a woman known in the west as "Lucy":

   About 3.5 million years ago, in this Great Rift Valley in Kush (Ethiopia), a woman of slight frame and short stature lived her life and passed away without so much as a gravestone surviving to mark her place. Most of the world knows her as "Lucy," named by her discoverers after a Beatles song. The locals call her *Dinquinesh*, meaning "You are a wonder!" In 1974 an American paleontological team found her skeletal remains at Hadar in the Afar portion of the Great Rift Valley. Including other sites in Ethiopia, Kenya, and Tanzania, this valley has furnished the

## Notes

world with more of the earliest human skeletal remains than any other region in the world. (10)

3. In his introduction to *Selected Essays of Wilson Harris*, Andrew Bundy uses this phrase to refer to the novels of Wilson Harris, whose association of images is reminiscent of the language of dreams. My own use of "dream book" is slightly different in that it does not refer to the end product of the creative process (i.e. the published book) but rather to its beginning and source.

4. Brathwaite lists that it was first written in Paris in 1953 and first published in *Bim* in 1955 (*DS* 45).

5. Like *obeah*, myalism is an aspect of African-Caribbean religion (mainly of Jamaica) dating back to the times of slavery. In "The African Presence in Caribbean Literature," Brathwaite describes "myal" as "the divination aspect of Afro-Caribbean religion" (201 n23). He stresses that it "had no connection whatever with Christianity" but was "a fragmented form of African religion, expressing, through dreams, visions, prophesying, and possession (*kumina*), what the establishment called 'hysteria' and later *pocomania:* 'a little madness'" (201–2). Leonard Barrett argues along similar lines: "Although the legitimate priests and priestesses were unable to do their work under slavery, they did not wholly forget their roles. They remained capable of casting and exorcising spells. Exorcism became the function by which they were best known and in this role became known as *myal*-men and *myal*-women" (18).

6. Of particular interest here is "Scapegoats or the Whole Lindisfarne Dream Warning" (1993), or the revised version, "Scapeghost(s) or the whole lindisfarne dream morning" (1999), where the island of Lindisfarne overlaps with Barbados.

7. In *Divine Horsemen*, Deren gives a description of Legba's dual nature. Often depicted with an erect phallus, he is also invoked at childbirth "as navel of the world, or as its womb" (96).

8. *Chad*

> This sacred lake
> is the soul
> of the world;
>
> winds whirl

> born in the soul
> of this dark water's world.
>
> This lake
> moulds
> the wars of the world;
>
> no peace in this world
> till the soul
> knows this dark water's
>
> world.
> Reeds whisper
> here in the morning;
>
> buffaloes blaze;
> and around these shores,
> man whirls
>
> in his dark rest-
> less haste; search-
> ing for hope; seek-
>
> ing his fate
> far from the shores
> of this lake. (*Arrivants* 105)

9. "Path of Words" is a term used by Benítez-Rojo in *The Repeating Island* with reference to the work of Alejo Carpentier, who attempts to create a "Path of Words" between Europe and America (184).

10. Compare to the section in Glissant's *Caribbean Discourse*, where he refers to the Caribbean as a "new Atlantis": "The oldest dream in Western culture is related, for example, to an island-continent, Atlantis. The hope for a Caribbean cultural identity must not be hampered by our people not achieving independence, so that the new Atlantis, our threatened but vital Caribbeanness, would disappear before taking root" (224).

11. Damballah and Ayida are also reminiscent of the Nommo serpent twins of Dogon mythology, the life-force of the universe (see my introduction).

## Notes

12. Brathwaite employs the rainbow as a major symbol in *Sun Poem* (1982) to illustrate this notion of migration as well as the cultural connection between Africa and the Caribbean.

13. See *The Arrivants* and *The Zea Mexican Diary* in particular, but also individual poems in *X/Self*, such as "The visibility trigger" and "The fapal state machine."

14. Bloch writes in vol. 3 of *The Principle of Hope*:

    It was the Naassenes or Ophites (naas, ophis = serpent), undoubtedly a Jewish heretical sect long before they appeared as a Christian-gnostic sect around 100 A.D. who definitively carried through the *transvaluation of the serpent of paradise in relation to Jesus, as the usurper of Yahweh*. They interpreted the serpent of Genesis as a life-creating principle in the lower world, but not only in the world-preserving, therefore evil sense. The serpent of paradise is at the same time the symbol of world-exploding reason; for it teaches man to eat of the tree of knowledge, it announces to the first men a kingdom which is higher than that of their creator and the creator of the world. It teaches them to break the law of the demiurge in order by knowledge of salvation to become like that highest god who is not Yahweh and who was not proclaimed again until Jesus came.... (*PH* 3: 1268)

15. In his notes to *Mother Poem*, Brathwaite writes: "... long before the Europeans, the Amerindian Arawaks lived here and we still stumble upon their artifacts. Indeed it is my instinct that certain features of our eastern landscape ... were ceremonial monuments for our ancestors" (*MP* 119).

16. A Savacou North edition of "Dream Haiti" appeared in 1995. A new version of the whole of *DreamStories* was published by New Directions in 2007 as *DS(2): DreamStories*.

17. Roberto Fernández Retamar gives an account of the history of the interlinked words Carib, cannibal and Caliban. Retamar states that the association of Carib and man-eating cannibal is first made in the navigation logbooks of Columbus. By the sixteenth century, the Caribs had come to represent bestial humanity in European thought, whereas the Arawaks, who were described as peaceful by Columbus, became associated with the notion of the noble savage (6–7).

18. In her discussion of the Caribbean imaginary and symbolic, Rondha Cobham uses the novel *Divina Trace* by Trinidadian author Robert Antoni to illustrate her argument. *Divina Trace* is literally divided into two halves by a mirror page, which tangibly demonstrates how the novel itself passes from the imaginary to the symbolic through a mirror stage. Although Brathwaite's mirror is entirely metaphorical, the principle is the same.

# CHAPTER SIX: "Oceans within": *Barabajan Poems, ConVERSations with Nathaniel Mackey* and the Utopian Space of the Text

1. *The Poet and his Place in Bajan Culture* is the title of the original lecture.

2. "Caliban's Guarden" is the first in a series of T. S. Eliot lectures that Brathwaite delivered at the University of Kent. The series is entitled *Conversations with Caliban*, which echoes *ConVERSations with Nathaniel Mackey* and, in turn, *Conversations with Ogotemmeli*, and points to Brathwaite's general engagement with the notion of dialogue and open-endedness.

3. The fact that *DreamStories* and *Barabajan Poems* were published within a year of each other suggests that they must have been developed more or less simultaneously. The earliest version of *Barabajan Poems* dates back to 1987, so the book spans almost the entire period of trauma, Brathwaite's "time of salt." Therefore, it appears justifiable to read *DreamStories* and *Barabajan Poems* within the same thematic context.

4. Brathwaite's statement expresses what James Walvin refers to as the "Atlantic world":

> Historians have become increasingly interested in the concept of an Atlantic world: a world that embraced the maritime and littoral societies of Europe, Africa and the Americas, and one in which slavery played a crucial role. The Atlantic system developed a gravitational pull that drew to it many more societies than those formally committed to African slavery. Even the economies of Asia were ultimately linked to African slavery. European ships, bound for the slave coast of Africa, brimmed not simply with produce from their home towns, their hinterland and from Europe, but also with goods transhipped from Asia. Firearms from Birmingham, French wines, Indian textiles, cowrie shells from the Maldives, food from Ireland, all were packed into the holds of the outbound ships, destined to be exchanged for Africans. (48–49)

## Notes

5.  Chapman's poem as quoted by Brathwaite:

    But on one well-remembered morn, there rose
    Or seemed to rise, no sun. No stars disclose,
    Nor straggling moonlight, the uncertain hour,
    But darkness reigns with undisputed power.
    Horror on horror! onward rolls the day,
    And yet there comes no solitary ray:
    The birds fly screaming round the night-wrapt walls;
    The obscene bat is wheeling through the halls;
    The affrighted herds in wild confusion run –
    All that has life bewails the veiled sun...

    Now from the heavens a strange portentous shower
    Is felt descending...
    Like Him of old, who scattered down the rain
    Of lightning on the Cities of the Plain...
    The helpless fall upon the ground and pray, –
    "If we must perish, let it be in day!"
    Affrighted crowds the distant churches throng;
    At mid-day torches gleam the roads along:
    Terrors, unmasked, upon the impious seize –
    Who never prayed before, are on their knees...
    [MJ Chapman, **Barbadoes** (London 1833), 2nd edition (1835), pp13-14]
    (*BP* 87)

Compare to Brathwaite's poem "The Dust" (*Rights of Passage*), which in *Barbajan Poems* is juxtaposed with Chapman's and conveys a similar atmosphere:

> **But it black black black
> from that mountain back
> in yuh face, in yuh food,
> in yuh eye
> In fac'
> Granny say, in de broad
> day light, even de white**

> o' we skylight went out An'
> if you hear people shout!
> how they can't find the way
>
> how they isn't have shelter
> can't pray to no priest or no leader
> an' God gone an' darken the day!
> . . . . . . . . . . . . . . . . .
> (*BP* 87–88)

6. Aimé Césaire's *Cahier d'un retour au pays natal* is another example of a volcano poem. In *Cahier*, the volcano is employed as a metaphor for the voice of the poet who cries out on behalf of "the mouths of those griefs which have no mouth" (89). Moreover, the destructive quality of the volcano Mont Pelée of Césaire's native Martinique is appropriated as an agent of liberation from colonial rule. Referring to the eruption of Mont Pelée in 1902, which destroyed the city of Saint-Pierre, Mireille Rosello writes in her introduction: "By reclaiming the image of the volcano as a symbol of life, Césaire suggests that the destruction of Saint-Pierre stood for the demise of a three century-long colonial power. Like slaves who 'stifled [their] cry' for centuries, and then violently rebelled against their masters, Césaire's poetry is volcanic ..." (60).

7. In "The Place of *Wide Sargasso Sea*" (1994), Peter Hulme attacks Brathwaite for his apparent racial exclusiveness, citing Brathwaite's reference to *Wide Sargasso Sea* in *Contradictory Omens*. In his response to Hulme, "A Post-Cautionary Tale of the Helen of Our Wars" (1995), Brathwaite explains that the passage refers to the context of black nationalism in which *Contradictory Omens* was written, its situational character being already indicated in "given the present structure":

> When WSS first appeared, as you will see from the List (above) it was we West Indians who paid it mind. It was 'ours' as it shd be But since in the 60s we were so race-consciously fragmented, some of us at least fought over the importance/ value / significance of its SMI, its ENIGMA. **CO** in fact, fr

> om *that point of view, is part of those uncivil civil wars w / in Caribb culture & I can't tell you how far we get beyond that yet.* (75)

Other critics, in response to the Hulme/Brathwaite debate, also point out that in the "present structure" of 1974 African identity was still marginalized and racial segregation was still an issue in the Caribbean islands, and in Barbados in particular: "In Barbados, Brathwaite's country, 1974 was not so long after virtual apartheid there, when hotels, sports facilities and clubs were effectively segregated, and white Barbadians dominated business and finance" (Savory, "Jean Rhys, Race and Caribbean/English Criticism" 33). In most of his work from the late 1980s and 1990s onwards, Brathwaite is far from excluding the white population of the Caribbean from his creole model (although African spirituality continues to function as the prime alternative to western exploitation). Therefore, in "A Post-Cautionary Tale" he rightly accuses Hulme of not having "*read my work — certainly none of it since the parts on WSS he quotes*" (70).

8. In *Caribbean Discourse*, Glissant tells of a similar survival of ancestral memory expressing itself in a wood carving by the Cuban sculptor Augustin Cárdenas:

   > ... his hands did not resist the hard, brown mahogany for long, even if it was not thick this time, and there soon emerged the undeniable figure of *an Ancestor who is broken in silence*. In it, the flatness of the original wood became patience and transparency, the tiny opening became the *eye of lineage*, lost time took shape in our consciousness. I like the fact that this work was so born of a twofold imperative. Those who admire it instinctively ask: "Is it African?" ... The poetics of Cárdenas ... connects with the tradition of oral celebration, the rhythm of the body, the continuities of frescoes, the gift of melody. From one work to the other, the same text is articulated. Structuring to this extent into discourse the art of the unique object, that is where Cárdenas is at his most striking. In this way he puts together a poetics of continuous time: the privileged moment yields to the rhythms of the voice. Memory is forced to abandon its diversions, where unexpected forms lurk and suddenly emerge. (240–41)

   Both Cárdenas and Bob'ob/Ogoun create "a poetics of continuous time," although the Cuban artist seems to do so consciously, whereas the Barbadian carpenter stumbles across his ancestral memory apparently by accident.

9. Into this resistance he includes the German emperor, himself the ruler of an empire-building nation. Bob'ob's cherishing of this icon of imperial Germany is probably more an assertion of anti-British or anti-American sentiment, related to his identification with black nationalism, rather than an affiliation with German race ideology. However, it may be interesting to mention that W.E.B. Du Bois found a prototype for his own views of black exceptionalism in the racial and national ideology of imperial Germany (Gilroy 133–35).

10. In *Poetics of Relation*, Édouard Glissant compares the ocean and the experience of the Middle Passage to the creation of an archive or text: "Navigating the green splendor of the sea ... still brings to mind, coming to light like seaweed, these lowest depths, these deeps, with their *punctuation* of scarcely corroded balls and chains" [emphasis mine] (6). Derek Walcott's reference to the Atlantic as archive in *Omeros* is even more direct when he describes the St Lucian fisherman Achille walking along the ocean floor between Africa and the Caribbean, observing "the parchment overhead / of crinkling water record[ing] three centuries / of the submerged archipelago" (155).

11. This, of course, is a play on the title of the collection of essays and poems on Brathwaite, *For the Geography of a Soul*, edited by Timothy J. Reiss.

12. In an autobiographical essay, writer Paule Marshall, herself of Barbadian descent, interprets the same island saying, handed down to her by her mother and her mother's friends, the "poets in the kitchen": "'The sea ain't got no back door,' they would say, meaning that it wasn't like a house where if there was a fire you could run out the back. Meaning that it was not to be trifled with. And meaning perhaps in a larger sense that man should treat all of nature with caution and respect" (2076).

13. Van Sertima mainly investigates the pre-Columbian connection between Africa and the Americas. Brathwaite's adding of the Pacific and Australian region illustrates his own idea of a global connection.

# CHAPTER SEVEN: "The spirits of GOLOKWATI ... have led me to this place": *Words Need Love Too* and *Born to Slow Horses*

1. Interestingly, the project that seeks to save the poet's space of writing, the website *Save CowPastor*, is a realized creole experiment itself by bringing together a community of poets in virtual reality. The threat to the poet's

## Notes

physical space of writing creates another space of a much wider dimension. As in *ConVERSations*, here again the computer, and by extension the internet, are utopian spaces. They offer the possibility as well as the realization of utopia. Virtual reality is, in fact, the closest manifestation of "concrete utopia" and the fullest realization of *Heimat* in Brathwaite's work.

2. Most of the writers listed are Caribbean or African-American, with the exception of William Butler Yeats. A variation on the last line of his poem "Among School Children," "how can we know the dancer from the dance," appears here (as well as in "Pixie") in creolized form. Yeats's most important role in this list of poets is his status as a writer of the Irish Revival, who succeeded in making the language of colonization his own and thus reclaiming it for his people, along with a reorientation towards Irish folk culture. In this sense, he is closely related to the cultural project of many Caribbean writers and most notably Brathwaite himself.

3. All references are to the online pdf version.

4. This is reminiscent of "Francina," which describes a similar event:

> In the park that was once green,
> had a lake, two red stone lions,
> a macaw, monkeys, humped hundred-
>
> year-old turtle with pale pink
> shell-fish eyes, the Mayor and Council,
> .........................
> have built a dance hall and a barbecue
> so that the city-sick electorate
>
> can brawl and stew their buttocks
> in thick saucy tunes and latest juke-
> box choices. The green is gone now,
>
> trees cut down, grass cruelled under-
> foot, the lake converted to a park-
> ing lot.... (*Arrivants* 214)

The second part of the poem states "Francina bought it" (*Arrivants* 215), although she is far too poor to afford it. In rescuing the turtle and thus a part of the island's past, Francina can be regarded as a Namsetoura/Sycorax figure.

5. Ritual marriage ensures the protection of a *loa*.

6. See, for example, Olive Senior, *Working Miracles: Women's Lives in the English-Speaking Caribbean* (1991). Most famously, George Lamming, in *In the Castle of My Skin*, states: "My father who had fathered only the idea of me had left me the sole liability of my mother who really fathered me" (3).

7. Of particular importance in this context, apart from Brathwaite's own work, is Eduardo Galeano's *The Open Veins of Latin America*.

8. In McSweeney's *Raintaxi* interview with him he states: "One thing about catastrophe, for me, is that it always seems to lead to a kind of magical realism. That moment of utter disaster, the very moment when it seems almost hopeless, too difficult to proceed, you begin to glimpse a kind of radiance on the other end of the maelstrom."

9. The work of Derek Walcott also frequently refers to landscape as text, for example in the opening lines of *Another Life*: "Verandahs, where the pages of the sea / are a book left open by an absent master..." (3).

10. "MMassaccourraamann" portrays two generations of Caribbean poets in the diaspora, one whose points of reference remain rooted in the Caribbean and one who begins to adjust his cultural metaphors to the new environment. In his Epilogue to *An Intellectual History of the Caribbean*, Torres-Saillant discusses this new generation of diasporic writers. He argues that there is enormous potential in these diaspora communities to produce "an influential cadre of intellects who will not judge their ancestral homelands more harshly than they do the Western societies where they live and work, but who recognize their diasporic citizenship as one that entails a 'double duty (with accountability both here and there)'" (252–53;Radhakrishnan 212).

11. Although aligning the female solely with the spiritual is creating a new binarism that feminists would object to, Brathwaite at least succeeds in subverting the western binarism of woman = body, man = mind by turning it on its head.

12. As early as "MR" (1997), Brathwaite refers to "golokwati" in lower case spelling loosely as a gathering of intellectuals and writers in order to create new visions or ways of thinking, implying that the conference at which he delivered "MR" would be such a "golokwati."

# Bibliography

As this study does not take an encylopedic approach to the work of Kamau Brathwaite, the bibliography is not exhaustive. In section 1, I have listed only those works by Brathwaite that are discussed or mentioned in this book. Likewise, in sections 2 – 4, I list only works cited here and some that I found were useful in providing context.

## 1. Works by Kamau Brathwaite

"An Alternative View of Caribbean History." *The Colonial Encounter: Language.* Powre above Powres 7. Mysore, India: The Centre for Commonwealth Literature and Research, University of Mysore, 1984. 43–65.

*Ancestors.* New York: New Directions, 2001.

"An excerpt from Limbo." *The Caribbean Writer* 14 (2000): 97–111.

"A Post-Cautionary Tale of the Helen of Our Wars." *Wasafiri* 22 (1995): 69–81.

April 29th [2005]. Online posting. *Save CowPastor.* 15 May 2006 <http://www.tomraworth.com/wordpress/?page_id=73>.

*Barabajan Poems 1492-1992.* New York: Savacou North, 1994.

*Black + Blues.* Benin City, Nigeria: Ethiope, 1977. Rev. ed. *Black + Blues* (New York: New Directions, 1995.

*Born to Slow Horses.* Middletown, CT: Wesleyan University Press, 2005.

"Caliban, Ariel, and Unprospero in the Conflict of Creolization: A Study of the Slave Revolt in Jamaica in 1831–32." *Comparative Perspectives on Slavery & the New World Plantation Societies.* Ed. Vera Rubin and Arthur Tuden. New York: New York Academy of Sciences, 1977. 41–62.

"Caliban's Guarden." *Wasafiri* 16 (1992): 2–6

"Caribbean Culture — Two Paradigms." *Missile and Capsule.* Ed. Jürgen Martini Bremen: Universität Bremen, 1983. 8–55

*Caribbean Man in Space and Time: A Bibliographical and Conceptual Approach.* Mona: Savacou, 1974.

*Contradictory Omens: Cultural Diversity and Integration in the Caribbean.* Mona: Savacou, 1974.

*ConVERSations with Nathaniel Mackey.* Staten Island, NY: We Press; Minneapolis, MN: Xcp: Cross-Cultural Poetics, 1999.

"Dream Haiti." New York: Savacou North, 1995.

*DreamStories.* Intro. Gordon Rohlehr. Longman Caribbean Writers. Harlow: Longman, 1994. Rev. ed. *DreamStories* (*DS 2*). New York: New Directions, 2007.

*Folk Culture of the Slaves in Jamaica.* 1971. Rev. ed. London: New Beacon, 1981.

"Forward." *Savacou* 3–4 (1970): 5–9.

"from Janice Whittle, with an extract from Kamau's reply." May 22nd [2005]. Online posting. *Save CowPastor.* 15 May 2006 <http://www.tomraworth.com/wordpress/ ?page_id=73>.

"from Kamau; reply to email." May 9th [2005]. Online posting. *Save CowPastor.* 15 May 2006 <http://www.tomraworth.com/ wordpress/?page_id=73>.

# Bibliography

"from Kamau: TWO SMALL VICTORIES." May 28th [2005]. Online posting. *Save CowPastor.* 2 May 2007 <http://tomraworth.com/wordpress/?page_id=73>.

*Gods of the Middle Passage.* Mona: Savacou, 1982.

*Golokwati 2000.* New York: Savacou North, 2002.

*History of the Voice: The Development of Nation Language in Anglophone Caribbean Poetry.* London/Port of Spain: New Beacon Books, 1984.

"History, the Caribbean Writer and *X/Self.*" *Crisis and Creativity in the New Literatures in English.* Ed. Geoffrey V. Davis and Hena Maes-Jelinek. Cross/Cultures: Readings in the Post/Colonial Literatures in English 1. Amsterdam/Atlanta, GA: Rodopi, 1990. 23–45

"Houses in the West Indian Novel." *Literary Half-Yearly* 17 (1976): 111–21.

*Islands.* London/Oxford: Oxford University Press 1969.

*Jah Music.* Mona: Savacou 1986.

"Jazz and the West Indian Novel." *Roots.* Ann Arbor: University of Michigan Press, 1993. 55–110.

"Kamau Brathwaite and CowPastor." 2006. Online posting. *Save CowPastor.* 22 May 2006 <http://tomraworth.com/wordpress/?p=66>.

*Kumina: The Spirit of African Survival in Jamaica.* Mona: Savacou, 1982. Rpt. of *Jamaica Journal* 42 (1978): 44–63.

"Letter from Kamau to the Jamaican poet and critic Mervyn Morris." May 19th [2005]. Online posting. *Save CowPastor.* 15 May 2006 <http://www.tomraworth.com/ wordpress/?page_id=73>.

Letter to Gordon Rohlehr. 13 Nov. 1993. Gordon Rohlehr. "Dream Journeys." *DreamStories.* By Kamau Brathwaite. Harlow: Longman, 1994.

*Masks.* London/Oxford: Oxford University Press 1968.

"Metaphors of Underdevelopment: A Proem for Hernan Cortez." *The Art of Kamau Brathwaite*. Ed. Stewart Brown. Bridgend, Wales: Seren, 1995. 232-53.

*Middle Passages*. Newcastle upon Tyne: Bloodaxe, 1992.

*Mother Poem*. Oxford/New York: Oxford University Press, 1977.

"MR." *Annals of Scholarship* 12.1-2 (1997): 1-28.

*MR (Magic Realism)*. New York: Savacou North, 2002.

"Nanny, Palmares & the Caribbean Maroon Connexion." *Maroon Heritage*. Ed. Kofi Agorsh. Mona: Canoe Press, 1994. 119-38.

"New Gods of the Middle Passage." *Caribbean Quarterly* 46.3-4 (2000): 12-58

"Newstead to Neustadt." *Kamau Brathwaite: 1994 Neustadt Prize for Literature*. Special Issue of *World Literature Today* 68.4 (1994): 653-60.

*Rights of Passage*. London/Oxford: Oxford University Press 1967.

*Roots*. Ann Arbor: University of Michigan Press, 1993.

*Save CowPastor*. 2006. 3 Dec. 2008. <http://tomraworth.com/wordpress/>.

"Scapegoats or the Whole Lindisfarne Dream Warning." *The Page*. Nov. 1993: 6-7.

"Scapeghost(s) or the whole lindisfarne dream morning." *Xcp: Cross-Cultural Poetics* 4 (1999): 9-27.

*Shar/Hurricane Poem*. Mona, Jamaica: Savacou, 1990.

*Sun Poem*. Oxford/New York: Oxford University Press, 1982.

"The African Presence in Caribbean Literature." *Roots*. Ann Arbor: University of Michigan Press, 1993. 190-258.

*The Arrivants: A New World Trilogy*. London/Oxford: Oxford University Press, 1973.

*The Colonial Encounter: Language*. Powre above Powres 7. Mysore, India: The Centre for Commonwealth Literature and Research, University of Mysore, 1984.

"The Controversial Tree of Time." *Bim* 30 (1960): 104–14.

*The Development of the Creole Society in Jamaica 1770–1820*. 1971. Intro. B. W. Higman. Kingston/Miami: Ian Randle, 2005.

*The Namsetoura Papers*. 19 Nov. 2008 <http://tomraworth.com/np.pdf>. 1–55. Rpt. of "The Namsetoura Papers." *Hambone* 17 (2004): [no pag.].

*The People Who Came*. 3 vols. 2nd ed. Series ed. Edward Brathwaite. San Juan, Trinidad: Longman Caribbean, 1986.

*The Poet and His Place in Bajan Culture*. Twelfth Sir Winston Scott Memorial Lecture. Bridgetown: Central Bank of Barbados, 1987.

*The Zea Mexican Diary 7 Sept 1926 – 7 Sept 1986*. Foreword Sandra Pouchet Paquet. Wisconsin Studies in American Autobiography. Madison, Wisconsin: The University of Wisconsin Press, 1993.

*Third World Poems*. Harlow: Longman, 1983.

"Timehri." *Is Massa Day Dead? Black Moods in the Caribbean*. Ed. Orde Coombs. Garden City, NY: Anchor Press/Doubleday, 1974. 29–45.

*Trench Town Rock*. Providence: Lost Roads, 1994. Rev. rept. of "Trench Town Rock." *Hambone*. 10 (Spring 1992). 123–201.

*Wars of Respect: Nanny and Sam Sharpe*. Mona: API for the National Heritage Week Committee, 1977.

"Words by Kamau Brathwaite." Kamau Brathwaite and the Caribbean Word: A North-South Counterpoint Conference. Bronx, NY: Hostos Community College, City University of New York. 24 Oct. 1992.

*Words Need Love Too*. Intro. Fabian Adekunle Badejo. Philipsburg, St. Martin: House of Nehesi, 2000.

*Words Need Love Too.* Intro. Stewart Brown. Cambridge: Salt, 2004.

"World Order Models: A Caribbean Perspective." *Caribbean Quarterly* 31 (1985): 53–63.

*X/Self.* Oxford/New York: Oxford University Press, 1987.

"Xtendting the CP Discourse: June 2005." 19 Nov. 2008. *Save CowPastor* <http:// tomraworth.com/xtend.pdf>. 1–13.

## 2. Secondary Sources and Contextual Material

Achebe, Chinua. *Morning Yet on Creation Day*: London/Nairobi: Heinemann, 1975.

_____ *Things Fall Apart.* 1958. Intro. Kwame Anthony Appiah. London: Everyman's Library, 1992.

"African Religions: an Overview." *The Encyclopedia of Religion.* Ed. Mircea Eliade et al. 16 vols. New York: Macmillan; London: Collier Macmillan, 1987. Vol. 1: 60–69.

"African Tricksters." *The Encyclopedia of Religion.* Ed. Mircea Eliade et al. 16 vols. New York: Macmillan; London: Collier Macmillan, 1987. Vol. 15: 46–48.

Agorsh, Kofi. Ed. *Maroon Heritage.* Mona: Canoe Press, 1994.

Alighieri, Dante. *The Divine Comedy*. Trans. with commentary Charles S. Singleton. *Inferno.* 1: Italian Text and Translation. 2: Commentary. Princeton, New Jersey: Princeton University Press, 1980.

Alleyne, Mervyn C. "The Role of Africa in the Construction of Identity in the Caribbean." *For the Geography of a Soul: Emerging Perspectives on Kamau Brathwaite.* Ed. Timothy J. Reiss. Trenton, NJ/Asmara, Eritrea: Africa World Press, 2001. 177–90

Allfrey, Phyllis. *Orchid House.* 1953. London: Virago, 1982.

Antoni, Robert. *Divina Trace.* Woodstock, NY: Overlook Press, 1992.

# Bibliography

Appiah, Kwame Anthony. Introduction. *Things Fall Apart*. By Chinua Achebe. 1958. London: Everyman's Library, 1992. viii–ix.

Arrom, José Juan, and Manuel A. García Arévalo. *Cimarrón*. Santo Domingo: Fundación García Arévalo, 1986.

Arrom, José Juan. "Cimarrón: Apuntes sobre sus primeras documentations y su probable origen." Arrom and Arévalo. 13–30.

Arthur, Charles and Michael Dash. Eds. *Libète: A Haiti Anthology*. London: The Latin America Bureau, 1999.

Ashcroft, Bill, Gareth Griffiths, Helen Tiffin. *The Empire Writes Back: Theory and Practice in Post-Colonial Literatures*. New Accents. London/New York: Routledge, 1989.

*Atlapedia Online: Countries A to Z*. 2008. 18 Nov. 2008 <http://www.atlapedia.com/ online/country_index.htm >.

Badejo, Fabian Adekunle. Introduction. *Words Need Love Too*. By Kamau Brathwaite. St Martin: House of Nehesi, 2000. ix–xx.

Barrett, Leonard E. *The Rastafarians: The Dreadlocks of Jamaica*. Kingston, Jamaica: Sangster's Book Store; London: Heinemann Educational, 1977.

Beckford, George, and Michael Witter. *Small Garden . . . Bitter Weed: The Political Economy of Struggle and Change in Jamaica*. 2nd ed. Morant Bay, Jamaica: Maroon Publishing House; London: Zed Books, 1982.

Benítez-Rojo, Antonio. *The Repeating Island: The Caribbean and the Postmodern Perspective*. 2nd ed. Trans. James E. Maraniss. Durham and London: Duke University Press, 1996.

Binder, Wolfgang. Ed. *Slavery in the Americas*. Würzburg: Königshausen und Neumann, 1993.

Bloch, Ernst. *The Principle of Hope*. Trans. Neville Plaice, Stephen Plaice and Paul Knight. 3 vols. Studies in Contemporary German Social Thought. Cambridge, MA: The MIT Press, 1995.

Bobb, June D. *Beating a Restless Drum: the Poetics of Kamau Brathwaite and Derek Walcott*. Trenton, NJ/Asmara Eritrea: Africa World Press, 1998.

Bob Marley: Home: The Official Website. 2008. 4 Dec. 2008. <http://web.bobmarley.com/index.jsp>.

Bob Marley Sound Archives. 13 Jan. 2003 <http://www.bobmarley.com>.

"Book." *A Dictionary of Symbols*. Ed. by Jean Chevalier and Alain Gheerbrant. Trans. John Buchanan-Brown. London: Penguin, 1996: 111–12.

*Books of Chilam Balam*. Trans. Alfredo Barrera Vásquez and Silvia Rendón. Colección popular 42. Mexico: Fondo de Cultura Económica, 1963.

Brathwaite, Doris Monica. *A Descriptive and Chronological Bibliography, 1950–1982, of the Work of Edward Kamau Brathwaite*. London: New Beacon Books, 1988.

Brontë, Charlotte. *Jane Eyre*. 1847. London: Penguin, 2003.

Brown, Karen McCarthy. *Mama Lola: A Vodou Priestess in Brooklyn*. Berkeley: University of California Press, 2001.

Brown, Stewart. Interview with Edward Kamau Brathwaite. *Kyk-over-al* 40 (1989): 84–93.

———. Introduction. *Words Need Love Too*. By Kamau Brathwaite. Cambridge: Salt, 2004. xiii–xxvi.

———. Ed. *The Art of Kamau Brathwaite*. Bridgend, Wales: Seren, 1995.

Bundy, Andrew. Introduction. *Selected Essays of Wilson Harris: The Unfinished Genesis of the Imagination*. Ed. Andrew Bundy. Readings in Postcolonial Literatures. London: Routledge, 1999. 1–34.

———. Ed. *Selected Essays of Wilson Harris: The Unfinished Genesis of the Imagination*. Readings in Postcolonial Literatures. London: Routledge, 1999.

Campbell, Horace *Rasta and Resistance: from Marcus Garvey to Walter Rodney*. Preface Eusi Kwayana. London: Hansib, 1985.

Caputi, Jane, "On the Lap of Necessity: A Mythic Reading of Teresa Brennan's Energetics Philosophy." *Hypatia: A Journal of Feminist Philosophy* 16.2 (2001): 1–26.

Carpentier, Alejo. *El Reino de Este Mundo.* 1949. Vol. 2. *Obras completas de Alejo Carpentier.* 12 vols. Mexico City: Siglo Veintiuno, 1989.

Castillo, Ana. Ed. *Goddess of the Americas La Diosa de las Américas: Writings on the Virgin of Guadalupe.* New York: Riverhead Books, 1996.

Césaire, Aimé. *Cahier d'un retour au pays natal / Notebook of a Return to My Native Land.* 1939. Trans. Mireille Rosello with Annie Pritchard. Intro. Mireille Rosello. French-English Bilingual Edition. Bloodaxe Contemporary French Poets: 4. Newcastle upon Tyne: Bloodaxe, 1995.

_____ *Une Tempête: d'après "La Tempête" de Shakespeare, adaption pour un theatre nègre.* Festival d'Hammamet 1969. Paris: Seuil, 1974.

Chang, Victor L. Introduction. *The Children of Sisyphus.* By Orlando Patterson, 1964. Longman Caribbean Writers. Harlow: Longman, 1986. vii–xviii.

Chapman, M. J. *Barbadoes.* London, 1833.

Chatfield, Adrian Francis. "Spiritual Identity and Experience in the Literature of the Anglophone Caribbean." Ph.D. thesis. University of Leeds, 1997.

Chevalier, Jean and Alain Gheerbrant. Eds. *A Dictionary of Symbols.* Trans. John Buchanan-Brown. London: Penguin, 1996.

Cisneros, Sandra. "Guadalupe the Sex Goddess." *Goddess of the Americas La Diosa de las Américas: Writings on the Virgin of Guadalupe.* Ed. Ana Castillo. New York: Riverhead Books, 1996.

Cixous, Hélène. *"Coming to Writing" and Other Essays.* Intro. Susan Rubin Suleiman. Ed. Deborah Jenson. Cambridge, MA: Harvard University Press, 1991.

Clendinnen, Inga. *Aztecs: An Interpretation.* Cambridge: Cambridge University Press, 1995.

Cobham, Rhonda. "Of Boloms, Mirrors, and Monkeymen: What's Real and What's Not in Robert Antoni's *Divina Trace.*" *Sisyphus and Eldorado: Magical and Other Realisms in Caribbean Literature.* Ed. Timothy J. Reiss. 2nd ed. Trenton, NJ/Asmara, Eritrea: Africa World Press, 2002. 25-56

Collymore, Frank A. *Notes for a Glossary of Words and Phrases of Barbadian Dialect.* 4th ed. [no place]: The Barbados National Trust Fund, 1970.

Coombs, Orde. Ed. *Is Massa Day Dead? Black Moods in the Caribbean.* Garden City, NY: Anchor Press/Doubleday, 1974.

Cordan, Wolfgang. Annotations. *Popol Vuh: Das Buch des Rates.* Mythos und Geschichte der Maya. Special ed. Munich: Diederichs, 1998.

Cortés, Hernán. *Cartas de relación.* Ed. Angel Delgado Gómez. Madrid : Clásicos Castalia, 1993.

Dabydeen, Cyril. *Stoning the Wind.* Toronto: Tsar, 1994.

Dash, J. Michael. "Libre sous la mer — Submarine Identities in the Work of Kamau Brathwaite and Édouard Glissant." *For the Geography of a Soul: Emerging Perspecives on Kamau Bratwaite.* Ed. Timothy J. Reiss. Trenton, NJ/Asmara Eritrea: Africa World Press, 2001. 191–200.

Davis, Geoffrey V. and Hena Maes-Jelinek. Eds. *Crisis and Creativity in the New Literatures in English.* Cross/Cultures: Readings in the Post/Colonial Literatures in English 1. Amsterdam/Atlanta, GA: Rodopi, 1990.

Dawes, Neville. *The Last Enchantment.* London: MacGibbon & Kee, 1960.

Dayan, Joan. "A New World Lament." *For the Geography of a Soul: Emerging Perspectives on Kamau Brathwaite.* Ed. Timothy J. Reiss. Trenton, NJ/Asmara Eritrea: Africa World Press, 2001. 333–42

———. "Erzulie: A Women's History of Haiti?" *Postcolonial Subjects: Francophone Women Writers.* Ed. Mary Jean Green et al. Minneapolis: University of Minnesota Press, 1996. 42–60.

———. "René Depestre and the Symbiosis of Poetry and Revolution." *Modern Language Studies* 10.1 (Winter 1979–80): 75–81.

Delany, Samuel R. *The Jewels of Aptor.* London: Gollancz, 1962.

Depestre, René. *A Rainbow for the Christian West.* Trans. Joan Dayan. Amherst: Massachuesetts Press, 1977.

Deren, Maya. *Divine Horsemen: The Living Gods of Haiti*. 1953. Preface Joseph Campbell. New York: McPherson; Documentext, 1970.

Díaz del Castillo, Bernal. *The Discovery and Conquest of Mexico*. Ed. Genaro García. Trans. Alfred Maudsley. Intro. Hugh Thomas. 2nd ed. New York: Da Capo Press, 2003.

Dos Santos, Juana Elbein, and Deoscoredes M. dos Santos. *Esu Bara Laroye: A Comparative Study*. Ibadan: Institute of African Studies, 1971.

Duane, O.B. *African Myths and Legends*. London: Brockhampton Press, 1998.

Duerden, Dennis. *African Art & Literature: The Invisible Present.* London: Heinemann, 1975.

"eastern Africa." *Encyclopaedia Britannica*. 2008. Encyclopaedia Britannica Online. 18 Nov. 2008 <http://search.eb.com.elib.tcd.ie/eb/article-37760>

Eliot, T. S. *Four Quartets*. 1944. London: Faber and Faber, 1959.

_____ *The Waste Land*. 1922. Faber Pocket Poetry. London: Faber and Faber, 1999.

*Encyclopaedia Britannica*. 2008. Encyclopaedia Britannica Online. 18 Nov. 2008. <http://search.eb.com.elib.tcd.ie/>.

*Encyclopedia Mythica*, 2008, Encyclopedia Mythica Online. 15 Nov. 2008 <http:// www.pantheon.org/ >

Estrada, Ezequiel Martínez. "El Nuevo Mundo, la Isla de Utopía y la Isla de Cuba" ("The New World, the Island of Utopia, and the Island of Cuba"). *Homenaje a Ezequiel Martínez Estrada, Casa de las Américas* 33 (1965).

Fenwick, M. J. and Vincent O. Cooper. "'Geological Connection/Poetic Perception:' An Interview with Kamau Brathwaite: Part I." *The Caribbean Writer* 14 (2000): 76-84.

Fleischmann, Ulrich. "Maroons, Writers, and History." *Slavery in the Americas*. Ed. Wolfgang Binder. Würzburg: Königshausen und Neumann, 1993. 565-79.

Freud, Sigmund. *The Interpretation of Dreams*. 1899. Trans. Joyce Cricks. Intro. and annot. Ritchie Robertson. Oxford World's Classics. Oxford/New York: Oxford University Press, 1999.

Fukuyama, Francis. *The End of History and the Last Man*. New York: Free Press, 1992.

Galeano, Eduardo. *The Open Veins of Latin America: Five Centuries of the Pillage of a Continent*. Trans. Cedric Belfrage. Foreword Isabel Allende. 25th anniversary ed. New York: Monthly Review Press, 1997.

Gates, Jr., Henry Louis. *The Signifying Monkey: A Theory of African-American Literary Criticism*. New York/ Oxford: Oxford University Press, 1989.

Gilroy, Paul. *The Black Atlantic: Modernity and Double Consciousness*. London/ New York: Verso, 1993.

Glissant, Édouard. *Caribbean Discourse: Selected Essays*. Trans. and intro. J. Michael Dash. Charlottesville: University Press of Virginia; Caraf Books, 1992.

———. *Poetics of Relation*. Trans. and intro. Betsy Wing. Ann Arbor: University of Michigan Press, 1997.

Graves, Robert. *The Greek Myths*. 1955. Combined ed. London: Penguin, 1992.

Green, Mary Jean, et al. Eds. *Postcolonial Subjects: Francophone Women Writers*. Minneapolis: University of Minnesota Press, 1996.

Greenblatt, Stephen. *Marvelous Possessions: The Wonder of the New World*. The Clarendon Lectures and the Carpenter Lectures 1988. Oxford: Clarendon, 1991.

Griaule, Marcel. *Conversations with Ogotemmeli: An Introduction to Dogon Religious Ideas*. Trans. and intro. Germaine Dieterlen. Foreword Daryll Forde. London/Oxford: Oxford University Press for the International African Institute, 1965.

Haley, Alex. *Roots: The Saga of an American Family*. London: Pan Books, 1978.

## Bibliography

Hall, Stuart, "Cultural Identity and Diaspora." *Contemporary Postcolonial Theory: A Reader*. Ed. Padmini Mongia. London/New York: Arnold, 1996. 110–21.

Handler, Jerome S. "An African-Type Burial, Newton Plantation Barbados." *African-American Archaeology: Newsletter of the African-American Archaeology Network.*. 15 (1995). Ed. Thomas R. Wheaton. The African Diaspora Archaeology Network. 19 Nov. 2008 <http://www.diaspora.uiuc.edu/A-AAnewsletter/newsletter15.html>.

Harris, Wilson. "Creoleness: The Crossroads of a Civilization?" *Selected Essays of Wilson Harris: The Unfinished Genesis of the Imagination*. Ed. Andrew Bundy. Readings in Postcolonial Literatures. London: Routledge, 1999. 237–47.

_____ *Eternity to Season*. 1954. London/Port of Spain: New Beacon Books, 1978.

_____ "Letter from Francisco Bone to W. H." *Selected Essays of Wilson Harris: The Unfinished Genesis of the Imagination*. Ed. Andrew Bundy. London: Routledge, 1999. 47–52.

_____ "New Preface to *Palace of the Peacock*." *Selected Essays of Wilson Harris: The Unfinished Genesis of the Imagination*. Ed. Andrew Bundy. London: Routledge, 1999. 53–57.

_____ *Palace of the Peacock*. London: Faber and Faber, 1960.

_____ *Selected Essays of Wilson Harris: The Unfinished Genesis of the Imagination*. Ed. Andrew Bundy. London: Routledge, 1999.

_____ *The Carnival Trilogy*. London: Faber and Faber, 1993.

_____ *The Mask of the Beggar*. London: Faber, 2003.

_____ "The Music of Living Landscapes" *Selected Essays of Wilson Harris: The Unfinished Genesis of the Imagination*. Ed. Andrew Bundy. London: Routledge, 1999. 40–46.

_____ *The Womb of Space: The Cross-Cultural Imagination*. Contributions in Afro-American and African Studies 73. Westport, CT/London: Greenwood Press, 1983.

Hart, George. Ed. *A Dictionary of Egyptian Gods and Goddesses*. London/New York: Routledge, 1986.

Hearne, John. *Stranger at the Gate*. London: Faber and Faber, 1956.

Herskovits, M.J. *Life In A Haitian Valley*. New York [n. pub.], 1937.

Higgins, Jr., Chester. *Feeling the Spirit: Searching the World for the People of Africa*. New York/Toronto: Bantam Books, 1994.

Higman, B. W. Introduction. *The Development of the Creole Society in Jamaica 1770–1820*. By Kamau Brathwaite. Kingston/Miami: Ian Randle, 2005. ix–xxxii.

*Hispanos Famosos*. 2006. 18 Nov. 2008 < http://coloquio.com/famosos/>.

"Horus." *A Dictionary of Egyptian Gods and Goddesses*. Ed. George Hart. London/New York: Routledge, 1986. 92–93.

Hulme, Peter. "The Place of *Wide Sargasso Sea*." *Wasafiri* 20 (1994): 5–11.

Huntington, Samuel P. *The Clash of Civilizations and the Remaking of World Order*. New York: Touchstone Books, 1998.

"Hurakan," *Encyclopedia Mythica*, 2008, Encyclopedia Mythica Online. 15 Nov. 2008 <http://www.pantheon.org/articles/h/hurakan.html>.

*I Ching, or, The Book of Changes*. Trans. Cary F. Baynes from Richard Wilhelm's translation. Foreword C.G. Jung. 3rd ed. London: Routledge & K. Paul, 1968.

"Jamaica." *Atlapedia Online: Countries A to Z*. 2008. 18 Nov. 2008 <http://www.atlapedia.com/online/countries/jamaica.htm>.

James, C.L.R. *The Black Jacobins: Toussaint L'Ouverture and the San Domingo Revolution*. 1938. 3rd rev. ed. London: Allison & Busby, 1980.

"John Crow." *The New Shorter Oxford English Dictionary*. Ed. Lesley Brown. 2 vols. Oxford: Clarendon Press, 1993. Vol. 1: 1452.

# Bibliography

Jones, Jonathan. "Too good for this world?" *The Guardian*. Saturday Review. 22 Sept. 2001: 5.

Jones, LeRoi. *The Dead Lecturer*. New York: Grove Press, 1964.

———— *The System of Dante's Hell*. London: MacGibbon & Kee, 1966.

Joyce, James. *Ulysses*. 1922. Intro. and notes Declan Kiberd. Annot. Students' ed. London: Penguin, 1992.

*Kamau Brathwaite: 1994 Neustadt Prize for Literature*. Special Issue of *World Literature Today* 68.4 (1994).

Khan, Ismith. *The Jumbie Bird*. 1961. Longman Caribbean Writers. Harlow: Longman, 1985.

Kincaid, Jamaica. *Annie John*. 1985. London: Vintage, 1997.

———— *At the Bottom of the River*. 1984. London: Vintage, 1997

———— *Lucy*. 1990. New York: Farrar Straus Giroux, 2002.

———— *The Autobiography of My Mother*. London: Vintage, 1996.

Lacan, Jacques. *Écrits: A Selection*. Trans. Alan Sheridan. London/New York: Routledge, 2001.

Lamming, George. *In the Castle of my Skin*. 1953. Intro. David Williams. Longman Caribbean Writers. Harlow: Longman, 1987.

———— *The Pleasures of Exile*. London: Michael Joseph, 1960.

———— *Season of Adventure*. London: Michael Joseph, 1960.

Lévi-Strauss, Claude. *The Raw and the Cooked: Introduction to the Science of Mythology I*. Trans. John and Doreen Weightman. London: Jonathan Cape, 1969.

Lewis, M. "Odomankoma Kyerema Se." *Caribbean Quarterly* 19.2 (1973): 65–69.

Lovelace, Earl. *The Wine of Astonishment*. 1982. Intro. Marjorie Thorpe. Caribbean Writers Series. London: Heinemann, 1986.

Mackey, Nathaniel. *Discrepant Engagement: Dissonance, Cross-Culturality, and Experimental Writing*. Cambridge Studies in American Literature and Culture. Cambridge: Cambridge University Press, 1993.

Mackey, Nathaniel. An Interview with Edward Kamau Brathwaite. *Hambone* 9 (Winter 1991): 42–59.

Malcolm X. *The Autobiography of Malcolm X*. With Alex Haley. 1964. Intro. M. S. Handler. Epilogue Alex Haley. New York: Ballantine Books, 1992.

Marley, Bob. "Trench Town Rock." *Bob Marley Sound Archives*. 13 Jan. 2003 <http://www.bobmarley.com/sounds>.

Marshall, Paule. "The Making of a Writer: From the Poets in the Kitchen." *The Norton Anthology of African American Literature*. Ed. Henry Louis Gates, Jr. and Nellie Y. McKay. New York/London: Norton, 1997. 2072–79.

Martini, Jürgen. Ed. *Missile and Capsule*. Bremen: Universität Bremen, 1983.

Maximilien, Louis. *Le Vodou Haitien, Rite Rada-Canzo*. Port-au-Prince, Haiti [n. pub.] 1945.

McDonald, Ian. *The Humming-Bird Tree*. London: Heinemann, 1969.

McMorris, Mark. "Provincial Subjects in the Classical Labyrinth: the Challenge to Tradition in Brathwaite's *X/Self*." *Journal of Commonwealth and Postcolonial Studies*. 6.1 (1999): 104–24.

McSweeney, Joyelle. "Poetics, Revelations, and Catastrophes: an Interview with Kamau Brathwaite." *Raintaxi Review of Books*. Online ed. (Fall 2005). 15 May 2006 <http://raintaxi.com/online/2005fall/brathwaite.shtml>.

Melville, Pauline. *The Ventriloquist's Tale*. London: Bloomsbury, 1997.

Mendlovitz, Saul H. Ed. *On the Creation of a Just World Order: Preferred Worlds of the 1990's*. New York: The Free Press, 1975.

Métraux, Alfred. *Voodoo in Haiti*. Trans. Hugo Charteris. Intro. Sidney W. Mintz. New York: Schocken Books, 1972.

## Bibliography

Meyerowitz, Eva. *The Sacred State of the Akan*. London: Faber and Faber, 1951.

Mongia, Padmini. Ed. *Contemporary Postcolonial Theory: A Reader*. London/New York: Arnold, 1996.

Mordecai, Pamela. "Images of Creativity and the Art of Writing in *The Arrivants.*" *For the Geography of a Soul: Emerging Perspectives on Kamau Brathwaite*. Ed. Timothy J. Reiss. Trenton, NJ/Asmara Eritrea: Africa World Press, 2001. 21–42

Morgan, Mary E. "Highway to Vision: The Sea Our Nexus." *Kamau Brathwaite: 1994 Neustadt Prize for Literature*. Special Issue of *World Literature Today* 68.4 (1994). 663–68

_____ "This Silver Feather." *For the Geography of a Soul: Emerging Perspectives on Kamau Brathwaite*. Ed. Timothy J. Reiss. Trenton, NJ/Asmara Eritrea: Africa World Press, 2001. 317–31.

More, Thomas. *Utopia*. 1516. Ed. George M. Logan and Robert M. Adams. Cambridge: Cambridge University Press, 1989.

Moreton, J. B. *Manners and Customs of the West India Islands*. London [n. pub.], 1790.

Naipaul, V. S. *A House for Mr Biswas*. 1961. London: Penguin, 1969.

_____ *The Loss of Eldorado: A History*. 1969. London: Penguin, 1973.

_____ *The Middle Passage*. 1961. London: Penguin, 1969.

*New Jerusalem Bible, The*. Pocket ed. London: Darton, Longman & Todd, 1990.

*New Shorter Oxford English Dictionary*, The. Ed. Lesley Brown. 2 vols. Oxford: Clarendon Press, 1993.

Ngũgĩ wa Thiong'o, "Kamau Brathwaite: The Voice of African Presence." *Kamau Brathwaite: 1994 Neustadt Prize for Literature*. Special Issue of *World Literature Today* 68.4 (1994). 677–79.

Nichols, Grace. *I Is a Long-Memoried Woman*. London: Karnak House, 1983.

Nkrumah, Kwame. *Neo-colonialism, The Last Stage of Imperialism.* London: Heinemann, 1965.

Norman, Alma. *The People Who Came.* Book One. 2nd ed. Series ed. Edward Brathwaite. San Juan, Trinidad: Longman Caribbean, 1986.

*Norton Anthology of African American Literature, The.* Ed. Henry Louis Gates, Jr. and Nellie Y. McKay. New York/London: Norton, 1997.

Okara, Gabriel. *The Voice.* 1964. Intro. Arthur Ravenscroft. African Writers Series. London: Heinemann, 1970.

Olson, Charles. "Projective Verse." *Collected Prose.* Ed. Donald Allen and Benjamin Friedlander. Intro. Robert Creeley. Berkeley/Los Angeles/ London: University of California Press, 1997. 239–49.

Pagnoulle, Christine. "'Labyrinth of past/present/future' in some of Kamau Brathwaite's recent Poems." *Crisis and Creativity in the New Literatures in English: Cross/Cultures.* Ed. Geoffrey V. Davis and Hena Maes-Jelinek. Amsterdam: Rodopi, 1990. 449–66.

Paquet, Sandra Pouchet. Foreword. *The Zea Mexican Diary.* By Kamau Brathwaite. v–xi.

Patterson, Orlando. *The Children of Sisyphus.* 1964. Introduction Victor L. Chang. Longman Caribbean Writers. Harlow: Longman, 1986.

Paul, Annie. Ed. *Caribbean Culture: Soundings on Kamau Brathwaite.* Kingston: UWI Press, 2007.

Plimpton, George. Ed. *The Paris Review Interviews: Beat Writers at Work.* Intro. Rick Moody. London: Harvill Press, 1999.

Pollard, Charles W. *New World Modernisms: T. S. Eliot, Derek Walcott, and Kamau Brathwaite.* New World Studies. Charlottesville/London: University of Virginia Press, 2004.

*Popol Vuh: Das Buch des Rates.* Mythos und Geschichte der Maya. Trans. and annot. Wolfgang Cordan. Special ed. Munich: Diederichs, 1998.

Price, Richard. Ed. *Maroon Societies: Rebel Slave Communities in the Americas.* 3rd ed. Baltimore/London: The Johns Hopkins University Press, 1996.

# Bibliography

"Quetzalcoatl." *The Encyclopedia of Religion.* Ed. Mircea Eliade et al, 16 vols. New York: Macmillan; London: Collier Macmillan, 1987. Vol. 12: 152–53.

Radhakrishnan, Rajogopalan. *Diasporic Mediations: Between Home and Location.* Minneapolis/London: University of Minnesota Press, 1996.

Reiss, Timothy J. *Against Autonomy: Global Dialects of Cultural Exchange.* Stanford: Stanford University Press, 2002.

———. Ed. *Sisyphus and Eldorado: Magical and Other Realisms in Caribbean Literature.* 2nd ed. Trenton, NJ/Asmara, Eritrea: Africa World Press, 2002.

———. Ed. *For the Geography of a Soul: Emerging Perspectives on Kamau Brathwaite.* Trenton, NJ/Asmara, Eritrea: Africa World Press, 2001.

———. "Realisms of the Fictive Imagination: Outsmarting Sisyphus, Amending Eldorado, Writing Caribbean." *Sisyphus and Eldorado: Magical and Other Realisms in Caribbean Literature.* 2nd ed. Ed. Timothy J. Reiss. Trenton, NJ/ Asmara, Eritrea: Africa World Press, 2002. 249–70.

Retamar, Roberto Fernández. *Caliban and Other Essays.* Trans. Edward Baker. Foreword Fredric Jameson. Minneapolis: University of Minnesota Press, 1989.

Reyhani, Roman O. "The Legality of the Use of White Phosphorus by the United States Military during the 2004 Fallujah Assaults." 24 Jan. 2007. *bepress Legal Series.* Working Paper 1959. 8 Nov. 2008 <http://law.bepress.com/expresso/eps/ 1959>.

Rigaud, Odette Mennesson, and Lorimer Denis. *Ceremonie En L'Honneur de Marinette.* Port-au-Prince: Bulletin Du Bureau d'Ethnologie, July 1947.

Rhys, Jean. *Wide Sargasso Sea.* 1966. London: Penguin, 1968.

Rodney, Walter. *Groundings With My Brothers.* London: Bogle-L'Ouverture, 1969.

Rohlehr, Gordon. "Dream Journeys." *Kamau Brathwaite: 1994 Neustadt Prize for Literature.* Special Issue of *World Literature Today* 68.4 (1994). 765–74.

_____ "Dream Journeys." Introduction. *DreamStories* By Kamau Brathwaite. iii–xvi.

_____ *My Strangled City and Other Essays.* Port of Spain: Longman Trinidad, 1992.

_____ *Pathfinder: Black Awakening in The Arrivants of Edward Kamau Brathwaite.* Tunapuna, Trinidad: private publication, 1981.

_____ "Songs of the Skeleton." *My Strangled City and Other Essays.* Port of Spain: Longman Trinidad, 1992. 270–323.

_____ "The Rehumanization of History: Regeneration of Spirit: Apocalypse and Revolution in Brathwaite's *The Arrivants* and *X/Self*." *The Shape of That Hurt and Other Essays.* Port-of-Spain: Longman Trinidad Limited, 1992. 247–92

_____ *The Shape of That Hurt and Other Essays.* Port-of-Spain: Longman Trinidad Limited, 1992.

Rosello, Mireille. Introduction. *Cahier d'un retour au pays natal / Notebook of a Return to My Native Land.* By Aimé Césaire. Trans. Mireille Rosello with Annie Pritchard. French-English Bilingual Edition. Bloodaxe Contemporary French Poets: 4. Newcastle upon Tyne: Bloodaxe, 1995. 9–68.

Rosenberg, Jim. "Poetics and Hypertext: Where are the Hypertext Poets?" 24 May 2002 <http://www.well.com/user/jer/ht_poetics.html>.

Rubin, Vera, and Arthur Tuden. Eds. *Comparative Perspectives on Slavery & the New World Plantation Societies.* New York: New York Academy of Sciences, 1977.

Savory, Elaine. "Jean Rhys, Race and Caribbean/English Criticism." *Wasafiri* 28 (1998): 33–34.

_____ "The Word Walking Among Us: Reading Kamau Brathwaite with William Blake." *For the Geography of a Soul: Emerging Perspectives on Kamau Brathwaite.* Ed. Timothy J. Reiss. Trenton, NJ/Asmara Eritrea: Africa World Press, 2001. 111–27.

_____ "Wordsongs & Wordwounds / Homecoming: Kamau Brathwaite's *Barabajan Poems.*" *Kamau Brathwaite: 1994 Neustadt Prize for Literature.* Special Issue of *World Literature Today* 68.4 (1994). 750–57.

## Bibliography

"Scarab." *A Dictionary of Symbols*. Ed. Jean Chevalier and Alain Gheerbrant. Trans. John Buchanan-Brown. London: Penguin, 1996. 833.

Senior, Olive. *Working Miracles: Women's Lives in the English-Speaking Caribbean*. London: James Curry, 1991.

Sernett, Milton. *Bound for the Promised Land: African American Religion and the Great Migration*. The C. Eric Lincoln Series on the Black Experience. Durham and London: Duke University Press, 1997.

Shakespeare, William. *The Tempest*. Ed. Frank Kermode. The Arden Shakespeare. 5th ed. London: Methuen, 1954.

Sharer, Robert J., and Loa P. Traxler. *The Ancient Maya*. 6th ed. Stanford: Stanford University Press, 2006.

Snyder, Gary. *The Old Ways: Six Essays*. San Francisco: City Lights Books, 1977.

———. *Turtle Island*. New York: New Directions, 1974.

Soyinka, Wole. *Myth, Literature and the African World*. Cambridge: Cambridge University Press, 1976.

Tatsumi, Takayuki. Interview with Samuel R. Delany. *Diacritics* 16.3 (1986): 27–45.

Taylor, John H. *Egyptian Coffins*. Aylesbury, Bucks: Shire Publications, 1989.

Thomas, Hugh. *The Conquest of Mexico*. London: Hutchinson, 1993.

Todorov, Tzvetan. *The Conquest of America: The Question of the Other*. Trans. Richard Howard. Foreword Anthony Pagden. Norman: University of Oklahoma Press, 1999.

Torres-Saillant, Silvio. *An Intellectual History of the Caribbean*. New York/Basingstoke: Palgrave Macmillan, 2006.

———. *Caribbean Poetics: Toward an Aesthetic of West Indian Literature*. Cambridge: Cambridge University Press, 1997.

"Trenchtown." *Bob Marley*. Places. 2002. 18 Nov. 2008 <http://www.manik.sk/bobmarley/places/index.html>.

"Trenchtown." The Life of Bob Marley. *Bob Marley Sound Archives*. 13 Jan. 2003 <http://www.bobmarley.com/life/trenchtown/>.

"Tricksters: An Overview." *The Encyclopedia of Religion*. Ed. Mircea Eliade et al. 16 vols. New York: Macmillan; London: Collier Macmillan, 1987. Vol. 15: 45–46.

Tuelon, Alan, "Nanny — Maroon Chieftainness." *Caribbean Quarterly* 19.4 (1973): [no pag.].

Van Sertima, Ivan: *They Came before Columbus: The African Presence in Ancient America*. London: Random House, 1976.

"Vasco Núñez de Balboa." *Hispanos Famosos*. 2006. 18 Nov. 2008 <http://coloquio.com/famosos/balboa.htm>.

Walcott, Derek. *Another Life*. London: Jonathan Cape, 1973.

———. *Omeros*. London: Faber and Faber, 1993.

Walmsley, Anne. "Her Stem Singing: Kamau Brathwaite's *The Zea Mexican Diary: 7 Sept 1926 – 7 Sept 1986*." *Kamau Brathwaite: 1994 Neustadt Prize for Literature*. Special Issue of *World Literature Today* 68.4 (1994). 747–49.

Walvin, James. "Slavery and the British." *History Today* 52.3 (2002): 48–54.

Warner, Marina. *Fantastic Metamorphoses, Other Worlds: Ways of Telling the Self*. The Clarendon Lectures in English 2001. Oxford: Oxford University Press, 2004.

Weinberger, Eliot. Interview with Gary Snyder. *The Paris Review Interviews: Beat Writers at Work*. Ed. George Plimpton. 276–300.

Wheeler, Elizabeth Anne. "Unthinkable Cities: Kingston and Los Angeles." Ph.D. thesis. University of California, Berkeley, 1996.

Wideman, John Edgar. *Damballah*. 1981. London: Flamingo, 1986.

Williams, Emily Allen. *The Critical Response to Kamau Brathwaite*. Critical Responses in Arts and Letters Series. Westport/CT: Greenwood, 2004.

Wilson-Tagoe, Nana. *Historical Thought and Literary Representation in West Indian Literature*. Gainesville: University Press of Florida; Barbados/Jamaica/Trinidad and Tobago: The Press University of the West Indies; Oxford: James Curry, 1998.

Wolf, Eric R. *Europe and the People Without History*. Cartographic illustrations Noël L. Diaz. Berkeley/Los Angeles/London: University of California Press, 1982.

Woolf, Virginia. *A Room of One's Own*. 1928. London: Penguin, 2004.

Yeats, W. B. *The Collected Poems of W. B. Yeats*. 1933. 2nd ed. London: Macmillan, 1950.

## 3. Films and Television Series

*Roots: television miniseries*. By Alex Haley. Writ. William Blinn, Ernest Kinoy, James Lee, and M. Charles Cohen. Dir. David Greene, John Erman, Marvin J. Chomsky, Gilbert Moses. ABC, New York. Broadcast 23 Jan. – 30 Jan. 1977.

*The Harder They Come*. Writ. Perry Henzell and Trevor D. Rhone. Prod. and dir. Perry Henzell. Title song Jimmy Cliff. New World Pictures, 1973.

## 4. Music

Davis, Miles. *Kind of Blue*. Rec. 1959. Sony, 1997.

Hawkins, Colman. *Body & Soul*. Rec. 1939–1956. RCA, 1996.

# Index

9/11 20, 215, 232, 233, 236-238, 240, 241

Abrahams, Carl 236
Achebe, Chinua 72, 73
Africa 3, 4, 9, 10, 13, 21, 24, 26, 30, 44, 54, 56, 57, 69, 73, 75, 77, 82-84, 89, 93, 96, 99, 104, 106, 110, 115-117, 133, 146, 147, 157, 158, 163-165, 168, 193-197, 200, 201, 209, 226, 230, 233, 240
Afro-creole 5, 7
Agoue 231
Akan 3, 143, 197, 216, 223
Akbal 28, 29, 31, 118
Allfrey, Phyllis 95
alter/native 7, 193, 200, 204
alter-Renaissance 53
Ananse 3, 23, 33, 35, 36, 99, 129, 142-144, 193, 214, 223
Anansi 143
*antillanité* 11
Anyaneanyane 87, 88, 242
Appiah, Kwame Anthony 72
archive 7, 91, 93-95, 97-99, 101, 103-105, 107, 109, 111, 112, 157, 158, 189, 202-204, 216, 224
arrived-at Being 10, 33, 36, 39, 62, 95, 106, 140, 161, 162, 164, 166, 204, 213, 242, 243
*Asantehene* 195, 196
*ase* 61
Ashanti 82, 88, 195, 196
*àshe* 61, 62
Atlantis 162-164
audioglyph 237
*àxé* 61, 212, 214, 239
Ayama 69, 73, 94
Ayida 164, 165
Aztec 25, 28, 29, 46, 47, 68, 105, 208, 211

Back-O-Wall 100
Bahamas 234
Bajan 158, 184, 185, 198-200, 230
Balboa, Vasco Nuñez 32, 190-193, 206

Barbados 7, 41, 42, 93, 162, 177, 183, 190, 192-194, 197-202, 216, 221, 228-230, 234, 237, 240, 241
Benítez-Rojo, Antonio 58, 158, 203
biosphere 47
Black Star Line Shipping Company 115
Bloch, Ernst 8-10, 25, 37, 49, 58, 63, 133, 134, 138, 142, 161, 191, 204, 230
Blue Mountains 51, 52, 55, 88, 89
Bob'ob 200-205
Bogle 235
book of life 103, 104
*Books of Chilam Balam* 46
Bosomtwi 226
Brathwaite, Kamau
 *Ancestors* 13, 19, 29, 40-46, 48, 49, 82, 88, 89, 99, 102, 146, 148, 153, 165, 194, 196, 208, 216
 "An excerpt from Limbo" 7, 61, 62, 72
 *Barabajan Poems* 2, 16, 75, 82, 95, 96, 111, 183, 184, 186-190, 192-198, 204, 206, 207, 209, 211, 212, 215, 216, 222, 228, 234
 *Born to Slow Horses* 87, 215, 231-233, 236, 240, 241, 243
 "Boy and the Sea" 216, 221, 222
 "Caliban's Guarden" 83, 192, 193
 *Caribbean Man in Space and Time* 10, 34, 84, 94, 200
 *Contradictory Omens* 199, 200
 *ConVERSations with Nathaniel Mackey* 6, 12, 51, 95, 140, 170, 207
 *DreamStories* 16, 40, 42, 81, 145-151, 153, 155-159, 161-163, 165, 167, 169, 171-177, 179, 181, 192, 201
 *Folk Culture of the Slaves in Jamaica*
 *Gods of the Middle Passage* 9, 112, 164, 201
 *Golokwati 2000* 16, 17, 183, 216
 "History, the Caribbean Writer and *X/Self*" 163
 "Houses in the West Indian Novel" 95
 *Islands* 11, 15, 34, 35, 41-43, 100, 163, 175, 192, 193, 195, 200, 203, 221
 *Jah Music* 64, 212, 231
 "Jazz and the West Indian Novel" 185
 *Kumina: The Spirit of African Survival in Jamaica* 53, 96, 240
 *Masks* 88, 99, 104, 107, 158, 162, 164, 194, 195, 197
 "Metaphors of Underdevelopment: A Proem for Hernan Cortez" 51, 52, 58
 *Middle Passages* 13, 54, 63, 64, 66, 72, 112, 121, 135, 138, 236
 *Mother Poem* 1, 4, 6, 19, 40-42, 45, 46, 48, 54, 59, 84, 152, 171, 220, 222, 230, 234

## Index

"MR" 14-16, 20, 21, 74, 85, 86, 101, 125-127, 132, 140, 141, 183, 238

"New Gods of the Middle Passage" 9

"Newstead to Neustadt" 60, 63, 81, 101

*Rights of Passage* 198

*Save CowPastor* 211, 216, 241

*Shar/Hurricane Poem* 60, 91, 93, 95, 97, 99, 101, 103, 105, 107, 109, 111, 113

*Sun Poem* 6, 19, 24, 40, 42, 59, 183, 197, 203, 222

"The African Presence in Caribbean Literature" 157

*The Arrivants* 19, 59, 88, 93, 152

*The Development of the Creole Society in Jamaica 1770–1820* 6

*The Namsetoura Papers* 222, 223, 225, 230

*The People Who Came* 10

*The Zea Mexican* 51, 53-55, 57-59, 61, 63, 65-67, 69, 71, 73, 75, 77, 79, 81, 83, 85, 87, 89, 92-94, 97, 101, 107, 113, 134, 145, 152, 153, 156, 166, 172, 200, 241, 242

*Third World Poems* 43

"Timehri" 8, 170, 190, 207-211, 234

*Trench Town Rock* 42, 61, 89, 95, 97, 100-103, 113-119, 121, 123, 125-127, 129, 131, 133-135, 137-145, 147, 175, 178, 197, 220, 231

*Wars of Respect: Nanny and Sam Sharpe* 57, 81, 82

*Words Need Love Too* 20, 175, 176, 212, 215-217, 219-221, 223, 230, 232, 243

"World Order Models: A Caribbean Perspective" 10, 21, 48, 53

*X/Self* 6, 13, 19-29, 31-45, 47-49, 51, 54, 58, 59, 72, 86, 87, 94, 102, 111, 114, 118, 131, 134, 146, 150, 163, 179, 183, 189, 191, 193, 215, 222, 226, 231-233, 236, 241

Brontë, Charlotte 161

Brown, Stewart 20, 215, 218, 219

Brown's Beach 197

Bussa Centre 216

Caliban 1, 2, 4, 13, 75, 136, 137, 178, 179, 181, 193, 200, 210, 219, 220, 225, 228

Cambridge 93, 183, 194, 216

Campbell, Horace 115-117, 122, 131, 144

Caribbean 1, 2, 4-16, 19-22, 24, 26, 33-36, 39-42, 49, 53-58, 65, 69, 73, 75, 76, 78, 80-84, 87, 89, 93-97, 99, 100, 102-104, 106, 110, 112, 117, 125, 129, 137-140, 146, 147, 149, 150, 152, 157, 158, 161-165, 167, 168, 171, 173, 174, 176, 177, 179-181, 186-188, 190, 192-201, 203-205, 207, 208, 215, 217, 219, 221, 223, 225-230, 232-236, 238, 240

Castro, Fidel 21

*cenote* 44, 47, 239

Césaire, Aimé 35

Chang, Victor L. 8, 12, 14, 22, 33, 38-40, 42, 43, 49, 63, 64, 71, 73, 77, 100, 102, 104, 107, 142, 143, 155, 164, 170, 172, 177, 180, 217, 218, 235, 236, 239
Chapman, M. J. 32, 198-200
Charlemagne 35, 150
Christ 3, 39, 49, 84, 131, 143
Christophe, Henri 34, 35, 178
circle 53, 71-73, 76, 80, 96, 107, 239
Cixous, Hélène 220
Cobham, Rhonda 13, 14, 39
Coke, Lester 127
Coltrane, John 237
Columbus, Christopher 8, 43, 53, 98, 149, 178, 208, 209, 233, 234, 236
concrete utopia 8, 10, 14, 15, 37, 50, 215, 230
Cortez, Hernan 25-33, 51, 53, 118, 191
CowPastor 7, 42, 59, 97, 172, 176, 187, 216, 217, 222-226, 230, 235, 240, 241
creole 1, 4-7, 9-11, 13, 14, 19, 21-25, 27, 29, 31, 33, 35-37, 39-41, 43, 45, 47-50, 52, 53, 56, 58, 59, 61, 63, 65, 89, 98, 102, 103, 105, 125, 133, 134, 142, 143, 152, 154, 158, 159, 161, 166, 168, 181, 187, 195, 200, 203, 215, 218, 220, 223, 231, 232, 236, 239, 240
creole cosmos 6, 7
creole experiment 1
creoleness 11

creolization 5, 6, 8, 10, 11, 20, 24, 25, 36, 42, 69, 164, 170, 191, 232
Cronus 28, 29, 31

Dabydeen, Cyril 235, 236
Damballah 40, 72, 76, 111, 112, 121, 164, 165, 170, 180, 203, 204, 211
Dante 117-119
Dantor 226-228
darkness of the lived moment 9, 62
Davis, Miles 212, 213
Dawes, Neville 142
Dayan, Joan 111, 121, 228
de/education 194, 195
Défilée 218, 219, 228
Delany, Samuel R. 152, 187, 203
Depestre, René 111
Deren, Maya 40, 96, 164, 165, 226, 238
Dessalines, Jean-Jacques 34, 218, 228
Dis 79, 85, 135, 138, 139, 143, 198, 224
Dogon 2
Doris Monica 12, 54
Dream Chad 87, 146, 149, 158, 171, 177, 222
dreamstories 16, 40, 42, 81, 145-151, 153, 155-159, 161-163, 165, 167, 169, 171-177, 179, 181, 192, 201
dreamstory 153, 158, 161, 164, 171, 175
Dungle 15, 96, 100, 115

dystopian 49, 53, 65, 66, 88, 101, 114, 135, 140, 143, 196, 236

East African Rift System 164
ecosystem 47
Egypt 99, 104, 106, 107, 164, 201, 208
Eldorado 15, 21, 32, 50, 66-68, 101, 191, 193, 195, 196, 210, 235
Eleuthera 234-236
Eliot, T. S. 181, 192, 240
*ens perfectissimum* 134
epic 92, 93, 98, 99
Epicenter 92
Erzulie 36, 37, 226, 228
Eshu 62, 101, 153, 154
Ethiopia 146, 201
Eucharist 3, 84
experiment of communion 63, 176
eye of Horus 106, 107
Fallujah 240, 241
Fenwick, M. J. 26
filth eater 40, 47, 49
Fukuyama, Francis 23


Garvey, Marcus 100, 114, 115, 117, 122, 133, 134, 202
Gates, Henry Louis 122, 144, 198, 207, 208, 214
Genesis 170, 231
Ghana 88, 99, 117, 156, 162, 183, 190, 194-197, 216, 241
Gikuyuland 173

*Gleaner* 117, 127, 136, 137
Glissant, Édouard 5, 11, 83, 187, 195, 205
Golokwati 16, 17, 99, 183, 215-217, 219, 221, 223, 225, 227, 229-231, 233, 235, 237, 239, 241-243
Gorée 162
Grand Chemin 39, 40, 72, 87, 165, 198, 203
Graves, Robert 28, 49
Great Migration 111
Great Rift Valley 146, 163
Griffin Poetry Prize 2006 232
Guanahani 234
Guantanamo Bay 233
Guevara, Che 21
Guinée 105, 153, 164, 231

Haile Selassie 21, 115, 121, 134, 144, 202
Haiti 35, 37, 164, 218, 226-228, 238
Haley, Alex, Roots 2
Hall, Stuart 4
Hannibal 24, 27, 33
*harmattan* 26, 233
Harris, Wilson 5, 10, 11, 15, 21, 25, 31, 33, 66, 185, 202, 203, 210, 211, 234, 235
Hawkins, Coleman 237, 239
*Heimat* 10, 34-36, 39, 40, 42, 49, 54, 63, 69, 80, 84, 87, 89, 95, 96, 106, 112, 114, 133, 144, 149, 161, 162, 175, 186, 191, 193, 203-205, 213, 222, 232, 235
Herron, Carolivia 92-94, 97

hieroglyphs 209
Higgins, Chester 146
Holy Spirit 27, 130
*houmfort* 39, 40, 50, 87, 91, 93, 95-97, 99, 101, 103, 105, 107, 109, 111, 112, 116, 122, 202-204, 223, 229, 242
Howell, Leonard 122
Hulme, Peter 200
humanization of religion 49, 144
Hunte, Julian 200
Huntington, Samuel P. 23
Hurakan 103
hurricane 12, 58, 60, 91-95, 97-99, 101, 103, 105, 107, 109-111, 113, 115, 157, 238
Hurricane Gilbert 91, 157, 238
hypertext 188, 189, 213

*I-Ching* 60, 63, 65
Inferno 113, 117-119, 129, 135
Irish Town 7, 12, 51, 52, 54, 55, 57, 58, 63-65, 69, 70, 72, 73, 85, 89, 95, 97, 101, 113, 130, 158-160, 168, 187, 189, 212, 216, 217, 223

Jamaica 6-9, 55, 83, 88, 91, 97, 122, 125, 127, 128, 157, 158, 168, 228, 230
Jamaica Labour Party (JLP) 125, 127, 128
jazz 111, 185, 186, 212, 213, 232, 237, 239
Jones, Jonathan 213
jumbie bird 65
Jura Mountains 233

Kamau 1, 3, 5, 7, 9, 11, 13, 15, 17, 60, 63, 69, 73, 75, 76, 79, 91, 172, 173, 180, 186, 187, 226, 240
Keats, John 32
Kilimanjaro 51, 52, 56, 58, 240
Kingston 12, 15, 41, 52, 58, 85, 95, 96, 113-115, 118, 122-125, 127, 129, 131, 138, 139, 143, 175, 177, 184, 239
Kingston poetry 127, 129, 177
Kumasi 195, 196
*kumina* 53, 96, 240

Lacan, Jacques 13, 42, 147
Lake Chad 158, 226
Latin America 15, 96, 229
Lazarus 135
Legba 3, 45, 61, 62, 76, 79, 101, 103, 143, 204
Lévi-Strauss 102
Lion of Judah 21, 121, 144
*loa* 24, 37-39, 61, 70, 76, 84, 87, 131, 147, 152, 153, 162, 164, 165, 170, 198, 201, 203, 204, 226-228, 231
Lucifer 150

Mackey, Nathaniel 6, 8, 12, 31, 51, 94, 95, 140, 170, 183, 184, 186, 207
Magellan 191
magical realism 14-17, 21, 230
Manley, Michael 128, 235
Marassa 165, 237, 238
Marley Manor 66, 113, 117, 118, 122, 124

## Index

Marley, Bob 66, 99, 100, 113, 115-119, 121, 122, 124, 127, 134, 140, 235, 237
*maronage* 57, 63, 85, 89, 116, 121, 167, 168, 172, 178, 229
maroon 4, 7, 14, 21, 51, 54-58, 63, 69, 70, 72, 73, 76, 81, 83, 89, 116, 121, 122, 140, 167-169, 172, 178, 179, 187, 193, 212, 217, 228, 229
Márquez, Gabriel Garcia 15, 16
Mayan 28, 44, 103, 220, 238
McKay, Claude 242
McSweeney, Joyelle 7, 9, 11, 12, 61, 80, 174, 222, 232, 237
Mendlovitz 10
messiah 21, 25, 37, 39, 129, 131, 133-135, 140, 142, 143, 170, 231
*métissage* 187
Mexican (Zea) 12, 40, 51, 53-55, 57-69, 71-73, 75-77, 79, 81, 83-89, 92-94, 97, 101, 106, 107, 113, 134, 140, 145-147, 152, 153, 156-159, 162, 165, 166, 171, 172, 180, 200, 212, 230, 239, 241, 242
Mictlan 29, 118
Mictlantecuhtli 28, 29
Middle Passage 9, 11-13, 33, 53, 61, 64, 66, 71, 78-80, 98, 105, 142, 162, 164, 173, 174, 179, 197, 201, 203, 235, 236
Mile&Quarter 192, 198, 204
missile 47, 218, 233, 234
*mkissi* 201-203, 209
Mkonde Plateau 163, 164
Mona 63, 91

montage 21, 32, 41, 114, 175, 181
Mordecai, Pamela 152
More, Thomas 8
Morgan, Mary 37, 63, 78, 80, 81, 91, 92, 139, 230
Mt Blanc 51, 52, 56, 58, 233

Naipaul, V. S. 15
*nam* 2-4, 9, 45, 82, 105-107, 129, 130, 146, 150-154, 156, 158, 165, 167, 168, 170-172, 176, 180, 193, 201, 203, 210, 223, 224, 227
Namsetoura 3, 5, 16, 42, 45, 215, 216, 219, 221-228, 230, 240-242
Nanny 57, 81, 83, 134, 228
nation language 5
neocolonial 7, 20, 21, 42, 53, 57, 58, 100, 114, 117, 123, 125, 129, 133, 146, 175, 195, 221
Neustadt Prize for Literature 1994
New World 5, 8, 10, 15, 21, 25, 29, 31-33, 53, 54, 88, 89, 104-106, 110, 111, 121, 125, 134, 135, 138, 144, 163, 164, 169, 170, 194, 197, 218, 240
New York 184, 239
Newton 225
Ngũgĩ wa Thiong'o 241
Nkrumah, Kwame 117
*Noche Triste* 27, 31
Nommo 2, 3, 201
Nyabingi 131
Nyame 3, 143, 144, 223

O'Grady 1, 4
Obatala 69, 71, 76, 80, 134
*obeah* 45, 107
Ogoun 201, 202, 204, 228
Ogun 71, 72
*ohemma* 81-83
*ohene* 82, 83
Olodumare 214
*omowale* 194, 195
Onyame 3
Orisa-nla 71, 72
Osei Tutu 195
*oumfô* 215, 224
Oxala 69
Oya 226

Pagnoulle, Christine 21, 22
Palmares 56, 57, 89
pangeneric 187
patois 5
Patterson, Orlando 15, 41, 95, 99, 100, 114
People's National Party (PNP) 127, 128
Petro 226
petroglyphs 207, 208
Pinnacle 122, 130, 140
plantation 1, 2, 21, 24, 35, 54-58, 89, 96, 149, 155, 167, 169, 171, 197, 203, 216, 225, 228, 229, 240, 241
Pollard, Charles 181
Pollock, Jackson 213
*Popol Vuh* 46
*poteau mitan* 39, 87, 203
precomposition 188, 189
Prospero 1, 4, 13, 14, 83, 154, 240

Quashie 144
Quetzalcoatl 29, 31, 191, 211

Rasta 115, 122, 131, 134
Rastafarianism 115, 117, 133
Rastafarians 21, 100, 115, 122, 130, 131, 140, 144
Raworth, Tom 216
reggae 116, 131
Reiss, Timothy J. 11, 14, 16, 61, 80, 210
Revelation to John 104
Rhys, Jean 95, 159-161
Rohlehr, Gordon 25, 40, 44, 45, 49, 60, 63, 88, 146, 172, 194
Roman empire 20, 23
Rosenberg, Jim 188, 189

*santería* 36, 201, 226
Savory, Elaine 14, 187, 209
scarab 46, 47, 49
Selvon, Sam 235
Senegal 162
Shango 96, 111
Signifyin(g) 127, 144
Simone, Nina 237
Sir Philip Sherlock Celebration Lecture 174
Sisyphus 15, 50, 95, 99-101, 103, 104, 110, 111, 114, 121, 129, 139, 161, 179, 221
Smith, Michael 114, 115, 176
Snyder, Gary 47, 195
Soyinka, Wole 69, 71, 204
St Lucia 26, 162
Stark 83, 184, 228

*Index*

*Sunday Gleaner* 117, 137
*sunsum* 197, 198
Sycorax 1-5, 12-14, 16, 35, 45, 54, 75, 83, 146, 150, 157, 176, 184, 192-194, 212, 220, 225, 226, 240
Sycorax video style, see video style

Tenochtitlan 25-27, 30, 31, 44, 68
*The Divine Comedy* 119, 153
Thomas, Hugh 31
Thyme Bottom 229
tidalectics 8, 9, 49, 52, 98
time of salt 12, 19, 59, 81, 230, 231
*timehri* 190, 207-211
Titans 25, 28, 29
Tivoli Gardens 100
Tlazolteotl 46
Torres-Saillant, Silvio 11, 14, 16, 174, 228
Toussaint l'Ouverture 34
transboundary 188
tree of life 103, 104, 161
Trench Town 42, 61, 89, 95, 97, 100-103, 113-119, 121-123, 125-127, 129, 131, 133-135, 137-145, 147, 149, 175, 176, 178, 197, 220, 231, 240
trickster 33, 41, 85, 129, 142, 154
Twelfth Sir Winston Scott Memorial Lecture 183
Twi 216, 223

udjat eye 106, 107
United States 20, 97, 115, 128, 173, 233, 239
utopia 8, 10, 14, 15, 22, 36, 37, 63, 114, 133, 138, 142, 162, 187, 191
utopian 5, 7, 8, 10, 12-16, 21, 25, 26, 33, 35-37, 40, 42, 49, 50, 58, 62, 63, 66, 70, 72, 74, 83, 87, 98, 100, 101, 111, 112, 114-117, 121, 124, 129, 133, 134, 140, 142, 144, 159-162, 164-167, 170, 183, 185, 187, 190-193, 195, 200, 203, 206, 211, 214, 229, 232, 234-236, 240, 241
utopian space 8, 14, 21, 35, 42, 58, 62, 72, 87, 112, 116, 124, 133, 144, 159, 161, 183, 187, 190, 191, 203, 206, 211, 214
Utterly Different 133

Vercingetorix 21, 23, 33
video style 13
Virgin Mary 37
Volta 198
voodoo 1, 13, 24, 36, 37, 39, 40, 70, 96, 101, 105, 111, 122, 125, 129, 131, 147, 153, 165, 170, 201, 202, 226, 231

Walcott, Derek 11, 210
Walmsley, Anne 69
Warner, Marina 218
Wheeler, Elizabeth 122, 123, 128, 129, 131, 134
Wideman, John Edgar 203

Williams, William Carlos 31, 208
Woolf, Virginia 83
World Trade Center 238, 240


Xango 24, 25, 36-39, 49


Yeats, W. B. 72, 210
Yemajaa 33, 34
Yoruba 57, 62, 69, 71, 153, 154,
    201, 204
Yucatan 28, 44, 163, 220, 238


Zion 166, 167, 202, 204
Zionism 89
zombie 125, 130, 131, 138

Printed in the United States
219143BV00001B/10/P